STUDENT SOLUTIONS MANUAL

LINEAR ALGEBRA WITH APPLICATIONS

SECOND EDITION

D0557275

OTTO BRETSCHER

Prentice
Hall

Upper Saddle River, New Jersey 07458

Executive Editor: George Lobell
Supplement Editor: Melanie Van Benthuysen
Assistant Managing Editor, Math Media Production: John Matthews
Production Editor: Barbara A. Till
Supplement Cover Manager: Paul Gourhan
Supplement Cover Designer: PM Workshop Inc.
Manufacturing Buyer: Lisa McDowell

Printed in the United States of America

10 9 8 7 6 5 4 3 2 1

ISBN   0-13-032856-1

Prentice-Hall International (UK) Limited, London
Prentice-Hall of Australia Pty. Limited, Sydney
Prentice-Hall Canada, Inc., Toronto
Prentice-Hall Hispanoamericana, S.A., Mexico City
Prentice-Hall of India Private Limited, New Delhi
Pearson Education Asia Pte. Ltd., Singapore
Prentice-Hall of Japan, Inc., Tokyo
Editora Prentice-Hall do Brazil, Ltda., Rio de Janeiro

Contents

Chapter 1

1.1

1.
$$\begin{vmatrix} x + 2y = 1 \\ 2x + 3y = 1 \end{vmatrix} \xrightarrow{} \begin{vmatrix} x + 2y = 1 \\ -y = -1 \end{vmatrix} \xrightarrow{\div(-1)}$$

$$\begin{vmatrix} x + 2y = 1 \\ y = 1 \end{vmatrix} \xrightarrow{-2 \times \text{2nd equation}} \begin{vmatrix} x = -1 \\ y = 1 \end{vmatrix}, \text{ so that } (x, y) = (-1, 1).$$

3.
$$\begin{vmatrix} 2x + 4y = 3 \\ 3x + 6y = 2 \end{vmatrix} \xrightarrow{\div 2} \begin{vmatrix} x + 2y = \frac{3}{2} \\ 3x + 6y = 2 \end{vmatrix} \xrightarrow{-3 \times \text{1st equation}} \begin{vmatrix} x + 2y = \frac{3}{2} \\ 0 = -\frac{5}{2} \end{vmatrix}$$

There is no solution.

5.
$$\begin{vmatrix} 2x + 3y = 0 \\ 4x + 5y = 0 \end{vmatrix} \xrightarrow{\div 2} \begin{vmatrix} x + \frac{3}{2}y = 0 \\ 4x + 5y = 0 \end{vmatrix} \xrightarrow{-4 \times \text{1st equation}}$$

$$\begin{vmatrix} x + \frac{3}{2}y = 0 \\ -y = 0 \end{vmatrix} \xrightarrow{\div(-1)} \begin{vmatrix} x + \frac{3}{2}y = 0 \\ y = 0 \end{vmatrix} \xrightarrow{-\frac{3}{2} \times \text{2nd equation}} \begin{vmatrix} x = 0 \\ y = 0 \end{vmatrix}, \text{ so that } (x, y) = (0, 0).$$

7.
$$\begin{vmatrix} x + 2y + 3z = 1 \\ x + 3y + 4z = 3 \\ x + 4y + 5z = 4 \end{vmatrix} \begin{matrix} \\ -I \\ -I \end{matrix} \xrightarrow{} \begin{vmatrix} x + 2y + 3z = 1 \\ y + z = 2 \\ 2y + 2z = 3 \end{vmatrix} \begin{matrix} -2(II) \\ \\ -2(II) \end{matrix} \xrightarrow{} \begin{vmatrix} x + z = -3 \\ y + z = 2 \\ 0 = -1 \end{vmatrix}$$

This system has no solution.

9.
$$\begin{vmatrix} x + 2y + 3z = 1 \\ 3x + 2y + z = 1 \\ 7x + 2y - 3z = 1 \end{vmatrix} \begin{matrix} \\ -3(I) \\ -7(I) \end{matrix} \xrightarrow{} \begin{vmatrix} x + 2y + 3z = 1 \\ -4y - 8z = -2 \\ -12y - 24z = -6 \end{vmatrix} \xrightarrow{\div(-4)} \begin{vmatrix} x + 2y + 3z = 1 \\ y + 2z = \frac{1}{2} \\ -12y - 24z = -6 \end{vmatrix} \begin{matrix} -2(II) \\ \\ +12(II) \end{matrix} \xrightarrow{}$$

$$\begin{vmatrix} x - z = 0 \\ y + 2z = \frac{1}{2} \\ 0 = 0 \end{vmatrix}$$

This system has infinitely many solutions: if we choose $z = t$, an arbitrary real number, then we get $x = z = t$ and $y = \frac{1}{2} - 2z = \frac{1}{2} - 2t$. Therefore, the general solution is $(x, y, z) = \left(t, \frac{1}{2} - 2t, t\right)$, where t is an arbitrary real number.

11.
$$\begin{vmatrix} x - 2y = 2 \\ 3x + 5y = 17 \end{vmatrix} \xrightarrow{-3(I)} \begin{vmatrix} x - 2y = 2 \\ 11y = 11 \end{vmatrix} \xrightarrow{\div 11} \begin{vmatrix} x - 2y = 2 \\ y = 1 \end{vmatrix} \xrightarrow{+2(II)} \begin{vmatrix} x = 4 \\ y = 1 \end{vmatrix},$$

so that $(x, y) = (4, 1)$.

(Diagram 1)

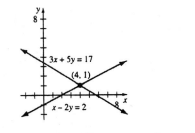

13. $\begin{vmatrix} x - 2y = 3 \\ 2x - 4y = 8 \end{vmatrix} \xrightarrow{\hspace{0.3cm}-2(I)\hspace{0.3cm}} \begin{vmatrix} x - 2y = 3 \\ 0 = 2 \end{vmatrix}$

This system has no solution.

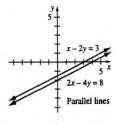

15. The system reduces to $\begin{vmatrix} x = 0 \\ y = 0 \\ z = 0 \end{vmatrix}$ so the unique solution is $(x, y, z) = (0, 0, 0)$. The three planes intersect at the origin.

17. $\begin{vmatrix} x + 2y = a \\ 3x + 5y = b \end{vmatrix} \xrightarrow{\hspace{0.3cm}-3(I)\hspace{0.3cm}} \begin{vmatrix} x + 2y = a \\ -y = -3a + b \end{vmatrix} \xrightarrow{\hspace{0.3cm}\div(-1)\hspace{0.3cm}} \begin{vmatrix} x + 2y = a \\ y = 3a - b \end{vmatrix} \xrightarrow{\hspace{0.3cm}-2(II)\hspace{0.3cm}}$

$\begin{vmatrix} x = -5a + 2b \\ y = 3a - b \end{vmatrix}$, so that $(x, y) = (-5a + 2b, \ 3a - b)$.

19. a. Note that the demand D_1 for product 1 increases with the increase of price P_2; likewise the demand D_2 for product 2 increases with the increase of price P_1. This indicates that the two products are competing; some people will switch if one of the products gets more expensive.

    b. Setting $D_1 = S_1$ and $D_2 = S_2$ we obtain the system $\begin{vmatrix} 70 - 2P_1 + P_2 = -14 + 3P_1 \\ 105 + P_1 - P_2 = -7 + 2P_2 \end{vmatrix}$, or

    $\begin{vmatrix} -5P_1 + P_2 = -84 \\ P_1 - 3P_2 = 112 \end{vmatrix}$, which yields the unique solution $P_1 = 26$ and $P_2 = 46$.

21. The total demand for the products of Industry A is 310 (the consumer demand) plus $0.3b$ (the demand from Industry B). The output a must meet this demand: $a = 310 + 0.3b$.

    Setting up a similar equation for Industry B we obtain the system $\begin{vmatrix} a = 310 + 0.3b \\ b = 100 + 0.5a \end{vmatrix}$ or

    $\begin{vmatrix} a - 0.3b = 310 \\ -0.5a + b = 100 \end{vmatrix}$, which yields the solution $a = 400$ and $b = 300$.

23. a. Substituting $\lambda = 5$ yields the system $\begin{vmatrix} 7x - y = 5x \\ -6x + 8y = 5y \end{vmatrix}$ or $\begin{vmatrix} 2x - y = 0 \\ -6x + 3y = 0 \end{vmatrix}$ or $\begin{vmatrix} 2x - y = 0 \\ 0 = 0 \end{vmatrix}$.

There are infinitely many solutions, of the form $(x, y) = \left(\dfrac{t}{2}, t \right)$, where t is an arbitrary real number.

b. Proceeding as in part (a), we find $(x, y) = \left(-\frac{1}{3}t, t \right)$.

c. Proceedings as in part (a), we find only the solution $(0, 0)$.

25. The system reduces to $\begin{vmatrix} x + z = 1 \\ y - 2z = -3 \\ 0 = k - 7 \end{vmatrix}$.

a. The system has solutions if $k - 7 = 0$, or $k = 7$.

b. If $k = 7$ then the system has infinitely many solutions.

c. If $k = 7$ then we can choose $z = t$ freely and obtain the solutions $(x, y, z) = (1 - t, -3 + 2t, t)$.

27. Let $x =$ the number of male children and $y =$ the number of female children.

Then the statement "Emile has twice as many sisters as brothers" translates into $y = 2(x - 1)$ and "Gertrude has as many brothers as sisters" translates into $x = y - 1$.

Solving the system $\begin{vmatrix} -2x + y = -2 \\ x - y = -1 \end{vmatrix}$ gives $x = 3$ and $y = 4$.

There are seven children in this family.

29. To assure that the graph goes through the point $(1, -1)$, we substitute $t = 1$ and $f(t) = -1$ into the equation $f(t) = a + bt + ct^2$ to give $-1 = a + b + c$.

Proceeding likewise for the two other points, we obtain the system $\begin{vmatrix} a + b + c = -1 \\ a + 2b + 4c = 3 \\ a + 3b + 9c = 13 \end{vmatrix}$.

The solution is $a = 1$, $b = -5$, and $c = 3$, and the polynomial is $f(t) = 1 - 5t + 3t^2$.

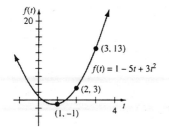

31. The given system reduces ro $\left| \begin{array}{l} x - z = \frac{-5a+2b}{3} \\ y + 2z = \frac{4a-b}{3} \\ 0 = a - 2b + c \end{array} \right|$.

This system has solutions (in fact infinitely many) if $a - 2b + c = 0$.
The points (a, b, c) with this property form a plane through the origin.

33. a.

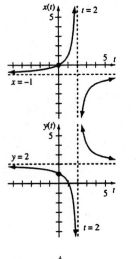

The two lines intersect unless $t = 2$ (in which case both lines have slope -1).
To draw a rough sketch of $x(t)$, note that

$$\lim_{t \to \infty} x(t) = \lim_{t \to -\infty} x(t) = -1 \left(\text{the line } x + \frac{t}{2}y = t \text{ becomes almost horizontal} \right)$$

and

$$\lim_{t \to 2^-} x(t) = \infty, \ \lim_{t \to 2^+} x(t) = -\infty.$$

Also note that $x(t)$ is positive if t is between 0 and 2, and negative otherwise.
Apply similar reasoning to $y(t)$.

b. $x(t) = \dfrac{-t}{t - 2}$, and $y(t) = \dfrac{2t - 2}{t - 2}$.

4

35. To eliminate the arbitrary constant t, we can solve the last equation for t to give $t = z - 2$, and substitute $z - 2$ for t in the first two equations, obtaining $\begin{vmatrix} x = 6 + 5(z-2) \\ y = 4 + 3(z-2) \end{vmatrix}$ or $\begin{vmatrix} x - 5z = -4 \\ y - 3z = -2 \end{vmatrix}$.
This system does the job.

37. Let us start by reducing the system:
$$\begin{vmatrix} x + 2y + 3z = 39 \\ x + 3y + 2z = 34 \\ 3x + 2y + z = 26 \end{vmatrix} \xrightarrow[\;-3(I)\;]{-I} \begin{vmatrix} x + 2y + 3z = 39 \\ y - z = -5 \\ -4y - 8z = -91 \end{vmatrix}$$

Note that the last two equations are exactly those we get when we substitute $x = 39 - 2y - 3z$: either

way, we end up with the system $\begin{vmatrix} y - z = -5 \\ -4y - 8z = -91 \end{vmatrix}$.

1.2

1. $\begin{bmatrix} 1 & 1 & -2 \vdots & 5 \\ 2 & 3 & 4 \vdots & 2 \end{bmatrix} \xrightarrow[-2(I)]{} \begin{bmatrix} 1 & 1 & -2 \vdots & 5 \\ 0 & 1 & 8 \vdots & -8 \end{bmatrix} \xrightarrow{-II} \begin{bmatrix} 1 & 0 & -10 \vdots & 13 \\ 0 & 1 & 8 \vdots & -8 \end{bmatrix}$

$\begin{vmatrix} x - 10z = 13 \\ y + 8z = -8 \end{vmatrix} \longrightarrow \begin{vmatrix} x = 13 + 10z \\ y = -8 - 8z \end{vmatrix}$

$\begin{bmatrix} x \\ y \\ z \end{bmatrix} = \begin{bmatrix} 13 + 10t \\ -8 - 8t \\ t \end{bmatrix}$, where t is an arbitrary real number.

3. $x = 4 - 2y - 3z$

y and z are free variables; let $y = s$ and $z = t$.

$\begin{bmatrix} x \\ y \\ z \end{bmatrix} = \begin{bmatrix} 4 - 2s - 3t \\ s \\ t \end{bmatrix}$, where s and t are arbitrary real numbers.

5. $\begin{bmatrix} 0 & 0 & 1 & 1 \vdots & 0 \\ 0 & 1 & 1 & 0 \vdots & 0 \\ 1 & 1 & 0 & 0 \vdots & 0 \\ 1 & 0 & 0 & 1 \vdots & 0 \end{bmatrix} \xrightarrow{I \leftrightarrow III} \begin{bmatrix} 1 & 1 & 0 & 0 \vdots & 0 \\ 0 & 1 & 1 & 0 \vdots & 0 \\ 0 & 0 & 1 & 1 \vdots & 0 \\ 1 & 0 & 0 & 1 \vdots & 0 \end{bmatrix} \xrightarrow[-(I)]{} \begin{bmatrix} 1 & 1 & 0 & 0 \vdots & 0 \\ 0 & 1 & 1 & 0 \vdots & 0 \\ 0 & 0 & 1 & 1 \vdots & 0 \\ 0 & -1 & 0 & 1 \vdots & 0 \end{bmatrix} \begin{matrix} -II \\ \\ \longrightarrow \\ +II \end{matrix}$

$\begin{bmatrix} 1 & 0 & -1 & 0 \vdots & 0 \\ 0 & 1 & 1 & 0 \vdots & 0 \\ 0 & 0 & 1 & 1 \vdots & 0 \\ 0 & 0 & 1 & 1 \vdots & 0 \end{bmatrix} \begin{matrix} +III \\ \xrightarrow{-III} \\ \\ -III \end{matrix} \begin{bmatrix} 1 & 0 & 0 & 1 \vdots & 0 \\ 0 & 1 & 0 & -1 \vdots & 0 \\ 0 & 0 & 1 & 1 \vdots & 0 \\ 0 & 0 & 0 & 0 \vdots & 0 \end{bmatrix}$

$$
\begin{vmatrix}
x_1 & & & + & x_4 & = & 0 \\
& x_2 & & - & x_4 & = & 0 \\
& & x_3 & + & x_4 & = & 0
\end{vmatrix}
\longrightarrow
\begin{vmatrix}
x_1 = -x_4 \\
x_2 = x_4 \\
x_3 = -x_4
\end{vmatrix}
$$

$$
\begin{bmatrix} x_1 \\ x_2 \\ x_3 \\ x_4 \end{bmatrix}
=
\begin{bmatrix} -t \\ t \\ -t \\ t \end{bmatrix},
\text{ where } t \text{ is an arbitrary real number.}
$$

7.
$$
\begin{bmatrix}
1 & 2 & 0 & 2 & 3 & \vdots & 0 \\
0 & 0 & 1 & 3 & 2 & \vdots & 0 \\
0 & 0 & 1 & 4 & -1 & \vdots & 0 \\
0 & 0 & 0 & 0 & 1 & \vdots & 0
\end{bmatrix}
\xrightarrow{-II}
\begin{bmatrix}
1 & 2 & 0 & 2 & 3 & \vdots & 0 \\
0 & 0 & 1 & 3 & 2 & \vdots & 0 \\
0 & 0 & 0 & 1 & -3 & \vdots & 0 \\
0 & 0 & 0 & 0 & 1 & \vdots & 0
\end{bmatrix}
\begin{array}{l} -2(III) \\ -3(III) \\ \xrightarrow{} \end{array}
$$

$$
\begin{bmatrix}
1 & 2 & 0 & 0 & 9 & \vdots & 0 \\
0 & 0 & 1 & 0 & 11 & \vdots & 0 \\
0 & 0 & 0 & 1 & -3 & \vdots & 0 \\
0 & 0 & 0 & 0 & 1 & \vdots & 0
\end{bmatrix}
\begin{array}{l} -9(IV) \\ -11(IV) \\ +3(IV) \\ \xrightarrow{} \end{array}
\begin{bmatrix}
1 & 2 & 0 & 0 & 0 & \vdots & 0 \\
0 & 0 & 1 & 0 & 0 & \vdots & 0 \\
0 & 0 & 0 & 1 & 0 & \vdots & 0 \\
0 & 0 & 0 & 0 & 1 & \vdots & 0
\end{bmatrix}
$$

$$
\begin{vmatrix}
x_1 + 2x_2 = 0 \\
x_3 = 0 \\
x_4 = 0 \\
x_5 = 0
\end{vmatrix}
\longrightarrow
\begin{vmatrix}
x_1 = -2x_2 \\
x_3 = 0 \\
x_4 = 0 \\
x_5 = 0
\end{vmatrix}
$$

$$
\text{Let } x_2 = t. \quad
\begin{bmatrix} x_1 \\ x_2 \\ x_3 \\ x_4 \\ x_5 \end{bmatrix}
=
\begin{bmatrix} -2t \\ t \\ 0 \\ 0 \\ 0 \end{bmatrix},
\text{ where } t \text{ is an arbitrary real number.}
$$

9.
$$
\begin{bmatrix}
0 & 0 & 0 & 1 & 2 & -1 & \vdots & 2 \\
1 & 2 & 0 & 0 & 1 & -1 & \vdots & 0 \\
1 & 2 & 2 & 0 & -1 & 1 & \vdots & 2
\end{bmatrix}
\xrightarrow{I \leftrightarrow II}
\begin{bmatrix}
1 & 2 & 0 & 0 & 1 & -1 & \vdots & 0 \\
0 & 0 & 0 & 1 & 2 & -1 & \vdots & 2 \\
1 & 2 & 2 & 0 & -2 & 1 & \vdots & 2
\end{bmatrix}
\begin{array}{l} \longrightarrow \\ -I \end{array}
$$

$$
\begin{bmatrix}
1 & 2 & 0 & 0 & 1 & -1 & \vdots & 0 \\
0 & 0 & 0 & 1 & 2 & -1 & \vdots & 2 \\
0 & 0 & 2 & 0 & -2 & 2 & \vdots & 2
\end{bmatrix}
\xrightarrow{II \leftrightarrow III}
\begin{bmatrix}
1 & 2 & 0 & 0 & 1 & -1 & \vdots & 0 \\
0 & 0 & 2 & 0 & -2 & 2 & \vdots & 2 \\
0 & 0 & 0 & 1 & 2 & -1 & \vdots & 2
\end{bmatrix}
\begin{array}{l} \div 2 \longrightarrow \end{array}
$$

$$
\begin{bmatrix}
1 & 2 & 0 & 0 & 1 & -1 & \vdots & 0 \\
0 & 0 & 1 & 0 & -1 & 1 & \vdots & 1 \\
0 & 0 & 0 & 1 & 2 & -1 & \vdots & 2
\end{bmatrix}
$$

$$\left| \begin{array}{l} x_1 + 2x_2 + x_5 - x_6 = 0 \\ \quad\quad\quad x_3 - x_5 + x_6 = 1 \\ \quad\quad\quad x_4 + 2x_5 - x_6 = 2 \end{array} \right| \longrightarrow \left| \begin{array}{l} x_1 = -2x_2 - x_5 + x_6 \\ x_3 = 1 + x_5 - x_6 \\ x_4 = 2 - 2x_5 + x_6 \end{array} \right|$$

Let $x_2 = r$, $x_5 = s$, and $x_6 = t$.

$$\begin{bmatrix} x_1 \\ x_2 \\ x_3 \\ x_4 \\ x_5 \\ x_6 \end{bmatrix} = \begin{bmatrix} -2r - s + t \\ r \\ 1 + s - t \\ 2 - 2s + t \\ s \\ t \end{bmatrix}, \text{ where } r, s \text{ and } t \text{ are arbitrary real numbers.}$$

11. The system reduces to $\left| \begin{array}{ccccc} x_1 & & + & 2x_3 & & = & 0 \\ & x_2 & - & 3x_3 & & = & 4 \\ & & & & x_4 & = & -2 \end{array} \right| \longrightarrow \left| \begin{array}{l} x_1 = -2x_3 \\ x_2 = 4 + 3x_3 \\ x_4 = -2 \end{array} \right|.$

Let $x_3 = t$.

$$\begin{bmatrix} x_1 \\ x_2 \\ x_3 \\ x_4 \end{bmatrix} = \begin{bmatrix} -2t \\ 4 + 3t \\ t \\ -2 \end{bmatrix}$$

13. The system reduces to $\left| \begin{array}{ccccc} x & & - & z & = & 0 \\ & y & + & 2z & = & 0 \\ & & & 0 & = & 1 \end{array} \right|$

There are no solutions.

15. The system reduces to $\left| \begin{array}{ccc} x & & & = & 4 \\ & y & & = & 2 \\ & & z & = & 1 \end{array} \right|.$

17. The system reduces to $\left| \begin{array}{ccccc} x_1 & & & & & = & -\dfrac{8221}{4340} \\[2mm] & x_2 & & & & = & \dfrac{8591}{8680} \\[2mm] & & x_3 & & & = & \dfrac{4695}{434} \\[2mm] & & & x_4 & & = & -\dfrac{459}{434} \\[2mm] & & & & x_5 & = & \dfrac{699}{434} \end{array} \right|$

19. $\begin{bmatrix} 0 \\ 0 \\ 0 \\ 0 \end{bmatrix}$ and $\begin{bmatrix} 1 \\ 0 \\ 0 \\ 0 \end{bmatrix}$

21. Four, namely $\begin{bmatrix} 0 & 0 \\ 0 & 0 \\ 0 & 0 \end{bmatrix}$, $\begin{bmatrix} 1 & k \\ 0 & 0 \\ 0 & 0 \end{bmatrix}$, $\begin{bmatrix} 0 & 1 \\ 0 & 0 \\ 0 & 0 \end{bmatrix}$, $\begin{bmatrix} 1 & 0 \\ 0 & 1 \\ 0 & 0 \end{bmatrix}$ (k is an arbitrary constant.)

23. We need to show that the matrix has the three properties listed on page 16.
    Property a holds by Step 2 of the Gauss-Jordan algorithm (page 17).
    Property b holds by Step 3 of the Gauss-Jordan algorithm.
    Property c holds by Steps 1 and 4 of the algorithm.

25. Yes; if A is transformed into B by a sequence of elementary row operations, then we can recover A from B by applying the inverse operations in the reversed order (compare with Exercise 24).

27. No; whatever elementary row operations you apply to $\begin{bmatrix} 1 & 2 & 3 \\ 4 & 5 & 6 \\ 7 & 8 & 9 \end{bmatrix}$, you cannot make the last column equal to zero.

29. Since the number of oxygen atoms remains constant, we must have $2a + b = 2c + 3d$.

    Considering hydrogen and nitrogen as well, we obtain the system $\begin{vmatrix} 2a & + & b & = & 2c & + & 3d \\ & & 2b & = & c & + & d \\ a & & & = & c & + & d \end{vmatrix}$

    or

    $\begin{vmatrix} 2a & + & b & - & 2c & - & 3d & = & 0 \\ & & 2b & - & c & - & d & = & 0 \\ a & & & - & c & - & d & = & 0 \end{vmatrix}$, which reduces to $\begin{vmatrix} a & & & - & 2d & = & 0 \\ & b & & - & d & = & 0 \\ & & c & - & d & = & 0 \end{vmatrix}$.

    The solutions are $\begin{bmatrix} a \\ b \\ c \\ d \end{bmatrix} = \begin{bmatrix} 2t \\ t \\ t \\ t \end{bmatrix}$.

    To get the smallest positive integers, we set $t = 1$:
    $2NO_2 + H_2O \longrightarrow HNO_2 + HNO_3$

31. Let $f(t) = a + bt + ct^2 + dt^3 + et^4$. Substituting the points in, we get

    $\begin{vmatrix} a & + & b & + & c & + & d & + & e & = & 1 \\ a & + & 2b & + & 4c & + & 8d & + & 16e & = & -1 \\ a & + & 3b & + & 9c & + & 27d & + & 81e & = & -59 \\ a & - & b & + & c & - & d & + & e & = & 5 \\ a & - & 2b & + & 4c & - & 8d & + & 16e & = & -29 \end{vmatrix}$

    This system has the unique solution $a = 1$, $b = -5$, $c = 4$, $d = 3$, and $e = -2$, so that $f(t) = 1 - 5t + 4t^2 + 3t^3 - 2t^4$.

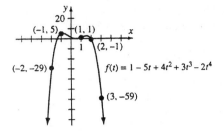

33. Let $f(t) = a + bt + ct^2 + dt^3$, so that $f'(t) = b + 2ct + 3dt^2$.

    Substituting the given points into $f(t)$ and $f'(t)$ we obtain the system

    $$\begin{vmatrix} a & + & b & + & c & + & d & = & 1 \\ a & + & 2b & + & 4c & + & 8d & = & 5 \\ & & b & + & 2c & + & 3d & = & 2 \\ & & b & + & 4c & + & 12d & = & 9 \end{vmatrix}$$

    This system has the unique solution $a = -5, b = 13, c = -10$, and $d = 3$, so that $f(t) = -5 + 13t - 10t^2 + 3t^3$.

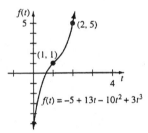

35. We need to solve the system $\begin{vmatrix} x_1 + x_2 + x_3 + x_4 = 0 \\ x_1 + 2x_2 + 3x_3 + 4x_4 = 0 \\ x_1 + 9x_2 + 9x_3 + 7x_4 = 0 \end{vmatrix}$,

    which reduces to $\begin{vmatrix} x_1 & & + & 0.25x_4 & = & 0 \\ & x_2 & - & 1.5x_4 & = & 0 \\ & & x_3 + & 2.25x_4 & = & 0 \end{vmatrix}$

    The solutions are of the form $\begin{bmatrix} x_1 \\ x_2 \\ x_3 \\ x_4 \end{bmatrix} = \begin{bmatrix} -0.25t \\ 1.5t \\ -2.25t \\ t \end{bmatrix}$, where t is an arbitrary real number.

37. Compare with the solution of Exercise 1.1.21.

    The diagram tells us that $\begin{vmatrix} x_1 = 0.2x_2 + 0.3x_3 + 320 \\ x_2 = 0.1x_1 + 0.4x_3 + 90 \\ x_3 = 0.2x_1 + 0.5x_2 + 150 \end{vmatrix}$ or $\begin{vmatrix} x_1 - 0.2x_2 - 0.3x_3 = 320 \\ -0.1x_1 + x_2 - 0.4x_3 = 90 \\ -0.2x_1 - 0.5x_2 + x_3 = 150 \end{vmatrix}$

    This system has the unique solution $x_1 = 500$, $x_2 = 300$, and $x_3 = 400$.

39. a. These components are zero because neither manufacturing not the energy sector directly require agricultural products.

    b. We have to solve the system $x_1\vec{v}_1 + x_2\vec{v}_2 + x_3\vec{v}_3 + \vec{b} = \vec{x}$ or

$$\begin{vmatrix} 0.707x_1 & & & & & = & 13.2 \\ -0.014x_1 & + & 0.793x_2 & - & 0.017x_3 & = & 17.6 \\ -0.044x_1 & + & 0.01x_2 & + & 0.784x_3 & = & 1.8 \end{vmatrix}$$

    The unique solution is approximately $x_1 = 18.67$, $x_2 = 22.60$, and $x_3 = 3.63$.

41. We know that $m_1\vec{v}_1 + m_2\vec{v}_2 = m_1\vec{w}_1 + m_2\vec{w}_2$ or $m_1(\vec{v}_1 - \vec{w}_1) + m_2(\vec{v}_2 - \vec{w}_2) = \vec{0}$

    or $\begin{vmatrix} -3m_1 + 2m_2 = 0 \\ -6m_1 + 4m_2 = 0 \\ -3m_1 + 2m_2 = 0 \end{vmatrix}$.

    We can conclude that $m_1 = \frac{2}{3}m_2$.

43. Plugging the data into the function $S(t)$ we obtain the system

$$\begin{vmatrix} a + \cos\left(\dfrac{2\pi \cdot 47}{365}\right) b + \sin\left(\dfrac{2\pi \cdot 47}{365}\right) c = 11.5 \\[2mm] a + \cos\left(\dfrac{2\pi \cdot 74}{365}\right) b + \sin\left(\dfrac{2\pi \cdot 74}{365}\right) c = 12 \\[2mm] a + \cos\left(\dfrac{2\pi \cdot 273}{365}\right) b + \sin\left(\dfrac{2\pi \cdot 273}{365}\right) c = 12 \end{vmatrix}$$

    The unique solution is approximately $a = 12.17$, $b = -1.15$, and $c = 0.18$, so that

$$S(t) = 12.17 - 1.15\cos\left(\frac{2\pi t}{365}\right) + 0.18\sin\left(\frac{2\pi t}{365}\right).$$

    The longest day is about 13.3 hours.

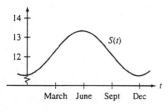

1.3

1. a. No solution, since the last row indicates $0 = 1$.

   b. The unique solution is $x = 5$, $y = 6$.

   c. Infinitely many solutions; the first variable can be chosen freely.

3. This matrix has rank 1 since its rref is $\begin{bmatrix} 1 & 1 & 1 \\ 0 & 0 & 0 \\ 0 & 0 & 0 \end{bmatrix}$.

5. a. $x \begin{bmatrix} 1 \\ 3 \end{bmatrix} + y \begin{bmatrix} 2 \\ 1 \end{bmatrix} = \begin{bmatrix} 7 \\ 11 \end{bmatrix}$

   b. The solution of the system in part (a) is $x = 3$, $y = 2$.

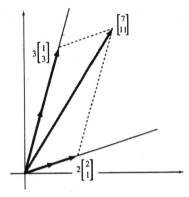

7. A unique solution, since there is only one parallelogram with sides along $\vec{v}_1$ and $\vec{v}_2$ and one vertex at the tip of $\vec{v}_3$.

9. $\begin{bmatrix} 1 & 2 & 3 \\ 4 & 5 & 6 \\ 7 & 8 & 9 \end{bmatrix} \begin{bmatrix} x \\ y \\ z \end{bmatrix} = \begin{bmatrix} 1 \\ 4 \\ 9 \end{bmatrix}$

11. Undefined since the two vectors do not have the same number of components.

13. $\begin{bmatrix} 1 & 2 \\ 3 & 4 \end{bmatrix} \begin{bmatrix} 7 \\ 11 \end{bmatrix} = 7 \begin{bmatrix} 1 \\ 3 \end{bmatrix} + 11 \begin{bmatrix} 2 \\ 4 \end{bmatrix} = \begin{bmatrix} 29 \\ 65 \end{bmatrix}$ or $\begin{bmatrix} 1 & 2 \\ 3 & 4 \end{bmatrix} \begin{bmatrix} 7 \\ 11 \end{bmatrix} = \begin{bmatrix} 1 \cdot 7 + 2 \cdot 11 \\ 3 \cdot 7 + 4 \cdot 11 \end{bmatrix} = \begin{bmatrix} 29 \\ 65 \end{bmatrix}$

15. $[1\ 2\ 3\ 4] \begin{bmatrix} 5 \\ 6 \\ 7 \\ 8 \end{bmatrix} = 5 \cdot 1 + 6 \cdot 2 + 7 \cdot 3 + 4 \cdot 8 = 70$ either way.

17. Undefined, since the matrix has three columns, but the vector has only two components.

19. $\begin{bmatrix} 1 & 1 & -1 \\ -5 & 1 & 1 \\ 1 & -5 & 3 \end{bmatrix} \begin{bmatrix} 1 \\ 2 \\ 3 \end{bmatrix} = 1 \begin{bmatrix} 1 \\ -5 \\ 1 \end{bmatrix} + 2 \begin{bmatrix} 1 \\ 1 \\ -5 \end{bmatrix} + 3 \begin{bmatrix} -1 \\ 1 \\ 3 \end{bmatrix} = \begin{bmatrix} 0 \\ 0 \\ 0 \end{bmatrix}$

21. $\begin{bmatrix} 158 \\ 70 \\ 81 \\ 123 \end{bmatrix}$

23. All variables are leading, that is, there is a leading one in each column of the rref: $\begin{bmatrix} 1 & 0 & 0 \\ 0 & 1 & 0 \\ 0 & 0 & 1 \\ 0 & 0 & 0 \end{bmatrix}$.

25. In this case, rref(A) has a row of zeros, so that $\text{rank}(A) < 4$; there will be a nonleading variable. The system $A\vec{x} = \vec{c}$ could have infinitely many solutions (for example, when $\vec{c} = \vec{0}$) or no solutions (for example, when $\vec{c} = \vec{b}$), but it cannot have a unique solution, by Fact 1.3.4.

27. a. True, since $\text{rref}[A \vdots \vec{b}]$ contains a row $[0\ 0\ \ldots\ 0\ \vdots\ 1]$.

    b. False; as a counterexample, consider the case when A is the zero matrix and $\vec{b}$ the zero vector.

29. True; if $A\vec{x} = \vec{b}$ is inconsistent then $\text{rank}[A \vdots \vec{b}] = \text{rank}(A) + 1$, since there will be an extra leading one in the last column of the augmented matrix:

    However, if $A\vec{x} = \vec{b}$ is consistent then $\text{rank}[A \vdots \vec{b}] = \text{rank}(A)$, since we do not have an extra leading one in the last column.

31. By Fact 1.3.4, rref $(A) = \begin{bmatrix} 1 & 0 & 0 & 0 \\ 0 & 1 & 0 & 0 \\ 0 & 0 & 1 & 0 \\ 0 & 0 & 0 & 1 \end{bmatrix}$.

33. The ith component of $A\vec{x}$ is $[0\ 0\ \ldots\ 1\ \ldots\ 0] \begin{bmatrix} x_1 \\ x_2 \\ \cdots \\ x_i \\ \cdots \\ x_n \end{bmatrix} = x_i$. (The 1 is in the ith position.)

    Therefore, $A\vec{x} = \vec{x}$.

35. Write $A = [\vec{v}_1\ \vec{v}_2\ \ldots\ \vec{v}_i\ \ldots\ \vec{v}_n]$, then

$$A\vec{e}_i = [\vec{v}_1\ \vec{v}_2\ \ldots\ \vec{v}_i\ \ldots\ \vec{v}_n] \begin{bmatrix} 0 \\ 0 \\ \cdots \\ 1 \\ \cdots \\ 0 \end{bmatrix} = 0\vec{v}_1 + 0\vec{v}_2 + \cdots + 1\vec{v}_i + \cdots + 0\vec{v}_n = \vec{v}_i = i\text{th column of } A.$$

37. We have to solve the system $\begin{vmatrix} x_1 & + & 2x_2 & & = & 2 \\ & & & x_3 & = & 1 \end{vmatrix}$ or $\begin{vmatrix} x_1 = 2 - 2x_2 \\ x_3 = 1 \end{vmatrix}$.

    Let $x_2 = t$. Then the solutions are of the form $\begin{bmatrix} x_1 \\ x_2 \\ x_3 \end{bmatrix} = \begin{bmatrix} 2 - 2t \\ t \\ 1 \end{bmatrix}$, where t is an arbitrary real number.

39. We will usually get $\text{rref}(A) = \begin{bmatrix} 1 & 0 & 0 & a \\ 0 & 1 & 0 & b \\ 0 & 0 & 1 & c \end{bmatrix}$, where $a, b,$ and c are arbitrary.

    (Compare with the summary at the end of Exercise 38.)

41. If $A\vec{x} = \vec{b}$ is a "random" system, then $\text{rref}(A)$ will usually be $\begin{bmatrix} 1 & 0 & 0 \\ 0 & 1 & 0 \\ 0 & 0 & 1 \end{bmatrix}$ (by Exercise 38), so that we will have a unique solution.

43. If $A\vec{x} = \vec{b}$ is a "random" system of equations with three unknowns, then $\text{rref}[A\,\vdots\,b]$ will usually be

    $\begin{bmatrix} 1 & 0 & 0 & \vdots & 0 \\ 0 & 1 & 0 & \vdots & 0 \\ 0 & 0 & 1 & \vdots & 0 \\ 0 & 0 & 0 & \vdots & 1 \end{bmatrix}$ (see the summary to Exercise 38), so that the system is inconsistent.

45. Write $A = [\vec{v}_1 \ \vec{v}_2 \ \dots \ \vec{v}_n]$ and $\vec{x} = \begin{bmatrix} x_1 \\ \dots \\ x_n \end{bmatrix}$. Then $A(k\vec{x}) = [\vec{v}_1 \ \dots \ \vec{v}_n] \begin{bmatrix} kx_1 \\ \dots \\ kx_n \end{bmatrix} = kx_1\vec{v}_1 + \dots + kx_n\vec{v}_n$

    and $k(A\vec{x}) = k(x_1\vec{v}_1 + \dots + x_n\vec{v}_n) = kx_1\vec{v}_1 + \dots + kx_n\vec{v}_n$. The two results agree, as claimed.

47. a. $\vec{x} = \vec{0}$ is a solution.

    b. This holds by part (a) and Fact 1.3.3.

    c. If $\vec{x}_1$ and $\vec{x}_2$ are solutions, then $A\vec{x}_1 = \vec{0}$ and $A\vec{x}_2 = \vec{0}$.

       Therefore, $A(\vec{x}_1 + \vec{x}_2) = A\vec{x}_1 + A\vec{x}_2 = \vec{0} + \vec{0} = \vec{0}$, so that $\vec{x}_1 + \vec{x}_2$ is a solution as well. Note that we have used Fact 1.3.7a.

    d. $A(k\vec{x}) = k(A\vec{x}) = k\vec{0} = \vec{0}$

       We have used Fact 1.3.7b.

49. a. This system has either infinitely many solutions (if the right-most column of $\text{rref}[A\,\vdots\,b]$ does not contain a leading one), or no solutions (if the right-most column *does* contain a leading one).

13

b. This system has either a unique solution (if $\text{rank}[A\vdots b] = 3$), or no solution (if $\text{rank}[A\vdots b] = 4$).

c. The right-most column of $\text{rref}[A\vdots b]$ must contain a leading one, so that the system has no solutions.

d. This system has infinitely many solutions, since there is one non-leading variable.

51. For $B\vec{x}$ to be defined, the number of columns of B, which is s, must equal the number of components of $\vec{x}$, which is p, so that we must have $s = p$. Then $B\vec{x}$ will be a vector in $\mathbb{R}^r$; for $A(B\vec{x})$ to be defined we must have $n = r$. Summary: We must have $s = p$ and $n = r$.

53. Yes; write $A = [\vec{v}_1 \ \ldots \ \vec{v}_n]$, $B = [\vec{w}_1 \ \ldots \ \vec{w}_n]$, and $\vec{x} = \begin{bmatrix} x_1 \\ \ldots \\ x_n \end{bmatrix}$.

Then $(A + B)\vec{x} = [\vec{v}_1 + \vec{w}_1 \ \ldots \ \vec{v}_n + \vec{w}_n] \begin{bmatrix} x_1 \\ \ldots \\ x_n \end{bmatrix} = x_1(\vec{v}_1 + \vec{w}_1) + \cdots + x_n(\vec{v}_n + \vec{w}_n)$ and

$A\vec{x} + B\vec{x} = [\vec{v}_1 \ \ldots \ \vec{v}_n] \begin{bmatrix} x_1 \\ \ldots \\ x_n \end{bmatrix} + [\vec{w}_1 \ \ldots \ \vec{w}_n] \begin{bmatrix} x_1 \\ \ldots \\ x_n \end{bmatrix} = x_1\vec{v}_1 + \cdots + x_n\vec{v}_n + x_1\vec{w}_1 + \cdots + x_n\vec{w}_n$.

The two results agree, as claimed.

55. We are looking for constants a and b such that $a \begin{bmatrix} 1 \\ 2 \\ 3 \end{bmatrix} + b \begin{bmatrix} 4 \\ 5 \\ 6 \end{bmatrix} = \begin{bmatrix} 7 \\ 8 \\ 9 \end{bmatrix}$.

The resulting system $\begin{vmatrix} a + 4b = 7 \\ 2a + 5b = 8 \\ 3a + 6b = 9 \end{vmatrix}$ has the unique solution $a = -1$, $b = 2$, so that $\begin{bmatrix} 7 \\ 8 \\ 9 \end{bmatrix}$ is indeed

a linear combination of the vector $\begin{bmatrix} 1 \\ 2 \\ 3 \end{bmatrix}$ and $\begin{bmatrix} 4 \\ 5 \\ 6 \end{bmatrix}$.

57. Pick a vector on each line, say $\begin{bmatrix} 2 \\ 1 \end{bmatrix}$ on $y = \dfrac{x}{2}$ and $\begin{bmatrix} 1 \\ 3 \end{bmatrix}$ on $y = 3x$.

Then write $\begin{bmatrix} 7 \\ 11 \end{bmatrix}$ as a linear combination of $\begin{bmatrix} 2 \\ 1 \end{bmatrix}$ and $\begin{bmatrix} 1 \\ 3 \end{bmatrix}$: $a \begin{bmatrix} 2 \\ 1 \end{bmatrix} + b \begin{bmatrix} 1 \\ 3 \end{bmatrix} = \begin{bmatrix} 7 \\ 11 \end{bmatrix}$.

The unique solution is $a = 2$, $b = 3$, so that the desired representation is $\begin{bmatrix} 7 \\ 11 \end{bmatrix} = \begin{bmatrix} 4 \\ 2 \end{bmatrix} + \begin{bmatrix} 3 \\ 9 \end{bmatrix}$.

$\begin{bmatrix} 4 \\ 2 \end{bmatrix}$ is on the line $y = \dfrac{x}{2}$; $\begin{bmatrix} 3 \\ 9 \end{bmatrix}$ is on line $y = 3x$.

True or False

1. T, by Definition on Page 16

3. F, by Example 3a of Section 1.3

5. T, by Fact 1.3.4.

7. F, by Fact 1.3.4

9. T, by Definition 1.3.6

11. F; The rank is 1

13. T; Let $A = \begin{bmatrix} -3 & 0 \\ -5 & 0 \\ -7 & 0 \end{bmatrix}$, for example.

15. T; The last component of the left-hand side is zero for all vectors $\vec{x}$.

17. T; Find rref

19. F; Consider the 4×3 matrix A that contains all zeroes, except for a 1 in the lower left corner.

21. F; Find rref to see that the rank is always 2.

23. F; Let $\vec{u} = \begin{bmatrix} 1 \\ 0 \end{bmatrix}, \vec{v} = \begin{bmatrix} 2 \\ 0 \end{bmatrix}, \vec{w} = \begin{bmatrix} 0 \\ 1 \end{bmatrix}$, for example.

25. F; Let $A = \begin{bmatrix} 0 & 1 & 0 \\ 0 & 0 & 1 \\ 0 & 0 & 0 \end{bmatrix}$ and $B = \begin{bmatrix} 1 & 0 & 0 \\ 0 & 1 & 0 \\ 0 & 0 & 0 \end{bmatrix}$, for example. We can apply elementary row operations to A all we want, we will always end up with a matrix that has all zeros in the first column.

27. F; The system $x = 2$, $y = 3$, $x + y = 5$ has a unique solution.

29. F; Let $A = \begin{bmatrix} 1 & 0 \\ 0 & 1 \\ 1 & 1 \end{bmatrix}$ and $\vec{b} = \begin{bmatrix} 2 \\ 3 \\ 5 \end{bmatrix}$, for example.

31. T; By Example 3c of Section 1.3, the equation $A\vec{x} = \vec{0}$ has the unique solution $\vec{x} = \vec{0}$. Now note that $A(\vec{v} - \vec{w}) = \vec{0}$, so that $\vec{v} - \vec{w} = \vec{0}$ and $\vec{v} = \vec{w}$.

33. F; Let $\vec{u} = \begin{bmatrix} 2 \\ 0 \end{bmatrix}$, $\vec{v} = \begin{bmatrix} 1 \\ 0 \end{bmatrix}$, $\vec{w} = \begin{bmatrix} 0 \\ 1 \end{bmatrix}$, for example.

35. F; Let $A = B = \begin{bmatrix} 1 & 0 \\ 0 & 1 \end{bmatrix}$, for example.

Chapter 2

2.1

1. Not a linear transformation, since $y_2 = x_2 + 2$ is not linear in our sense.

3. Not linear, since $y_2 = x_1 x_3$ is nonlinear

5. By Fact 2.1.2, the three columns of the 2×3 matrix A are $T(\tilde{e}_1), T(\tilde{e}_2)$, and $T(\tilde{e}_3)$, so that
$$A = \begin{bmatrix} 7 & 6 & -13 \\ 11 & 9 & 17 \end{bmatrix}.$$

7. Note that $x_1 \bar{v}_1 + \cdots + x_n \bar{v}_n = [\bar{v}_1 \ldots \bar{v}_n] \begin{bmatrix} x_1 \\ \cdots \\ x_n \end{bmatrix}$, so that T is indeed linear, with matrix $[\bar{v}_1 \ \bar{v}_2 \ \cdots \ \bar{v}_n]$.

9. We have to attempt to solve the equation $\begin{bmatrix} y_1 \\ y_2 \end{bmatrix} = \begin{bmatrix} 2 & 3 \\ 6 & 9 \end{bmatrix} \begin{bmatrix} x_1 \\ x_2 \end{bmatrix}$ for x_1 and x_2. Reducing the system
$$\begin{vmatrix} 2x_1 & + & 3x_2 & = & y_1 \\ 6x_1 & + & 9x_2 & = & & y_2 \end{vmatrix} \text{ we obtain } \begin{vmatrix} x_1 + 1.5x_2 = 0.5y_1 \\ 0 = -3y_1 + y_2 \end{vmatrix}.$$
No unique solution (x_1, x_2) can be found for a given (y_1, y_2); the matrix is noninvertible.

11. We have to attempt to solve the equation $\begin{bmatrix} y_1 \\ y_2 \end{bmatrix} = \begin{bmatrix} 1 & 2 \\ 3 & 9 \end{bmatrix} \begin{bmatrix} x_1 \\ x_2 \end{bmatrix}$ for x_1 and x_2. Reducing the system $\begin{vmatrix} x_1 & + & 2x_2 & = & y_1 \\ 3x_1 & + & 9x_2 & = & & y_2 \end{vmatrix}$ we find that $\begin{vmatrix} x_1 & = & 3y_1 - \frac{2}{3}y_2 \\ x_2 & = & -y_1 + \frac{1}{3}y_2 \end{vmatrix}$. The inverse matrix is $\begin{bmatrix} 3 & -\frac{2}{3} \\ -1 & \frac{1}{3} \end{bmatrix}.$

13. a. First suppose that $a \neq 0$. We have to attempt to solve the equation $\begin{bmatrix} y_1 \\ y_2 \end{bmatrix} = \begin{bmatrix} a & b \\ c & d \end{bmatrix} \begin{bmatrix} x_1 \\ x_2 \end{bmatrix}$ for x_1 and x_2.

$$\begin{vmatrix} ax_1 & + & bx_2 & = & y_1 \\ cx_1 & + & dx_2 & = & & y_2 \end{vmatrix} \xrightarrow{\div a_1} \begin{vmatrix} x_1 & + & \frac{b}{a}x_2 & = & \frac{1}{a}y_1 \\ cx_1 & + & dx_2 & = & & y_2 \end{vmatrix} -c(I)$$

$$\begin{vmatrix} x_1 & + & \frac{b}{a}x_2 & = & \frac{1}{a}y_1 \\ & & (d - \frac{bc}{a})x_2 & = & -\frac{c}{a}y_1 & + & y_2 \end{vmatrix}$$

$$\begin{vmatrix} x_1 & + & \frac{b}{a}x_2 & = & \frac{1}{a}y_1 \\ & & (\frac{ad-bc}{a})x_2 & = & -\frac{c}{a}y_1 & + & y_2 \end{vmatrix}$$

We can solve this system for x_1 and x_2 if (and only if) $ad - bc \neq 0$, as claimed.

If $a = 0$, then we have to consider the system

$$\left| \begin{array}{rcl} & bx_2 & = & y_1 \\ cx_1 & + \; dx_2 & = & y_2 \end{array} \right| \xrightarrow{I \leftrightarrow II} \left| \begin{array}{rcl} cx_1 & + \; dx_2 & = & y_2 \\ & bx_2 & = & y_1 \end{array} \right|$$

We can solve for x_1 and x_2 provided that both b and c are nonzero, that is if $bc \neq 0$. Since $a = 0$, this means that $ad - bc \neq 0$, as claimed.

b. First suppose that $ad - bc \neq 0$ and $a \neq 0$. Let $D = ad - bc$ for simplicity. We continue our work in part (a):

$$\left| \begin{array}{rcl} x_1 & + \; \frac{b}{a}x_2 & = & \frac{1}{a}y_1 \\ & \frac{D}{a}x_2 & = & -\frac{c}{a}y_1 & + \; y_2 \end{array} \right| \cdot \frac{a}{D}$$

$$\left| \begin{array}{rcl} x_1 & + \; \frac{b}{a}x_2 & = & \frac{1}{a}y_1 \\ & x_2 & = & -\frac{c}{D}y_1 & + \; \frac{a}{D}y_2 \end{array} \right| -\frac{b}{a}(II)$$

$$\left| \begin{array}{rcl} x_1 & = & (\frac{1}{a} + \frac{bc}{aD})y_1 & - \; \frac{b}{D}y_2 \\ x_2 & = & -\frac{c}{D}y_1 & + \; \frac{b}{D}y_2 \end{array} \right|$$

$$\left| \begin{array}{rcl} x_1 & = & \frac{d}{D}y_1 & - \; \frac{b}{D}y_2 \\ x_2 & = & -\frac{c}{D}y_1 & + \; \frac{a}{D}y_2 \end{array} \right|$$

$$\left(\text{Note that } \frac{1}{a} + \frac{bc}{aD} = \frac{D + bc}{aD} = \frac{ad}{aD} = \frac{d}{D}. \right)$$

It follows that $\begin{bmatrix} a & b \\ c & d \end{bmatrix}^{-1} = \dfrac{1}{ad - bc} \begin{bmatrix} d & -b \\ -c & a \end{bmatrix}$, as claimed. If $ad - bc \neq 0$ and $a = 0$, then we have to solve the system

$$\left| \begin{array}{rcl} cx_1 + dx_2 = y_2 & \div c \\ bx_2 = y_1 & \div b \end{array} \right|$$

$$\left| \begin{array}{rcl} x_1 + \frac{d}{c}x_2 = \frac{1}{c}y_2 \\ x_2 = \frac{1}{b}y_1 \end{array} \right| -\frac{d}{c}(II)$$

$$\left| \begin{array}{rcl} x_1 & = & -\frac{d}{bc}y_1 & + \frac{1}{c}y_2 \\ x_2 & = & \frac{1}{b}y_1 \end{array} \right|$$

It follows that $\begin{bmatrix} a & b \\ c & d \end{bmatrix}^{-1} = \begin{bmatrix} -\frac{d}{bc} & \frac{1}{c} \\ \frac{1}{b} & 0 \end{bmatrix} = \dfrac{1}{ad - bc} \begin{bmatrix} d & -b \\ -c & a \end{bmatrix}$ (recall that $a = 0$), as claimed.

15. By Exercise 13(a), the matrix $\begin{bmatrix} a & -b \\ b & a \end{bmatrix}$ is invertible if (and only if) $a^2 + b^2 \neq 0$, which is the case unless $a = b = 0$. If $\begin{bmatrix} a & -b \\ b & a \end{bmatrix}$ is invertible, then its inverse is $\dfrac{1}{a^2 + b^2} \begin{bmatrix} a & b \\ -b & a \end{bmatrix}$, by Exercise 13(b).

17

17. If $A = \begin{bmatrix} -1 & 0 \\ 0 & -1 \end{bmatrix}$, then $A\vec{x} = -\vec{x}$ for all $\vec{x}$ in $\mathbb{R}^2$, so that A represents a reflection about the origin. This transformation is its own inverse: $A^{-1} = A$.

19. If $A = \begin{bmatrix} 1 & 0 \\ 0 & 0 \end{bmatrix}$, then $A \begin{bmatrix} x_1 \\ x_2 \end{bmatrix} = \begin{bmatrix} x_1 \\ 0 \end{bmatrix}$, so that A represents the orthogonal projection onto the $\cdot\vec{e}_1$ axis. This transformation is not invertible, since the equation $A\vec{x} = \begin{bmatrix} 1 \\ 0 \end{bmatrix}$ has infinitely many solutions $\vec{x}$.

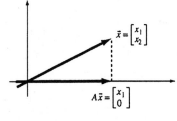

21. Compare with Example 5.

    If $A = \begin{bmatrix} 0 & 1 \\ -1 & 0 \end{bmatrix}$, then $A \begin{bmatrix} x_1 \\ x_2 \end{bmatrix} = \begin{bmatrix} x_2 \\ -x_1 \end{bmatrix}$. Note that the vectors $\vec{x}$ and $A\vec{x}$ are perpendicular and have the same length. If $\vec{x}$ is in the first quadrant, then $A\vec{x}$ is in the fourth. Therefore, A represents the rotation through an angle of $90°$ in the clockwise direction. The inverse $A^{-1} = \begin{bmatrix} 0 & -1 \\ 1 & 0 \end{bmatrix}$ represents the rotation through $90°$ in the counterclockwise direction

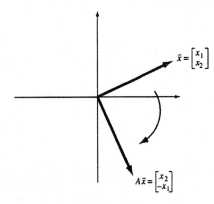

23. Compare with Exercise 21.

    Note that $A = 2 \begin{bmatrix} 0 & 1 \\ -1 & 0 \end{bmatrix}$, so that A represents a rotation through an angle of $90°$ in the clockwise direction, followed by a dilation by the factor of 2.

The inverse $A^{-1} = \begin{bmatrix} 0 & -\frac{1}{2} \\ \frac{1}{2} & 0 \end{bmatrix}$ represents a rotation through an angle of 90° in the counterclockwise direction, followed by a dilation by the factor of $\frac{1}{2}$.

25. The matrix represents a dilation by the factor of 2.

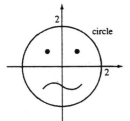

27. Matrix represents a reflection in the $\vec{e}_1$ axis.

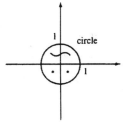

29. Matrix represents a reflection in the origin. Compare with Exercise 17.

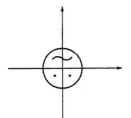

31. The image must be reflected in the $\vec{e}_2$ axis, that is $\begin{bmatrix} x_1 \\ x_2 \end{bmatrix}$ must be transformed into $\begin{bmatrix} -x_1 \\ x_2 \end{bmatrix}$: This can be accomplished by means of the linear transformation $T(\vec{x}) = \begin{bmatrix} -1 & 0 \\ 0 & 1 \end{bmatrix} \vec{x}.$

33. By Fact 2.1.2, $A = \begin{bmatrix} T\begin{bmatrix} 1 \\ 0 \end{bmatrix} & T\begin{bmatrix} 0 \\ 1 \end{bmatrix} \end{bmatrix}$. Now consider the figure below.

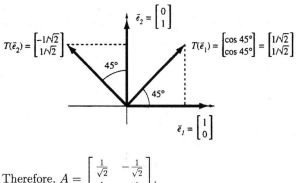

Therefore, $A = \begin{bmatrix} \frac{1}{\sqrt{2}} & -\frac{1}{\sqrt{2}} \\ \frac{1}{\sqrt{2}} & \frac{1}{\sqrt{2}} \end{bmatrix}$.

35. We want to find a matrix $A = \begin{bmatrix} a & b \\ c & d \end{bmatrix}$ such that $A \begin{bmatrix} 5 \\ 42 \end{bmatrix} = \begin{bmatrix} 89 \\ 52 \end{bmatrix}$ and $A \begin{bmatrix} 6 \\ 41 \end{bmatrix} = \begin{bmatrix} 88 \\ 53 \end{bmatrix}$. This

amounts to solving the system $\begin{vmatrix} 5a + 42b & = 89 \\ 6a + 41b & = 88 \\ & 5c + 42d = 52 \\ & 6c + 41d = 53 \end{vmatrix}$.

(Here we really have two systems with two unknowns each.)

The unique solution is $a = 1$, $b = 2$, $c = 2$, and $d = 1$, so that $A = \begin{bmatrix} 1 & 2 \\ 2 & 1 \end{bmatrix}$.

37. Since $\vec{x} = \vec{v} + k(\vec{w} - \vec{v})$, we have $T(\vec{x}) = T(\vec{v} + k(\vec{w} - \vec{v})) = T(\vec{v}) + k(T(\vec{w}) - T(\vec{v}))$, by Exercise 36. Since k is between 0 and 1, the tip of this vector $T(\vec{x})$ is on the line segment connecting the tips of $T(\vec{v})$ and $T(\vec{w})$.

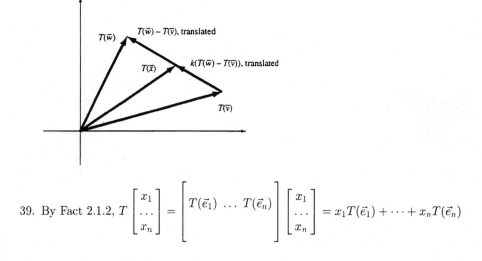

39. By Fact 2.1.2, $T \begin{bmatrix} x_1 \\ \dots \\ x_n \end{bmatrix} = \begin{bmatrix} T(\vec{e}_1) & \dots & T(\vec{e}_n) \end{bmatrix} \begin{bmatrix} x_1 \\ \dots \\ x_n \end{bmatrix} = x_1 T(\vec{e}_1) + \dots + x_n T(\vec{e}_n)$

41. These linear transformations are of the form $[y] = [a \ b] \begin{bmatrix} x_1 \\ x_2 \end{bmatrix}$, or $y = ax_1 + bx_2$. The graph of such a function is a plane through the origin.

43. a. $T(\vec{x}) = \begin{bmatrix} 2 \\ 3 \\ 4 \end{bmatrix} \cdot \begin{bmatrix} x_1 \\ x_2 \\ x_3 \end{bmatrix} = 2x_1 + 3x_2 + 4x_3 = [2 \ 3 \ 4] \begin{bmatrix} x_1 \\ x_2 \\ x_3 \end{bmatrix}$

   The transformation is indeed linear, with matrix [2 3 4].

   b. If $\vec{v} = \begin{bmatrix} v_1 \\ v_2 \\ v_3 \end{bmatrix}$, then T is linear with matrix $[v_1 \ v_2 \ v_3]$, as in part (a).

   c. Let $[a \ b \ c]$ be the matrix of T. Then $T \begin{bmatrix} x_1 \\ x_2 \\ x_3 \end{bmatrix} = [a \ b \ c] \begin{bmatrix} x_1 \\ x_2 \\ x_3 \end{bmatrix} = ax_1 + bx_2 + cx_3 = \begin{bmatrix} a \\ b \\ c \end{bmatrix} \cdot \begin{bmatrix} x_1 \\ x_2 \\ x_3 \end{bmatrix}$,

   so that $\vec{v} = \begin{bmatrix} a \\ b \\ c \end{bmatrix}$ does the job.

45. False; as a counterexample consider the linear transformation $T \begin{bmatrix} x_1 \\ x_2 \\ x_3 \end{bmatrix} = \begin{bmatrix} x_1 \\ x_2 \\ 0 \end{bmatrix}$, the orthogonal

   projection onto the $\vec{e}_1 - \vec{e}_2$ plane.
   Let $\vec{v} = \vec{e}_1$ and $\vec{w} = \vec{e}_2$.
   Then $T(\vec{v} \times \vec{w}) = T(\vec{e}_1 \times \vec{e}_2) = T(\vec{e}_3) = \vec{0}$, but $T(\vec{v}) \times T(\vec{w}) = T(\vec{e}_1) \times T(\vec{e}_2) = \vec{e}_1 \times \vec{e}_2 = \vec{e}_3$.

2.2

1. See Example 2.

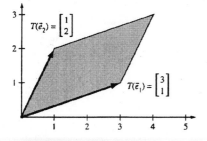

3. Compare with Example 2.
   If $\vec{x}$ is in the unit square in $\mathbb{R}^2$, then $\vec{x} = x_1 \vec{e}_1 + x_2 \vec{e}_2$ with $0 \le x_1, \ x_2 \le 1$, so that
   $T(\vec{x}) = T(x_1 \vec{e}_1 + x_2 \vec{e}_2) = x_1 T(\vec{e}_1) + x_2 T(\vec{e}_2)$.

The image of the unit square is a parallelogram in $\mathbb{R}^3$; two of its sides are $T(\vec{e}_1)$ and $T(\vec{e}_2)$, and the origin is one of its vertices.

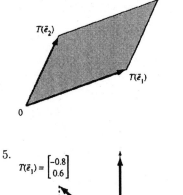

5. $T(\vec{e}_1) = \begin{bmatrix} -0.8 \\ 0.6 \end{bmatrix}$

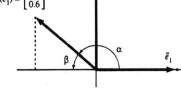

Note that $\sin\beta = 0.6$ so that $\beta = \arcsin(0.6) \approx 0.6435$, and $a = \pi - \beta \approx 2.498$.

7. By Fact 2.2.7, $\text{ref}_L \begin{bmatrix} 1 \\ 1 \\ 1 \end{bmatrix} = 2\left(\vec{u} \cdot \begin{bmatrix} 1 \\ 1 \\ 1 \end{bmatrix}\right)\vec{u} - \begin{bmatrix} 1 \\ 1 \\ 1 \end{bmatrix}$, where $\vec{u}$ is a unit vector on L. To get $\vec{u}$, we

normalize $\begin{bmatrix} 2 \\ 1 \\ 2 \end{bmatrix}$:

$\vec{u} = \dfrac{1}{3}\begin{bmatrix} 2 \\ 1 \\ 2 \end{bmatrix}$, so that $\text{ref}_L \begin{bmatrix} 1 \\ 1 \\ 1 \end{bmatrix} = 2\dfrac{5}{3} \cdot \dfrac{1}{3}\begin{bmatrix} 2 \\ 1 \\ 2 \end{bmatrix} - \begin{bmatrix} 1 \\ 1 \\ 1 \end{bmatrix} = \begin{bmatrix} \frac{11}{9} \\ \frac{1}{9} \\ \frac{11}{9} \end{bmatrix}$.

9. Examine the effect this transformation has on the unit square (compare with Example 6):

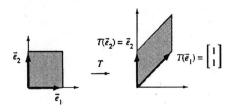

This is a shear parallel to the $\vec{e}_2$ axis.

22

11. In Exercise 10 we found the matrix $A = \begin{bmatrix} 0.64 & 0.48 \\ 0.48 & 0.36 \end{bmatrix}$ of the projection onto the line L. By Fact 2.2.6,

    $\text{ref}_L \vec{x} = 2(\text{proj}_L \vec{x}) - \vec{x} = 2A\vec{x} - \vec{x} = (2A - I_2)\vec{x}$, so that the matrix of the reflection is

    $2A - I_2 = \begin{bmatrix} 0.28 & 0.96 \\ 0.96 & -0.28 \end{bmatrix}$.

13. By Fact 2.2.6,

    $$\text{ref}_L \begin{bmatrix} x_1 \\ x_2 \end{bmatrix} = 2\left(\begin{bmatrix} u_1 \\ u_2 \end{bmatrix} \cdot \begin{bmatrix} x_1 \\ x_2 \end{bmatrix} \right) \begin{bmatrix} u_1 \\ u_2 \end{bmatrix} - \begin{bmatrix} x_1 \\ x_2 \end{bmatrix}$$

    $$= 2(u_1 x_1 + u_2 x_2) \begin{bmatrix} u_1 \\ u_2 \end{bmatrix} - \begin{bmatrix} x_1 \\ x_2 \end{bmatrix} = \begin{bmatrix} (2u_1^2 - 1)x_1 + 2u_1 u_2 x_2 \\ 2u_1 u_2 x_1 + (2u_2^2 - 1)x_2 \end{bmatrix}.$$

    The matrix is $\begin{bmatrix} 2u_1^2 - 1 & 2u_1 u_2 \\ 2u_1 u_2 & 2u_2^2 - 1 \end{bmatrix}$.

15. Proceeding as in Exercise 13, we find that A is the matrix whose ijth entry is $2u_i u_j$ if $i \neq j$ and $u_i^2 - 1$ if $i = j$:

    $$A = \begin{bmatrix} u_1^2 - 1 & 2u_1 u_2 & \dots & 2u_1 u_n \\ 2u_2 u_1 & u_2^2 - 1 & \dots & 2u_2 u_n \\ \vdots & \vdots & \ddots & \vdots \\ 2u_n u_1 & 2u_n u_2 & \dots & u_n^2 - 1 \end{bmatrix}$$

17. a.

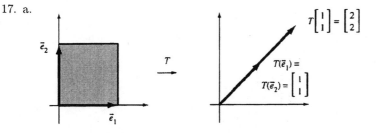

The image is a "collapsed parallelogram"; it is just the line segment from $\begin{bmatrix} 0 \\ 0 \end{bmatrix}$ to $\begin{bmatrix} 2 \\ 2 \end{bmatrix}$.

b. The figure below shows that the matrix of the projection onto the line through $\begin{bmatrix} 1 \\ 1 \end{bmatrix}$ is $\begin{bmatrix} \frac{1}{2} & \frac{1}{2} \\ \frac{1}{2} & \frac{1}{2} \end{bmatrix}$.

Therefore $\begin{bmatrix} 1 & 1 \\ 1 & 1 \end{bmatrix} = 2 \begin{bmatrix} \frac{1}{2} & \frac{1}{2} \\ \frac{1}{2} & \frac{1}{2} \end{bmatrix}$ represents this projection followed by a dilation by 2.

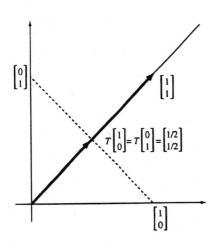

19. $T(\vec{e}_1) = \vec{e}_1$, $T(\vec{e}_2) = \vec{e}_2$, and $T(\vec{e}_3) = \vec{0}$, so that the matrix is $\begin{bmatrix} 1 & 0 & 0 \\ 0 & 1 & 0 \\ 0 & 0 & 0 \end{bmatrix}$.

21. $T(\vec{e}_1) = \vec{e}_2$, $T(\vec{e}_2) = -\vec{e}_1$, and $T(\vec{e}_3) = \vec{e}_3$, so that the matrix is $\begin{bmatrix} 0 & -1 & 0 \\ 1 & 0 & 0 \\ 0 & 0 & 1 \end{bmatrix}$.

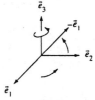

23. $T(\vec{e}_1) = \vec{e}_3$, $T(\vec{e}_2) = \vec{e}_2$, and $T(\vec{e}_3) = \vec{e}_1$, so that the matrix is $\begin{bmatrix} 0 & 0 & 1 \\ 0 & 1 & 0 \\ 1 & 0 & 0 \end{bmatrix}$.

25. The matrix $A = \begin{bmatrix} 1 & k \\ 0 & 1 \end{bmatrix}$ represents a shear parallel to the $\vec{e}_1$ axis, and its inverse $A^{-1} = \begin{bmatrix} 1 & -k \\ 0 & 1 \end{bmatrix}$ represents such a shear as well, but "the other way."

27. Yes; let us verify the two requirements expressed in Fact 2.2.1. Write $F(\vec{x}) = L(T(\vec{x}))$.

    a. $F(\vec{v} + \vec{w}) = L(T(\vec{v} + \vec{w})) = L(T(\vec{v}) + T(\vec{w})) = L(T(\vec{v})) + L(T(\vec{w})) = F(\vec{v}) + F(\vec{w})$

    b. $F(k\vec{v}) = L(T(k\vec{v})) = L(kT(\vec{v})) = kL(T(\vec{v})) = kF(\vec{v})$

29. To check that L is linear, we verify the two parts of Fact 2.2.1.

    a. Use the hint and apply L on both sides of the equation $\vec{x} + \vec{y} = T(L(\vec{x}) + L(\vec{y}))$:
    $L(\vec{x} + \vec{y}) = L(T(L(\vec{x}) + L(\vec{y}))) = L(\vec{x}) + L(\vec{y})$, as claimed.

    b. $L(k\vec{x}) = L(kT(L(\vec{x})) = L(T(kL(\vec{x}))) = kL(\vec{x})$, as claimed.
    $\quad\quad\quad\uparrow\quad\quad\quad\quad\quad\quad\uparrow$

    $\vec{x} = T(L(\vec{x}))\quad\quad T$ is linear.

31. Write $A = [\vec{v}_1 \ \vec{v}_2 \ \vec{v}_3]$; then $A\vec{x} = [\vec{v}_1 \ \vec{v}_2 \ \vec{v}_3] \begin{bmatrix} x_1 \\ x_2 \\ x_3 \end{bmatrix} = x_1\vec{v}_1 + x_2\vec{v}_2 + x_3\vec{v}_3$.

    We must choose $\vec{v}_1, \vec{v}_2$, and $\vec{v}_3$ in such a way that $x_1\vec{v}_1 + x_2\vec{v}_2 + x_3\vec{v}_3$ is perpendicular to $\vec{w} = \begin{bmatrix} 1 \\ 2 \\ 3 \end{bmatrix}$

    for all x_1, x_2, and x_3. This is the case if (and only if) all the vectors $\vec{v}_1, \vec{v}_2$, and $\vec{v}_3$ are perpendicular to $\vec{w}$, that is, if $\vec{v}_1 \cdot \vec{w} = \vec{v}_2 \cdot \vec{w} = \vec{v}_3 \cdot \vec{w} = 0$.

    For example, we can choose $\vec{v}_1 = \begin{bmatrix} -2 \\ 1 \\ 0 \end{bmatrix}$ and $\vec{v}_2 = \vec{v}_3 = \vec{0}$, so that $A = \begin{bmatrix} -2 & 0 & 0 \\ 1 & 0 & 0 \\ 0 & 0 & 0 \end{bmatrix}$.

33. Geometrically, we can find the representation $\vec{v} = \vec{v}_1 + \vec{v}_2$ by means of a parallelogram:

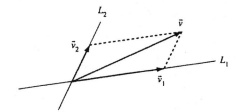

    To show the existence and uniqueness of this representation algebraically, choose a nonzero vector $\vec{w}_1$ in L_1 and a nonzero $\vec{w}_2$ in L_2. Then the system $x_1\vec{w}_1 + x_2\vec{w}_2 = \vec{0}$ or $[\vec{w}_1 \ \vec{w}_2] \begin{bmatrix} x_1 \\ x_2 \end{bmatrix} = \vec{0}$ has only the solution $x_1 = x_2 = 0$ (if $x_1\vec{w}_1 + x_2\vec{w}_2 = \vec{0}$ then $x_1\vec{w}_1 = -x_2\vec{w}_2$ is both in L_1 and in L_2, so that it must be the zero vector).

Therefore, the system $x_1\vec{w}_1 + x_2\vec{w}_2 = \vec{v}$ or $\begin{bmatrix} \vec{w}_1 & \vec{w}_2 \end{bmatrix} \begin{bmatrix} x_1 \\ x_2 \end{bmatrix} = \vec{v}$ has a unique solution x_1, x_2 for all $\vec{v}$ in $\mathbb{R}^2$ (by Fact 1.3.4). Now set $\vec{v}_1 = x_1\vec{w}_1$ and $\vec{v}_2 = x_2\vec{w}_2$ to obtain the desired representation $\vec{v} = \vec{v}_1 + \vec{v}_2$. (Compare with Exercise 1.3.57.)

To show that the transformation $T(\vec{v}) = \vec{v}_1$ is linear, we will verify the two parts of Fact 2.2.1.

Let $\vec{v} = \vec{v}_1 + \vec{v}_2$, $\vec{w} = \vec{w}_1 + \vec{w}_2$, so that $\vec{v} + \vec{w} = (\vec{v}_1 + \vec{w}_1) + (\vec{v}_2 + \vec{w}_2)$ and $k\vec{v} = k\vec{v}_1 + k\vec{v}_2$.

$$\begin{array}{cccccccc} \uparrow & \uparrow & \uparrow & \uparrow & & \uparrow & \uparrow & & \uparrow & \uparrow \\ \text{in} L_1 & \text{in} L_2 & \text{in} L_1 & \text{in} L_2 & & \text{in} L_1 & \text{in} L_2 & & \text{in} L_1 & \text{in} L_2 \end{array}$$

a. $T(\vec{v} + \vec{w}) = \vec{v}_1 + \vec{w}_1 = T(\vec{v}) + T(\vec{w})$, and

b. $T(k\vec{v}) = k\vec{v}_1 = kT(\vec{v})$, as claimed.

35. If the vectors $\vec{v}_1$ and $\vec{v}_2$ are defined as shown in the figure below, then the parallelogram P consists of all vectors of the form $\vec{v} = c_1\vec{v}_1 + c_2\vec{v}_2$, where $0 \le c_1,\ c_2 \le 1$. The image of P consists of all vectors of the form $T(\vec{v}) = T(c_1\vec{v}_1 + c_2\vec{v}_2) = c_1T(\vec{v}_1) + c_2T(\vec{v}_2)$. These vectors form the parallelogram shown below.

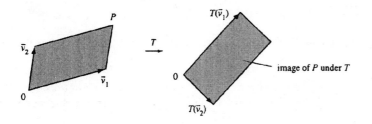

37. Write $\vec{w}$ as a linear combination of $\vec{v}_1$ and $\vec{v}_2 : \vec{w} = c_1\vec{v}_1 + c_2\vec{v}_2$.

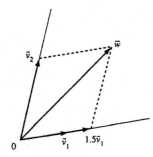

Measurements show that we have *roughly* $\vec{w} = 1.5\vec{v}_1 + \vec{v}_2$.

Therefore, by linearity, $T(\vec{w}) = T(1.5\vec{v}_1 + \vec{v}_2) = 1.5T(\vec{v}_1) + T(\vec{v}_2)$.

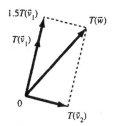

39. $T\begin{bmatrix} x_1 \\ x_2 \end{bmatrix} = \begin{bmatrix} x_1 \\ x_2 \end{bmatrix} + (ax_1 + bx_2)\begin{bmatrix} -b \\ a \end{bmatrix} = \begin{bmatrix} (1-ab)x_1 - b^2x_2 \\ a^2x_1 + (ab+1)x_2 \end{bmatrix} = \begin{bmatrix} 1-ab & -b^2 \\ a^2 & 1+ab \end{bmatrix}\begin{bmatrix} x_1 \\ x_2 \end{bmatrix}$

    The matrix of T is $\begin{bmatrix} 1-ab & -b^2 \\ a^2 & 1+ab \end{bmatrix}$.

41.

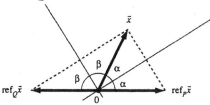

$\text{ref}_Q\vec{x} = -\text{ref}_P\vec{x}$ since $\text{ref}_Q\vec{x}$, $\text{ref}_P\vec{x}$, and $\vec{x}$ all have the same length, and $\text{ref}_Q\vec{x}$ and $\text{ref}_P\vec{x}$ enclose an angle of $2\alpha + 2\beta = 2(\alpha + \beta) = \pi$.

43. Since $\vec{y} = A\vec{x}$ is obtained from $\vec{x}$ by a rotation through α in the counterclockwise direction, $\vec{x}$ is obtained from $\vec{y}$ by a rotation through α in the *clockwise* direction, that is, a rotation through $-\alpha$.

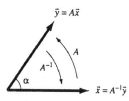

Therefore, the matrix of the inverse transformation is $A^{-1} = \begin{bmatrix} \cos(-\alpha) & -\sin(-\alpha) \\ \sin(-\alpha) & \cos(-\alpha) \end{bmatrix} = \begin{bmatrix} \cos\alpha & \sin\alpha \\ -\sin\alpha & \cos\alpha \end{bmatrix}$. You can use the formula in Exercise 2.1.13b to check this result.

45. Since $\vec{v}_1$ and $\vec{v}_2$ are not parallel, any vector $\vec{x}$ in $\mathbb{R}^2$ can be written as a linear combination of $\vec{v}_1$ and $\vec{v}_2$: $\vec{x} = c_1\vec{v}_1 + c_2\vec{v}_2$.
    Then $T(\vec{x}) = T(c_1\vec{v}_1 + c_2\vec{v}_2) = c_1T(\vec{v}_1) + c_2T(\vec{v}_2) = c_1L(\vec{v}_1) + c_2L(\vec{v}_2) = L(c_1\vec{v}_1 + c_2\vec{v}_2) = L(\vec{x})$, as claimed.

47. Write $T \begin{bmatrix} x_1 \\ x_2 \end{bmatrix} = \begin{bmatrix} a & b \\ c & d \end{bmatrix} \begin{bmatrix} x_1 \\ x_2 \end{bmatrix} = \begin{bmatrix} ax_1 + bx_2 \\ cx_1 + dx_2 \end{bmatrix}$.

a. $f(t) = \left(T \begin{bmatrix} \cos t \\ \sin t \end{bmatrix} \right) \cdot \left(T \begin{bmatrix} -\sin t \\ \cos t \end{bmatrix} \right) = \begin{bmatrix} a\cos t + b\sin t \\ c\cos t + d\sin t \end{bmatrix} \cdot \begin{bmatrix} -a\sin t + b\cos t \\ -c\sin t + d\cos t \end{bmatrix}$.

   $= (a\cos t + b\sin t)(-a\sin t + b\cos t) + (c\cos t + e\sin t)(-c\sin t + d\cos t)$

   This function $f(t)$ is continuous, since $\cos(t)$, $\sin(t)$, and constant functions are continuous, and sums and products of continuous functions are continuous.

b. $f\left(\dfrac{\pi}{2}\right) = T \begin{bmatrix} 0 \\ 1 \end{bmatrix} \cdot T \begin{bmatrix} -1 \\ 0 \end{bmatrix} = -\left(T \begin{bmatrix} 0 \\ 1 \end{bmatrix} \cdot T \begin{bmatrix} 1 \\ 0 \end{bmatrix} \right)$

   $\uparrow$

   T is linear

   $f(0) = T \begin{bmatrix} 1 \\ 0 \end{bmatrix} \cdot T \begin{bmatrix} 0 \\ 1 \end{bmatrix} = T \begin{bmatrix} 0 \\ 1 \end{bmatrix} \cdot T \begin{bmatrix} 1 \\ 0 \end{bmatrix}$

   The claim follows.

c. By part (b), the numbers $f(0)$ and $f\left(\dfrac{\pi}{2}\right)$ have different signs (one is positive and the other negative), or they are both zero. Since $f(t)$ is continuous, by part (a), we can apply the intermediate value theorem.

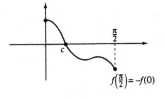

$f\left(\tfrac{\pi}{2}\right) = -f(0)$

d. Note that $\begin{bmatrix} \cos(t) \\ \sin(t) \end{bmatrix}$ and $\begin{bmatrix} -\sin(t) \\ \cos(t) \end{bmatrix}$ are perpendicular unit vectors, for any t. If we set

   $\vec{v}_1 = \begin{bmatrix} \cos(c) \\ \sin(c) \end{bmatrix}$, $\vec{v}_2 = \begin{bmatrix} -\sin(c) \\ \cos(c) \end{bmatrix}$, with the number c we found in part (c), then $f(c) = T(\vec{v}_1) \cdot$

   $T(\vec{v}_2) = 0$, so that $T(\vec{v}_1)$ and $T(\vec{v}_2)$ are perpendicular, as claimed. Note that $T(\vec{v}_1)$ or $T(\vec{v}_2)$ may be zero.

49. If $\vec{x} = \begin{bmatrix} \cos(t) \\ \sin(t) \end{bmatrix}$ then $T(\vec{x}) = \begin{bmatrix} 5 & 0 \\ 0 & 2 \end{bmatrix} \begin{bmatrix} \cos(t) \\ \sin(t) \end{bmatrix} = \begin{bmatrix} 5\cos(t) \\ 2\sin(t) \end{bmatrix} = \cos(t) \begin{bmatrix} 5 \\ 0 \end{bmatrix} + \sin(t) \begin{bmatrix} 0 \\ 2 \end{bmatrix}$.

   These vectors form an ellipse; consider the characterization of an ellipse given in the footnote on page 64, with $\vec{w}_1 = \begin{bmatrix} 5 \\ 0 \end{bmatrix}$ and $\vec{w}_2 = \begin{bmatrix} 0 \\ 2 \end{bmatrix}$.

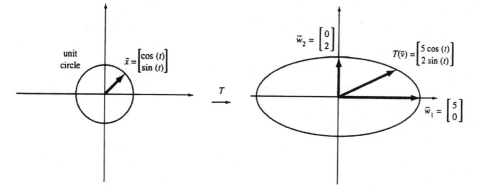

51. Consider the linear transformation T with matrix $A = [\vec{w}_1 \quad \vec{w}_2]$, that is,

$$T\begin{bmatrix} x_1 \\ x_2 \end{bmatrix} = A\begin{bmatrix} x_1 \\ x_2 \end{bmatrix} = [\vec{w}_1 \quad \vec{w}_2]\begin{bmatrix} x_1 \\ x_2 \end{bmatrix} = x_1\vec{w}_1 + x_2\vec{w}_2.$$

The curve C is the image of the unit circle under the transformation T: if $\vec{v} = \begin{bmatrix} \cos(t) \\ \sin(t) \end{bmatrix}$ is on the unit circle, then $T(\vec{v}) = \cos(t)\vec{w}_1 + \sin(t)\vec{w}_2$ is on the curve C. Therefore, C is an ellipse, by Exercise 50.

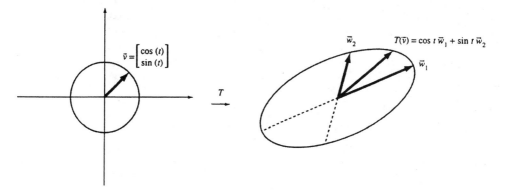

2.3

1. rref $\begin{bmatrix} 2 & 3 & \vdots & 1 & 0 \\ 5 & 8 & \vdots & 0 & 1 \end{bmatrix} = \begin{bmatrix} 1 & 0 & \vdots & 8 & -3 \\ 0 & 1 & \vdots & -5 & 2 \end{bmatrix}$, so that $\begin{bmatrix} 2 & 3 \\ 5 & 8 \end{bmatrix}^{-1} = \begin{bmatrix} 8 & -3 \\ -5 & 2 \end{bmatrix}$.

3. rref $\begin{bmatrix} 0 & 2 & \vdots & 1 & 0 \\ 1 & 1 & \vdots & 0 & 1 \end{bmatrix} = \begin{bmatrix} 1 & 0 & \vdots & -\frac{1}{2} & 1 \\ 0 & 1 & \vdots & \frac{1}{2} & 0 \end{bmatrix}$, so that $\begin{bmatrix} 0 & 2 \\ 1 & 1 \end{bmatrix}^{-1} = \begin{bmatrix} -\frac{1}{2} & 1 \\ \frac{1}{2} & 0 \end{bmatrix}$.

5. rref $\begin{bmatrix} 1 & 2 & 2 \\ 1 & 3 & 1 \\ 1 & 1 & 3 \end{bmatrix} = \begin{bmatrix} 1 & 0 & 4 \\ 0 & 1 & -1 \\ 0 & 0 & 0 \end{bmatrix}$, so that the matrix is not invertible, by Fact 2.3.3.

7. rref $\begin{bmatrix} 1 & 2 & 3 \\ 0 & 0 & 2 \\ 0 & 0 & 3 \end{bmatrix} = \begin{bmatrix} 1 & 2 & 0 \\ 0 & 0 & 1 \\ 0 & 0 & 0 \end{bmatrix}$, so that the matrix is not invertible, by Fact 2.3.3.

9. rref $\begin{bmatrix} 1 & 1 & 1 \\ 1 & 1 & 1 \\ 1 & 1 & 1 \end{bmatrix} = \begin{bmatrix} 1 & 1 & 1 \\ 0 & 0 & 0 \\ 0 & 0 & 0 \end{bmatrix}$, so that the matrix is not invertible, by Fact 2.3.3.

11. Use Fact 2.3.5; the inverse is $\begin{bmatrix} 1 & 0 & -1 \\ 0 & 1 & 0 \\ 0 & 0 & 1 \end{bmatrix}$.

13. Use Fact 2.3.5; the inverse is $\begin{bmatrix} 1 & 0 & 0 & 0 \\ -2 & 1 & 0 & 0 \\ 1 & -2 & 1 & 0 \\ 0 & 1 & -2 & 1 \end{bmatrix}$.

15. Use Fact 2.3.5; the inverse is $\begin{bmatrix} -6 & 9 & -5 & 1 \\ 9 & -1 & -5 & 2 \\ -5 & -5 & 9 & -3 \\ 1 & 2 & -3 & 1 \end{bmatrix}$

17. We make an attempt to solve for x_1 and x_2 in terms of y_1 and y_2:

$$\begin{vmatrix} x_1 + 2x_2 & = & y_1 \\ 4x_1 + 8x_2 & = & y_2 \end{vmatrix} \xrightarrow{-4(I)} \begin{vmatrix} x_1 + 2x_2 = y_1 \\ 0 = -4y_1 + y_2 \end{vmatrix}.$$

This system has no solutions (x_1, x_2) for some (y_1, y_2), and infinitely many solutions for others; the transformation is not invertible.

19. Solving for $x_1, x_2,$ and x_3 in terms of $y_1, y_2,$ and y_3 we find that

$x_1 = 3y_1 - \frac{5}{2}y_2 + \frac{1}{2}y_3$

$x_2 = -3y_1 + 4y_2 - y_3$

$x_3 = y_1 - \frac{3}{2}y_2 + \frac{1}{2}y_3$

21. $f(x) = x^2$ is not invertible, since the equation $f(x) = x^2 = 1$ has two solutions $x = \pm 1$.

23. Note that $f'(x) = 3x^2 + 1$ is always positive; this implies that the function $f(x) = x^3 + x$ is increasing throughout. Therefore, the equation $f(x) = b$ has *at most* one solution x for all b.
Now observe that $\lim_{x \to \infty} f(x) = \infty$ and $\lim_{x \to -\infty} f(x) = -\infty$; this implies that the equation $f(x) = b$ has at least one solution x for a given b (for a careful proof, use the intermediate value theorem; compare with Exercise 2.2.47c).

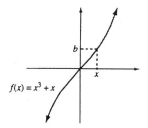

$f(x) = x^3 + x$

25. Invertible, with inverse $\begin{bmatrix} x_1 \\ x_2 \end{bmatrix} = \begin{bmatrix} \sqrt[3]{y_2} \\ y_2 \end{bmatrix}$

27. Not invertible, since the equation $\begin{bmatrix} x_1 + x_2 \\ x_1 x_2 \end{bmatrix} = \begin{bmatrix} 0 \\ 1 \end{bmatrix}$ has no solution.

29. Use Fact 2.3.3:

$$\begin{bmatrix} 1 & 1 & 1 \\ 1 & 2 & k \\ 1 & 4 & k^2 \end{bmatrix} \begin{array}{c} \longrightarrow \\ -I \\ -I \end{array} \begin{bmatrix} 1 & 1 & 1 \\ 0 & 1 & k-1 \\ 0 & 3 & k^2-1 \end{bmatrix} \begin{array}{c} -II \\ \longrightarrow \\ -3(II) \end{array} \begin{bmatrix} 1 & 0 & 2-k \\ 0 & 1 & k-1 \\ 0 & 0 & k^2-3k+2 \end{bmatrix}$$

The matrix is invertible if (and only if) $k^2 - 3k + 2 = (k-2)(k-1) \neq 0$, in which case we can further reduce it to I_3. Therefore, the matrix is invertible if $k \neq 1$ and $k \neq 2$.

31. Use Fact 2.3.3; first assume that $a \neq 0$.

$$\begin{bmatrix} 0 & a & b \\ -a & 0 & c \\ -b & -c & 0 \end{bmatrix} \xrightarrow{I \leftrightarrow II} \begin{bmatrix} -a & 0 & c \\ 0 & a & b \\ -b & -c & 0 \end{bmatrix} \xrightarrow{\div(-a)} \begin{bmatrix} 1 & 0 & -\frac{c}{a} \\ 0 & a & b \\ -b & -c & 0 \end{bmatrix} \xrightarrow[+b(I)]{} \begin{bmatrix} 1 & 0 & -\frac{c}{a} \\ 0 & a & b \\ 0 & -c & -\frac{bc}{a} \end{bmatrix} \xrightarrow{\div a}$$

$$\begin{bmatrix} 1 & 0 & -\frac{c}{a} \\ 0 & 1 & \frac{b}{a} \\ 0 & -c & -\frac{bc}{a} \end{bmatrix} \xrightarrow[+c(II)]{} \begin{bmatrix} 1 & 0 & -\frac{c}{a} \\ 0 & 1 & \frac{b}{a} \\ 0 & 0 & 0 \end{bmatrix}$$

Now consider the case when $a = 0$:

$$\begin{bmatrix} 0 & 0 & b \\ 0 & 0 & c \\ -b & -c & 0 \end{bmatrix} \xrightarrow{I \leftrightarrow III} \begin{bmatrix} -b & -c & 0 \\ 0 & 0 & c \\ 0 & 0 & b \end{bmatrix}:$$ The second entry on the diagonal of rref will be 0.

It follows that the matrix $\begin{bmatrix} 0 & a & b \\ -a & 0 & c \\ -b & -c & 0 \end{bmatrix}$ is noninvertible, regardless of the values of $a, b,$ and c.

33. Use Fact 2.3.6.

The requirement $A^{-1} = A$ means that $-\dfrac{1}{a^2 + b^2} \begin{bmatrix} -a & -b \\ -b & a \end{bmatrix} = \begin{bmatrix} a & b \\ b & -a \end{bmatrix}$. This is the case if (and only if) $a^2 + b^2 = 1$.

35. a. A is invertible if (and only if) all its diagonal entries, $a, d,$ and $f,$ are nonzero.

    b. As in part (a): if all the diagonal entries are nonzero.

    c. Yes, A^{-1} will be upper triangular as well; as you construct rref$[A \vdots I_n]$, you will perform only the following row operations:

    - divide rows by scalars

    - subtract a multiple of the jth row from the ith row, where $j > i$.

    Applying these operations to I_n, you end up with an upper triangular matrix.

    d. As in part (b): if all diagonal entries are nonzero.

37. Make an attempt to solve the linear transformation $\vec{y} = (cA)\vec{x} = c(A\vec{x})$ for $\vec{x}$:

    $$A\vec{x} = \frac{1}{c}\vec{y}, \text{ so that } \vec{x} = A^{-1}\left(\frac{1}{c}\vec{y}\right) = \left(\frac{1}{c}A^{-1}\right)\vec{y}.$$

    This shows that cA is indeed invertible, with $(cA)^{-1} = \frac{1}{c}A^{-1}$.

39. Suppose the ijth entry of M is k, and all other entries are as in the identity matrix. Then we can find rref$[M \vdots I_n]$ by subtracting k times the jth row from the ith row. Therefore, M is indeed invertible, and M^{-1} differs from the identity matrix only at the ijth entry; that entry is $-k$.

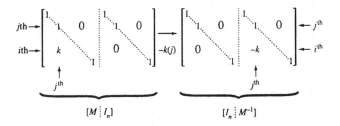

41. a. Invertible: the transformation is its own inverse.

    b. Not invertible: the equation $T(\vec{x}) = \vec{b}$ has infinitely many solutions if $\vec{b}$ is on the plane, and none otherwise.

    c. Invertible: The inverse is dilation by $\frac{1}{5}$ (that is, a contraction by 5). If $\vec{y} = 5\vec{x}$, then $\vec{x} = \frac{1}{5}\vec{y}$.

    d. Invertible: The inverse is a rotation about the same axis through the same angle in the opposite direction.

43. We make an attempt to solve the equation $\vec{y} = A(B\vec{x})$ for $\vec{x}$:
    $B\vec{x} = A^{-1}\vec{y}$, so that $\vec{x} = B^{-1}(A^{-1}\vec{y})$.

45. a. Each of the three row divisions requires 3 operations, and each of the six row subtractions requires three operations as well; altogether, we have $3 \cdot 3 + 6 \cdot 3 = 9 \cdot 3 = 3^3 = 27$ operations.

b. Suppose we have already taken care of the first m columns: $[A \vdots I_n]$ has been reduced to

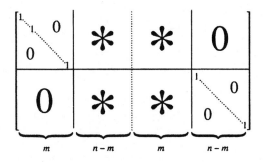

$$\underbrace{\qquad}_{m} \quad \underbrace{\qquad}_{n-m} \quad \underbrace{\qquad}_{m} \quad \underbrace{\qquad}_{n-m}$$

Here, the stars represent arbitrary entries.

Suppose the $(m+1)$th entry on the diagonal is k. Dividing the $(m+1)$th row by k requires n operations: $n - m - 1$ to the left of the dotted line $\left(\text{not counting the computation } \dfrac{k}{k} = 1\right)$, and $m + 1$ to the right of the dotted line $\left(\text{including } \dfrac{1}{k}\right)$. Now the matrix has the form

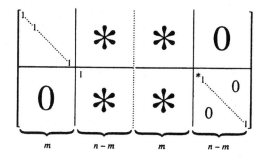

$$\underbrace{\qquad}_{m} \quad \underbrace{\qquad}_{n-m} \quad \underbrace{\qquad}_{m} \quad \underbrace{\qquad}_{n-m}$$

Eliminating each of the other $n - 1$ components of the $(m+1)$th column now requires n operations ($n - m - 1$ to the left of the dotted line, and $m + 1$ to the right). Altogher, it requires $n + (n-1)n = n^2$ operations to process the mth column. To process all n columns requires $n \cdot n^2 = n^3$ operations.

c. The inversion of a 12×12 matrix requires $12^3 = 4^3 3^3 = 64 \cdot 3^3$ operations, that is, 64 times as much as the inversion of a 3×3 matrix. If the inversion of a 3×3 matrix takes one second, then the inversion of a 12×12 matrix takes 64 seconds.

47. Let $f(x) = x^2$; the equation $f(x) = 0$ has the unique solution $x = 0$.

49. a. $A = \begin{bmatrix} 0.293 & 0 & 0 \\ 0.014 & 0.207 & 0.017 \\ 0.044 & 0.01 & 0.216 \end{bmatrix}$, $I_3 - A = \begin{bmatrix} 0.707 & 0 & 0 \\ -0.014 & 0.793 & -0.017 \\ -0.044 & -0.01 & 0.784 \end{bmatrix}$

$$(I_3 - A)^{-1} = \begin{bmatrix} 1.41 & 0 & 0 \\ 0.0267 & 1.26 & 0.0274 \\ 0.0797 & 0.0161 & 1.28 \end{bmatrix}$$

b. We have $\vec{b} = \begin{bmatrix} 1 \\ 0 \\ 0 \end{bmatrix}$, so that $\vec{x} = (I_3 - A)^{-1}\vec{e}_1 =$ first column of $(I_3 - A)^{-1} \approx \begin{bmatrix} 1.41 \\ 0.0267 \\ 0.0797 \end{bmatrix}$.

c. As illustrated in part (b), the ith column of $(I_3 - A)^{-1}$ gives the output vector required to satisfy a consumer demand of 1 unit on industry i, in the absence of any other consumer demands. In particular, the ith diagonal entry of $(I_3 - A)^{-1}$ gives the output of industry i required to satisfy this demand. Since industry i has to satisfy the consumer demand of 1 as well as the interindustry demand, its total output will be at least 1.

d. Suppose the consumer demand increases from $\vec{b}$ to $\vec{b} + \vec{e}_2$ (that is, the demand on manufacturing increases by one unit). Then the output must change from $(I_3 - A)^{-1}\vec{b}$ to
$(I_3 - A)^{-1}(\vec{v} + \vec{e}_2) = (I_3 - A)^{-1}\vec{b} + (I_3 - A)^{-1}\vec{e}_2 = (I_3 - A)^{-1}\vec{b} +$ (second column of $(I_3 - A)^{-1}$).
The components of the second column of $(I_3 - A)^{-1}$ tells us by how much each industry has to increase its output.

e. The ijth entry of $(I_n - A)^{-1}$ gives the required increase of the output x_i of industry i to satisfy an increase of the consumer demand b_j on industry j by one unit. In the language of multivariable calculus, this quantity is $\dfrac{\partial x_i}{\partial b_j}$.

2.4

1. $\begin{bmatrix} 4 & 6 \\ 3 & 4 \end{bmatrix}$

3. Undefined.

5. $\begin{bmatrix} a & b \\ c & d \\ 0 & 0 \end{bmatrix}$

7. $\begin{bmatrix} -1 & 1 & 0 \\ 5 & 3 & 4 \\ -6 & -2 & -4 \end{bmatrix}$

9. $\begin{bmatrix} 0 & 0 \\ 0 & 0 \end{bmatrix}$

11. $[10]$

13. $[h]$

15. $\begin{bmatrix} 1 & 0 \\ 0 & 1 \end{bmatrix}$; Fact 2.4.9 applies to square matrices only.

17. Not necessarily true; $(A+B)^2 = (A+B)(A+B) = A^2 + AB + BA + B^2 \neq A^2 + 2AB + B^2$ if $AB \neq BA$.

19. Not necessarily true; consider the case $A = I_n$ and $B = -I_n$.

21. True; $ABB^{-1}A^{-1} = AI_nA^{-1} = AA^{-1} = I_n$.

23. True; $(ABA^{-1})^3 = ABA^{-1}ABA^{-1}ABA^{-1} = AB^3A^{-1}$.

25. True; $(A^{-1}B)^{-1} = B^{-1}(A^{-1})^{-1} = B^{-1}A$ (use Fact 2.4.8).

27. $\left[\begin{array}{c|c} \begin{bmatrix} 1 & 0 \\ 0 & 1 \end{bmatrix} \begin{bmatrix} 1 \\ 2 \end{bmatrix} + \begin{bmatrix} 0 \\ 0 \end{bmatrix}[3] & \begin{bmatrix} 1 & 0 \\ 0 & 1 \end{bmatrix} \begin{bmatrix} 0 \\ 0 \end{bmatrix} + \begin{bmatrix} 0 \\ 0 \end{bmatrix}[4] \\ \hline \begin{bmatrix} 1 & 3 \end{bmatrix} \begin{bmatrix} 1 \\ 2 \end{bmatrix} + [4][3] & \begin{bmatrix} 1 & 3 \end{bmatrix} \begin{bmatrix} 0 \\ 0 \end{bmatrix} + [4][4] \end{array}\right] = \left[\begin{array}{c|c} \begin{bmatrix} 1 \\ 2 \end{bmatrix} & \begin{bmatrix} 0 \\ 0 \end{bmatrix} \\ \hline [19] & [16] \end{array}\right] = \begin{bmatrix} 1 & 0 \\ 2 & 0 \\ 19 & 16 \end{bmatrix}$

29. The columns of B must be solutions of the system $\begin{bmatrix} 1 & 3 \\ 2 & 6 \end{bmatrix} \vec{x} = \begin{bmatrix} 0 \\ 0 \end{bmatrix}$. One possible solution is

    $B = \begin{bmatrix} 3 & 0 \\ -1 & 0 \end{bmatrix}$.

31. The two columns of A must be solutions of the linear systems $B\vec{x} = \begin{bmatrix} 1 \\ 0 \end{bmatrix}$ and $B\vec{x} = \begin{bmatrix} 0 \\ 1 \end{bmatrix}$, respectively. Each of these systems has *infinitely many solutions*. One possible solution is

    $A = \begin{bmatrix} 2 & -1 \\ -1 & 1 \\ 0 & 0 \end{bmatrix}$.

33. By Fact 1.3.3, there is a nonzero $\vec{x}$ such that $B\vec{x} = \vec{0}$ and therefore $AB\vec{x} = \vec{0}$. By Fact 2.3.4b, the 3×3 matrix AB is not invertible.

35. a. Consider a solution $\vec{x}$ of the equation $A\vec{x} = \vec{0}$.
    Multiply both sides by B from the left: $BA\vec{x} = B\vec{0} = \vec{0}$, so that $\vec{x} = \vec{0}$ (since $BA = I_m$).
    It follows that $\vec{x} = \vec{0}$ is the only solution of $A\vec{x} = \vec{0}$.

    b. $\vec{x} = A\vec{b}$ is a solution, since $B\vec{x} = BA\vec{b} = \vec{b}$ (because $BA = I_m$).

    c. rank$(A) = m$, by part (a) (all variables are leading).
    rank$(B) = m$, by part (b) (compare with Example 13, Section 1.3).

    d. $m = $ rank$(B) \leq$ (number of columns of B) $= n$

37. We need to find all matrices $X = \begin{bmatrix} a & b \\ c & d \end{bmatrix}$ such that $\begin{bmatrix} a & b \\ c & d \end{bmatrix}\begin{bmatrix} 1 & 0 \\ 0 & 2 \end{bmatrix} = \begin{bmatrix} 1 & 0 \\ 0 & 2 \end{bmatrix}\begin{bmatrix} a & b \\ c & d \end{bmatrix}$, or,

$\begin{bmatrix} a & 2b \\ c & 2d \end{bmatrix} = \begin{bmatrix} a & b \\ 2c & 2d \end{bmatrix}$. This is the case if $b = 0$ and $c = 0$. This means that X must be a *diagonal matrix*, $X = \begin{bmatrix} a & 0 \\ 0 & d \end{bmatrix}$.

39. By Exercise 37, X must be diagonal, of the form $X = \begin{bmatrix} a & 0 \\ 0 & d \end{bmatrix}$. X must also commute with $\begin{bmatrix} 0 & 1 \\ 0 & 0 \end{bmatrix}$,

so that $\begin{bmatrix} a & 0 \\ 0 & d \end{bmatrix}\begin{bmatrix} 0 & 1 \\ 0 & 0 \end{bmatrix} = \begin{bmatrix} 0 & a \\ 0 & 0 \end{bmatrix}$ must equal $\begin{bmatrix} 0 & 1 \\ 0 & 0 \end{bmatrix}\begin{bmatrix} a & 0 \\ 0 & d \end{bmatrix} = \begin{bmatrix} 0 & d \\ 0 & 0 \end{bmatrix}$. It follows that we must

have $a = d$, so that X must be of the form $\begin{bmatrix} a & 0 \\ 0 & a \end{bmatrix}$, that is, a scalar multiple of the identity matrix.

41. a. $D_\alpha D_\beta$ and $D_\beta D_\alpha$ are the same transformation, namely, a rotation through $\alpha + \beta$.

   b. $D_\alpha D_\beta = \begin{bmatrix} \cos\alpha & -\sin\alpha \\ \sin\alpha & \cos\alpha \end{bmatrix}\begin{bmatrix} \cos\beta & -\sin\beta \\ \sin\beta & \cos\beta \end{bmatrix}$

   $= \begin{bmatrix} \cos\alpha\cos\beta - \sin\alpha\sin\beta & -\cos\alpha\sin\beta - \sin\alpha\cos\beta \\ \sin\alpha\cos\beta + \cos\alpha\sin\beta & -\sin\alpha\sin\beta + \cos\alpha\cos\beta \end{bmatrix}$

   $= \begin{bmatrix} \cos(\alpha+\beta) & -\sin(\alpha+\beta) \\ \sin(\alpha+\beta) & \cos(\alpha+\beta) \end{bmatrix}$

   $D_\beta D_\alpha$ yields the same answer.

43. Let A represent the rotation through $120°$; then A^3 represents the rotation through $360°$, that is $A^3 = I_2$.

   $A = \begin{bmatrix} \cos(120°) & -\sin(120°) \\ \sin(120°) & \cos(120°) \end{bmatrix} = \begin{bmatrix} -\frac{1}{2} & -\frac{\sqrt{3}}{2} \\ \frac{\sqrt{3}}{2} & -\frac{1}{2} \end{bmatrix}$

45. We want A such that $A\vec{v}_i = \vec{w}_i$, for $i = 1, 2, \ldots, n$, or $A[\vec{v}_1\ \vec{v}_2\ \ldots\ \vec{v}_n] = [\vec{w}_1\ \vec{w}_2\ \ldots\ \vec{w}_n]$, or $AS = B$. Multiplying by S^{-1} from the right we find the unique solution $A = BS^{-1}$.

47. Use the result of Exercise 45, with $S = \begin{bmatrix} 3 & 1 \\ 1 & 2 \end{bmatrix}$ and $B = \begin{bmatrix} 6 & 3 \\ 2 & 6 \end{bmatrix}$;

   $A = BS^{-1} = \frac{1}{5}\begin{bmatrix} 9 & 3 \\ -2 & 16 \end{bmatrix}$.

49. Let A be the matrix of T and C the matrix of L. We want that $AP_0 = P_1$, $AP_1 = P_3$, and $AP_2 = P_2$.

We can use the result of Exercise 45, with $S = \begin{bmatrix} 1 & 1 & -1 \\ 1 & -1 & 1 \\ 1 & -1 & -1 \end{bmatrix}$ and $B = \begin{bmatrix} 1 & -1 & -1 \\ -1 & -1 & 1 \\ -1 & 1 & -1 \end{bmatrix}$.

Then $A = BS^{-1} = \begin{bmatrix} 0 & 0 & 1 \\ -1 & 0 & 0 \\ 0 & -1 & 0 \end{bmatrix}$.

Using an analogous approach, we find that $C = \begin{bmatrix} 0 & 1 & 0 \\ 1 & 0 & 0 \\ 0 & 0 & 1 \end{bmatrix}$.

51. Let E be an elementary $n \times n$ matrix (obtained from I_n by a certain elementary row operation), and let F be the elementary matrix obtained from I_n by the reversed row operation. Our work in Exercise 50 (parts (a) to (c)) shows that $EF = I_n$, so that E is indeed invertible, and $E^{-1} = F$ is an elementary matrix as well.

53. a. Let $S = E_1 E_2 \ldots E_p$ in Exercise 52(a).

By Exercise 51, the elementary matrices E_i are invertible: now use Fact 2.4.8 repeatedly to see that S is invertible.

b. $A = \begin{bmatrix} 2 & 4 \\ 4 & 8 \end{bmatrix}^{\div 2}$, represented by $\begin{bmatrix} \frac{1}{2} & 0 \\ 0 & 1 \end{bmatrix}$

$\begin{bmatrix} 1 & 2 \\ 4 & 8 \end{bmatrix}_{-4(I)}$, represented by $\begin{bmatrix} 1 & 0 \\ -4 & 1 \end{bmatrix}$

$\mathrm{rref}(A) = \begin{bmatrix} 1 & 2 \\ 0 & 0 \end{bmatrix}$

Therefore, $\mathrm{rref}(A) = \begin{bmatrix} 1 & 2 \\ 0 & 0 \end{bmatrix} = \begin{bmatrix} 1 & 0 \\ -4 & 1 \end{bmatrix} \begin{bmatrix} \frac{1}{2} & 0 \\ 0 & 1 \end{bmatrix} \begin{bmatrix} 2 & 4 \\ 4 & 8 \end{bmatrix} = E_1 E_2 A = SA$, where

$S = \begin{bmatrix} 1 & 0 \\ -4 & 1 \end{bmatrix} \begin{bmatrix} \frac{1}{2} & 0 \\ 0 & 1 \end{bmatrix} = \begin{bmatrix} \frac{1}{2} & 0 \\ -2 & 1 \end{bmatrix}$.

(There are other correct answers.)

55. $\begin{bmatrix} 1 & k \\ 0 & 1 \end{bmatrix}$ represents a shear parallel to the $\vec{e}_1$ axis, $\begin{bmatrix} 1 & 0 \\ k & 1 \end{bmatrix}$ represents a shear parallel to the $\vec{e}_2$ axis,

$\begin{bmatrix} k & 0 \\ 0 & 1 \end{bmatrix}$ represents a "dilation in $\vec{e}_1$ direction" (leaving the $\vec{e}_2$ component unchanged),

$\begin{bmatrix} 1 & 0 \\ 0 & k \end{bmatrix}$ represents a "dilation in $\vec{e}_2$ direction" (leaving the $\vec{e}_1$ component unchanged), and

$\begin{bmatrix} 0 & 1 \\ 1 & 0 \end{bmatrix}$ represents the reflection in the line spanned by $\begin{bmatrix} 1 \\ 1 \end{bmatrix}$.

57. Let A and B be two lower triangular $n \times n$ matrices. We need to show that the ijth entry of AB is 0 whenever $i < j$.

    This entry is the dot product of the ith row of A and the jth column of B,

    $$[a_{i1} \ a_{i2} \ldots a_{ii} \ 0 \ldots 0] \cdot \begin{bmatrix} 0 \\ \vdots \\ 0 \\ b_{jj} \\ \vdots \\ b_{nj} \end{bmatrix}, \text{ which is indeed 0 if } i < j.$$

59. a. Write the system $L\vec{y} = \vec{b}$ in components:

    $$\begin{vmatrix} y_1 & & & & & = -3 \\ -3y_1 & + & y_2 & & & = 14 \\ y_1 & + & 2y_2 & + & y_3 & = 9 \\ -y_1 & + & 8y_2 & - & 5y_3 & + & y_4 & = 33 \end{vmatrix}, \text{ so that } y_1 = -3, \ y_2 = 14 + 3y_1 = 5,$$

    $y_3 = 9 - y_1 - 2y_2 = 2$, and $y_4 = 33 + y_1 - 8y_2 + 5y_3 = 0$:

    $$\vec{y} = \begin{bmatrix} -3 \\ 5 \\ 2 \\ 0 \end{bmatrix}.$$

    b. Proceeding as in part (a) we find that $\vec{x} = \begin{bmatrix} 1 \\ -1 \\ 2 \\ 0 \end{bmatrix}$.

61. a. Write $L = \begin{bmatrix} L^{(m)} & 0 \\ L_3 & L_4 \end{bmatrix}$ and $U = \begin{bmatrix} U^{(m)} & U_2 \\ 0 & U_4 \end{bmatrix}$. Then $A = LU = \begin{bmatrix} L^{(m)}U^{(m)} & L^{(m)}U_2 \\ L_3U^{(m)} & L_3U_2 + L_4U_4 \end{bmatrix}$, so that $A^{(m)} = L^{(m)}U^{(m)}$, as claimed.

    b. By Exercise 34, the matrices L and U are both invertible. By Exercise 2.3.35, the diagonal entries of L and U are all nonzero. For any m, the matrices $L^{(m)}$ and $U^{(m)}$ are triangular, with nonzero diagonal entries, so that they are invertible. By Fact 2.4.8, the matrix $A^{(m)} = L^{(m)}U^{(m)}$ is invertible as well.

    c. Using the hint, we write $A = \begin{bmatrix} A^{(n-1)} & \vec{v} \\ \vec{w} & k \end{bmatrix} = \begin{bmatrix} L' & 0 \\ \vec{x} & t \end{bmatrix} \begin{bmatrix} U' & \vec{y} \\ 0 & s \end{bmatrix}.$

    We are looking for a column vector $\vec{y}$, a row vector $\vec{x}$, and scalars t and s satisfying these equations. The following equations need to be satisfied: $\vec{v} = L'\vec{y}$, $\vec{w} = \vec{x}U'$, and $k = \vec{x}\vec{y} + ts$. We find that $\vec{y} = (L')^{-1}\vec{v}$, $\vec{x} = \vec{w}(U')^{-1}$, and $ts = k - \vec{w}(U')^{-1}(L')^{-1}\vec{v}$.

We can choose, for example, $s = 1$ and $t = k - \vec{w}(U')^{-1}(L')^{-1}\vec{v}$, proving that A does indeed have an LU factorization.

Alternatively, one can show that if all principal submatrices are invertible then no row swaps are required in the Gauss-Jordan Algorithm. In this case, we can find an LU-factorization as outlined in Exercise 58.

63. We will prove that $A(C + D) = AC + AD$, repeatedly using Fact 1.3.7a: $A(\vec{x} + \vec{y}) = A\vec{x} + A\vec{y}$.
Write $B = [\vec{v}_1 \ \ldots \ \vec{v}_n]$ and $C = [\vec{w}_1 \ \ldots \ \vec{w}_n]$. Then
$A(C + D) = A[\vec{v}_1 + \vec{w}_1 \cdots \vec{v}_n + \vec{w}_n] = [A\vec{v}_1 + A\vec{w}_1 \ \cdots \ A\vec{v}_n + A\vec{w}_n]$, and
$AC + AD = A[\vec{v}_1 \ \cdots \ \vec{v}_n] + A[\vec{w}_1 \ \cdots \ \vec{w}_n] = [A\vec{v}_1 + A\vec{w}_1 \ \cdots A\vec{v}_n + A\vec{w}_n]$.
The results agree.

65. Suppose A_{11} is a $p \times p$ matrix and A_{22} is a $q \times q$ matrix. For B to be the inverse of A we must have $AB = I_{p+q}$. Let us partition B the same way as A:

$B = \begin{bmatrix} B_{11} & B_{12} \\ B_{21} & B_{22} \end{bmatrix}$, where B_{11} is $p \times p$ and B_{22} is $q \times q$.

Then $AB = \begin{bmatrix} A_{11} & 0 \\ 0 & A_{22} \end{bmatrix} \begin{bmatrix} B_{11} & B_{12} \\ B_{21} & B_{22} \end{bmatrix} = \begin{bmatrix} A_{11}B_{11} & A_{11}B_{12} \\ A_{22}B_{21} & A_{22}B_{22} \end{bmatrix} = \begin{bmatrix} I_p & 0 \\ 0 & I_q \end{bmatrix}$ means that

$A_{11}B_{11} = I_p, \ A_{22}B_{22} = I_q, \ A_{11}B_{12} = 0, \ A_{22}B_{21} = 0$.
This implies that A_{11} and A_{22} are invertible, and $B_{11} = A_{11}^{-1}, \ B_{22} = A_{22}^{-1}$.
This in turn implies that $B_{12} = 0$ and $B_{21} = 0$.
We summarize: A is invertible if (and only if) both A_{11} and A_{22} are invertible; in this case

$A^{-1} = \begin{bmatrix} A_{11}^{-1} & 0 \\ 0 & A_{22}^{-1} \end{bmatrix}$.

67. Write A in terms of its rows: $A = \begin{bmatrix} \vec{w}_1 \\ \vec{w}_2 \\ \ldots \\ \vec{w}_n \end{bmatrix}$ (suppose A is $n \times m$).

We can think of this as a partition into n

$1 \times m$ matrices. Now $AB = \begin{bmatrix} \vec{w}_1 \\ \vec{w}_2 \\ \ldots \\ \vec{w}_n \end{bmatrix} B = \begin{bmatrix} \vec{w}_1 B \\ \vec{w}_2 B \\ \ldots \\ \vec{w}_n B \end{bmatrix}$ (a product of partitioned matrices).

We see that the ith row of AB is the product of the ith row of A and the matrix B.

69. Suppose A_{11} is a $p \times p$ matrix. Since A_{11} is invertible, $\text{rref}(A) = \begin{bmatrix} I_p & A_{12} & * \\ 0 & 0 & \text{rref}(A_{23}) \end{bmatrix}$, so that

$\text{rank}(A) = p + \text{rank}(A_{23}) = \text{rank}(A_{11}) + \text{rank}(A_{23})$.

71. Multiplying both sides with A^{-1} we find that $A = I_n$: The identity matrix is the only invertible matrix with this property.

73. The ijth entry of AB is $\displaystyle\sum_{k=1}^{n} a_{ik}b_{kj}$. Then $\displaystyle\sum_{k=1}^{n} a_{ik}b_{kj} \leq \sum_{k=1}^{n} sb_{kj} = s\left(\sum_{k=1}^{n} b_{kj}\right) \leq sr$.

$\qquad\qquad\qquad\qquad\qquad\qquad\uparrow \qquad\qquad\qquad\qquad\uparrow$

$\qquad\qquad\qquad\qquad$ since $a_{ik} \leq s$ this is $\leq r$, as it is the

$\qquad\qquad\qquad\qquad\qquad\qquad\qquad\qquad$ jth column sum of B.

75. a. The components of the jth column of the technology matrix A give the demands industry J_j makes on the other industries, per unit output of J_j. The fact that the jth column sum is less than 1 means that industry J_j *adds value* to the products it produces.

   b. A productive economy can satisfy any consumer demand $\vec{b}$, since the equation $(I_n - A)\vec{x} = \vec{b}$ can be solved for the output vector $\vec{x}$: $\vec{x} = (I_n - A)^{-1}\vec{b}$ (compare with Exercise 2.3.49).

   c. The output $\vec{x}$ required to satisfy a consumer demand $\vec{b}$ is
   $\vec{x} = (I_n - A)^{-1}\vec{b} = (I_n + A + A^2 + \cdots + A^m + \cdots)\,\vec{b} = \vec{b} + A\vec{b} + A^2\vec{b} + \cdots + A^m\vec{b} + \cdots$.
   To interpret the terms in this series, keep in mind that whatever output $\vec{v}$ the industries produce generates an interindustry demand of $A\vec{v}$.
   The industries first need to satisfy the consumer demand, $\vec{b}$. Producing the output $\vec{b}$ will generate an interindustry demand, $A\vec{b}$. Producing $A\vec{b}$ in turn generates an extra interindustry demand, $A(A\vec{b}) = A^2\vec{b}$, and so forth.
   For a simple example, see Exercise 2.3.50; also read the discussion of "chains of interindustry demands" in the footnote to Exercise 2.3.49.

77. a. $A^{-1} = \begin{bmatrix} 0 & 0 & 1 \\ 1 & 0 & 0 \\ 0 & 1 & 0 \end{bmatrix}$ and $B^{-1} = \begin{bmatrix} 1 & 0 & 0 \\ 0 & 0 & 1 \\ 0 & 1 & 0 \end{bmatrix}$.

   Matrix A^{-1} transforms a wife's clan into her husband's clan, and B^{-1} transforms a child's clan into the mother's clan.

   b. B^2 transforms a women's clan into the clan of a child of her daughter.

   c. AB transforms a woman's clan into the clan of her daughter-in-law (her son's wife), while BA transforms a man's clan into the clan of his children. The two transformations are different.

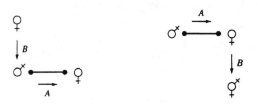

   d. The matrices for the four given diagrams (in the same order) are $BB^{-1} = I_3$,

40

$$BAB^{-1} = \begin{bmatrix} 0 & 0 & 1 \\ 1 & 0 & 0 \\ 0 & 1 & 0 \end{bmatrix}, \ B(BA)^{-1} = \begin{bmatrix} 0 & 1 & 0 \\ 0 & 0 & 1 \\ 1 & 0 & 0 \end{bmatrix}, \ BA(BA)^{-1} = I_3.$$

e. Yes; since $BAB^{-1} = A^{-1} = \begin{bmatrix} 0 & 0 & 1 \\ 1 & 0 & 0 \\ 0 & 1 & 0 \end{bmatrix}$, in the second case in part (d) the cousin belongs to Bueya's husband's clan.

79. $g(f(x)) = x$, for all x, so that $g \circ f$ is the identity, but $f(g(x)) = \begin{cases} x & \text{if } x \text{ is even} \\ x+1 & \text{if } x \text{ is odd} \end{cases}$.

True or False

1. T; The matrix is $\begin{bmatrix} 1 & -1 \\ -1 & 1 \end{bmatrix}$.

3. T, by Fact 2.3.3.

5. F, by Fact 2.4.3.

7. F; Matrix AB will be 3×5, by Definition 2.4.1b.

9. T, by Fact 2.2.3.

11. F, by Fact 2.3.6. Note that the determinant is 0.

13. T; The shear matrix $A = \begin{bmatrix} 1 & \frac{1}{2} \\ 0 & 1 \end{bmatrix}$ works.

15. T; The equation $\det(A) = k^2 - 6k + 10 = 0$ has no real solution.

17. F; Note that $\det(A) = (k-2)^2 + 9$ is always positive, so that A is invertible for all values of k.

19. F; Consider $A = I_2$ (or any other invertible 2×2 matrix).

21. F; For any 2×2 matrix A, the two columns of $A \begin{bmatrix} 1 & 1 \\ 1 & 1 \end{bmatrix}$ will be identical.

23. T; Note that $\begin{bmatrix} -1 & 2 \\ -2 & 3 \end{bmatrix} \begin{bmatrix} 1 \\ 1 \end{bmatrix} = \begin{bmatrix} 1 \\ 1 \end{bmatrix}$ and $\begin{bmatrix} -1 & 2 \\ -2 & 3 \end{bmatrix} \begin{bmatrix} 0 \\ 1 \end{bmatrix} = \begin{bmatrix} 2 \\ 3 \end{bmatrix} = \begin{bmatrix} 0 \\ 1 \end{bmatrix} + 2 \begin{bmatrix} 1 \\ 1 \end{bmatrix}$, so that it's a shear parallel to the line spanned by vector $\begin{bmatrix} 1 \\ 1 \end{bmatrix}$.

25. T; The product is $\det(A)I_2$.

27. T; Note that the matrix $\begin{bmatrix} 0 & -1 \\ 1 & 0 \end{bmatrix}$ represents a rotation through $\pi/2$. Thus $n = 4$ (or any multiple of 4) works.

29. F; If matrix A has two identical rows, then so does AB, for any matrix B. Thus AB cannot be I_n, so that A fails to be invertible.

31. F; Consider the matrix A that represents a rotation through the angle $2\pi/17$.

33. T; We have $(5A)^{-1} = \frac{1}{5}A^{-1}$.

35. T; Note that $A^2B = AAB = ABA = BAA = BA^2$.

37. F; Consider $A = I_2$ and $B = -I_2$.

39. F; Consider matrix $\begin{bmatrix} 0 & 0 & 1 \\ 0 & 1 & 0 \\ 1 & 0 & 0 \end{bmatrix}$, for example.

41. T; If you reflect twice in a row (across the same line), you will get the original vector back: $A(A\vec{x}) = \vec{x}$, or, $A^2\vec{x} = \vec{x} = I_2\vec{x}$. Thus $A^2 = I_2$ and $A^{-1} = A$.

43. T; Let $A = \begin{bmatrix} 1 & 0 & 0 \\ 0 & 1 & 0 \end{bmatrix}$, $B = \begin{bmatrix} 1 & 0 \\ 0 & 1 \\ 0 & 0 \end{bmatrix}$, for example.

45. T; We can rewrite the given equation as $A^2 + 3A = -4I_3$ and $-\frac{1}{4}(A + 3I_3)A = I_3$. By Fact 2.4.9, matrix A is invertible, with $A^{-1} = -\frac{1}{4}(A + 3I_3)$.

47. T; If we shear parallel to line L, then the vector $A\vec{x} - \vec{x}$ is parallel to L, for all $\vec{x}$, by part b of Definition 2.2.4. By part a, we have $A(A\vec{x} - \vec{x}) = A\vec{x} - \vec{x}$, or $(A^2 - 2A + I_2)\vec{x} = \vec{0}$. Since this holds for all vectors $\vec{x}$ in $\mathbb{R}^2$, the equation $A^2 - 2A + I_2 = 0$ must hold.

49. F; Since there are only eight entries that are not 1, there will be at least two rows that contain only ones. Having two identical rows, the matrix will be non-invertible.

Chapter 3

3.1

1. Find all $\vec{x}$ such that $A\vec{x} = \vec{0}$:

$$\begin{bmatrix} 1 & 2 & \vdots & 0 \\ 3 & 4 & \vdots & 0 \end{bmatrix} \longrightarrow \begin{bmatrix} 1 & 0 & \vdots & 0 \\ 0 & 1 & \vdots & 0 \end{bmatrix}, \text{ so that } x_1 = x_2 = 0.$$

$\ker(A) = \{\vec{0}\}$.

3. Find all $\vec{x}$ such that $A\vec{x} = \vec{0}$; note that all $\vec{x}$ in $\mathbb{R}^2$ satisfy the equation, so that $\ker(A) = \mathbb{R}^2 = \text{span}(\vec{e}_1, \vec{e}_2)$.

5. Find all $\vec{x}$ such that $A\vec{x} = \vec{0}$.

$$\begin{bmatrix} 1 & 1 & 1 & \vdots & 0 \\ 1 & 2 & 3 & \vdots & 0 \\ 1 & 3 & 5 & \vdots & 0 \end{bmatrix} \longrightarrow \begin{bmatrix} 1 & 0 & -1 & \vdots & 0 \\ 0 & 1 & 2 & \vdots & 0 \\ 0 & 0 & 0 & \vdots & 0 \end{bmatrix} ; \begin{matrix} x_1 = x_3 \\ x_2 = -2x_3 \end{matrix} ; \begin{bmatrix} x_1 \\ x_2 \\ x_3 \end{bmatrix} = \begin{bmatrix} t \\ -2t \\ t \end{bmatrix}$$

$$\ker(A) = \text{span} \begin{bmatrix} 1 \\ -2 \\ 1 \end{bmatrix}.$$

7. Find all $\vec{x}$ such that $A\vec{x} = \vec{0}$. Since $\text{rref}(A) = I_3$ we have $\ker(A) = \{\vec{0}\}$.

9. Find all $\vec{x}$ such that $A\vec{x} = \vec{0}$. Solving this system yields $\ker(A) = \{\vec{0}\}$.

11. Solving the system $A\vec{x} = \vec{0}$ we find that $\ker(A) = \text{span} \begin{bmatrix} -2 \\ 3 \\ 1 \\ 0 \end{bmatrix}.$

13. Solving the system $A\vec{x} = \vec{0}$ we find that $\ker(A) = \text{span} \left(\begin{bmatrix} -2 \\ 1 \\ 0 \\ 0 \\ 0 \\ 0 \end{bmatrix}, \begin{bmatrix} -3 \\ 0 \\ -2 \\ -1 \\ 1 \\ 0 \end{bmatrix}, \begin{bmatrix} 0 \\ 0 \\ 0 \\ 0 \\ 0 \\ 1 \end{bmatrix} \right).$

15. By Fact 3.1.3, the image of A is the span of the columns of A:

$$\text{im}(A) = \text{span} \left(\begin{bmatrix} 1 \\ 1 \end{bmatrix}, \begin{bmatrix} 1 \\ 2 \end{bmatrix}, \begin{bmatrix} 1 \\ 3 \end{bmatrix}, \begin{bmatrix} 1 \\ 4 \end{bmatrix} \right).$$

Since any two of these vectors span all of $\mathbb{R}^2$ already, we can write

$$\text{im}(A) = \text{span}\left(\begin{bmatrix} 1 \\ 1 \end{bmatrix}, \begin{bmatrix} 1 \\ 2 \end{bmatrix}\right).$$

17. By Fact 3.1.3, $\text{im}(A) = \text{span}\left(\begin{bmatrix} 1 \\ 3 \end{bmatrix}, \begin{bmatrix} 2 \\ 4 \end{bmatrix}\right) = \mathbb{R}^2$ (the whole plane).

19. Since the four column vectors of A are parallel, we have $\text{im}(A) = \text{span}\begin{bmatrix} 1 \\ -2 \end{bmatrix}$, a line in $\mathbb{R}^2$.

21. By Fact 3.1.3, $\text{im}(A) = \text{span}\left(\begin{bmatrix} 4 \\ 1 \\ 5 \end{bmatrix}, \begin{bmatrix} 7 \\ 9 \\ 6 \end{bmatrix}, \begin{bmatrix} 3 \\ 2 \\ 8 \end{bmatrix}\right).$

It is hard to tell by inspection whether this span is a plane in $\mathbb{R}^3$ or all of $\mathbb{R}^3$; we need to find out whether the third column vector is a linear combination of the first two.

$$\begin{bmatrix} 4 & 7 & 3 \\ 1 & 9 & 2 \\ 5 & 6 & 8 \end{bmatrix} \longrightarrow \begin{bmatrix} 1 & 0 & 0 \\ 0 & 1 & 0 \\ 0 & 0 & 1 \end{bmatrix}$$

This shows that the third column vector is not contained in the span of the first two, so that $\text{im}(A) = \mathbb{R}^3$.

23. $\text{im}(T) = \mathbb{R}^2$ and $\ker(T) = \{\vec{0}\}$, since T is invertible (see Summary 3.1.8).

25. $\text{im}(T) = \mathbb{R}^2$ and $\ker(T) = \{\vec{0}\}$, since T is invertible (see Summary 3.1.8).

27. Let $f(x) = x^3 - x = x(x^2 - 1) = x(x-1)(x+1)$.
Then $\text{im}(f) = \mathbb{R}$, by Exercise 26, but the function fails to be invertible since the equation $f(x) = 0$ has three solutions, $x = 0$, 1, and -1.

29. Use spherical coordinates (see any good text on multivariable calculus): $f\begin{bmatrix} \phi \\ \theta \end{bmatrix} = \begin{bmatrix} \sin(\phi)\cos(\theta) \\ \sin(\phi)\sin(\theta) \\ \cos(\phi) \end{bmatrix}$

31. The plane $x + 3y + 2z = 0$ is spanned by the two vectors $\begin{bmatrix} -2 \\ 0 \\ 1 \end{bmatrix}$ and $\begin{bmatrix} -3 \\ 1 \\ 0 \end{bmatrix}$, for example. Therefore, $A = \begin{bmatrix} -2 & -3 \\ 0 & 1 \\ 1 & 0 \end{bmatrix}$ does the job. There are many other correct answers.

33. The plane is the kernel of the linear transformation $T\begin{bmatrix} x \\ y \\ z \end{bmatrix} = x + 2y + 3z$ from $\mathbb{R}^3$ to $\mathbb{R}$.

35. $\text{kernel}(T) = \{\vec{x} : T(\vec{x}) = \vec{v} \cdot \vec{x} = 0\}$ = the plane with normal vector $\vec{v}$.

    $\text{im}(T) = \mathbb{R}$, since for every real number k there is a vector $\vec{x}$ such that $T(\vec{x}) = k$, namely, $\vec{x} = \dfrac{k}{\vec{v} \cdot \vec{v}}\vec{v}$.

37. $A = \begin{bmatrix} 0 & 1 & 0 \\ 0 & 0 & 1 \\ 0 & 0 & 0 \end{bmatrix}$, $A^2 = \begin{bmatrix} 0 & 0 & 1 \\ 0 & 0 & 0 \\ 0 & 0 & 0 \end{bmatrix}$, $A^3 = \begin{bmatrix} 0 & 0 & 0 \\ 0 & 0 & 0 \\ 0 & 0 & 0 \end{bmatrix}$, so that

    $\ker(A) = \text{span}(\vec{e}_1)$, $\ker(A^2) = \text{span}(\vec{e}_1, \vec{e}_2)$, $\ker(A^3) = \mathbb{R}^3$, and
    $\text{im}(A) = \text{span}(\vec{e}_1, \vec{e}_2)$, $\text{im}(A^2) = \text{span}(\vec{e}_1)$, $\text{im}(A^3) = \{\vec{0}\}$.

39. a. If a vector $\vec{x}$ is in $\ker(B)$, that is, $B\vec{x} = \vec{0}$, then $\vec{x}$ is also in $\ker(AB)$, since $AB(\vec{x}) = A(B\vec{x}) = A\vec{0} = \vec{0}$:
    $\ker(B) \subseteq \ker(AB)$.
    Exercise 37 (with $A = B$) illustrates that these kernels need not be equal.

    b. If a vector $\vec{y}$ is in $\text{im}(AB)$, that is $\vec{y} = AB\vec{x}$ for some $\vec{x}$, then $\vec{y}$ is also in $\text{im}(A)$, since we can write
    $\vec{y} = A(B\vec{x})$:
    $\text{im}(AB) \subseteq \text{im}(A)$.
    Exercise 37 (with $A = B$) illustrates that these images need not be equal.

41. a. $\text{rref}(A) = \begin{bmatrix} 1 & \frac{4}{3} \\ 0 & 0 \end{bmatrix}$, so that $\ker(A) = \text{span}\begin{bmatrix} -4 \\ 3 \end{bmatrix}$.

    $\text{im}(A) = \text{span}\begin{bmatrix} 0.36 \\ 0.48 \end{bmatrix} = \text{span}\begin{bmatrix} 3 \\ 4 \end{bmatrix}$.
    Note that $\text{im}(A)$ and $\ker(A)$ are perpendicular lines.

    b. $A^2 = A$
    If $\vec{v}$ is in $\text{im}(A)$ with $\vec{v} = A\vec{x}$, then $A\vec{v} = A^2\vec{x} = A\vec{x} = \vec{v}$.

    c.
    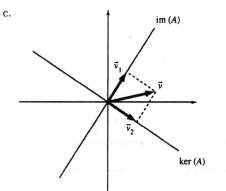

Any vector $\vec{v}$ in $\mathbb{R}^2$ can be written uniquely as $\vec{v} = \vec{v}_1 + \vec{v}_2$, where $\vec{v}_1$ is in $\text{im}(A)$ and $\vec{v}_2$ is in $\ker(A)$. Then $A\vec{v} = A\vec{v}_1 + A\vec{v}_2 = \vec{v}_1$ ($A\vec{v}_1 = \vec{v}_1$ by part b, $A\vec{v}_2 = \vec{0}$ since $\vec{v}_2$ is in $\ker(A)$), so that A represents the *orthogonal projection* onto $\text{im}(A) = \text{span}\begin{bmatrix} 3 \\ 4 \end{bmatrix}$.

43. Using our work in Exercise 42 as a guide, we come up with the following procedure to express the image of an $m \times n$ matrix A as the kernel of a matrix B:
If $\text{rank}(A) = m$, let B be the $m \times m$ zero matrix.
If $r = \text{rank}(A) < m$, let B be the $(m - r) \times m$ matrix obtained by omitting the first r rows and the first n columns of $\text{rref}[A \vdots I_m]$.

45. As we solve the system $A\vec{x} = \vec{0}$, we obtain r leading variables and $n - r$ nonleading variables. The "general vector" in $\ker(A)$ can be written as a linear combination of $n - r$ vectors, with the nonleading variables as coefficients. (See Example 12, where $n - r = 5 - 3 = 2$.)

47. $\text{im}(T) = L_2$ and $\ker(T) = L_1$.

49. If $\vec{v}$ and $\vec{w}$ are in $\ker(T)$, then $T(\vec{v} + \vec{w}) = T(\vec{v}) + T(\vec{w}) = \vec{0} + \vec{0} = \vec{0}$, so that $\vec{v} + \vec{w}$ is in $\ker(T)$ as well.
If $\vec{v}$ is in $\ker(T)$ and k is an arbitrary scalar, then $T(k\vec{v}) = kT(\vec{v}) = k\vec{0} = \vec{0}$, so that $k\vec{v}$ is in $\ker(T)$ as well.

51. We need to find all $\vec{x}$ such that $AB\vec{x} = \vec{0}$. If $AB\vec{x} = \vec{0}$, then $B\vec{x}$ is in $\ker(A) = \{\vec{0}\}$, so that $B\vec{x} = \vec{0}$. Since $\ker(B) = \{\vec{0}\}$, we can conclude that $\vec{x} = \vec{0}$. It follows that $\ker(AB) = \{\vec{0}\}$.

53. a. Using the equation $1 + 1 = 0$ (or $-1 = 1$), we can write the general vector $\vec{x}$ in $\ker(H)$ as

$$\vec{x} = \begin{bmatrix} x_1 \\ x_2 \\ x_3 \\ x_4 \\ x_5 \\ x_6 \\ x_7 \end{bmatrix} = \begin{bmatrix} p+r+s \\ p+q+s \\ p+q+r \\ p \\ q \\ r \\ s \end{bmatrix} = p\underset{\underset{\vec{v}_1}{\uparrow}}{\begin{bmatrix} 1 \\ 1 \\ 1 \\ 1 \\ 0 \\ 0 \\ 0 \end{bmatrix}} + q\underset{\underset{\vec{v}_2}{\uparrow}}{\begin{bmatrix} 0 \\ 1 \\ 1 \\ 0 \\ 1 \\ 0 \\ 0 \end{bmatrix}} + r\underset{\underset{\vec{v}_3}{\uparrow}}{\begin{bmatrix} 1 \\ 0 \\ 1 \\ 0 \\ 0 \\ 1 \\ 0 \end{bmatrix}} + s\underset{\underset{\vec{v}_4}{\uparrow}}{\begin{bmatrix} 1 \\ 1 \\ 0 \\ 0 \\ 0 \\ 0 \\ 1 \end{bmatrix}}$$

b. $\ker(H) = \text{span}(\vec{v}_1, \vec{v}_2, \vec{v}_3, \vec{v}_4)$ by part (a), and $\text{im}(M) = \text{span}(\vec{v}_1, \vec{v}_2, \vec{v}_3, \vec{v}_4)$ by Fact 3.1.3, so that $\text{im}(M) = \ker(H)$. $M\vec{x}$ is in $\text{im}(M) = \ker(H)$, so that $H(M\vec{x}) = \vec{0}$.

3.2

1. Not a subspace, since W does not contain the zero vector.

3. $W = \text{im} \begin{bmatrix} 1 & 2 & 3 \\ 4 & 5 & 6 \\ 7 & 8 & 9 \end{bmatrix}$ is a subspace of $\mathbb{R}^3$, by Fact 3.2.2.

5. We have subspaces $\{\vec{0}\}$, $\mathbb{R}^3$, and all lines and planes (through the origin). To prove this, mimic the reasoning in Example 3.

7. Yes; we need to show that W contains the zero vector. We are told that W is nonempty, so that it contains some vector $\vec{v}$. Since W is closed under scalar multiplication, it will contain the vector $0\vec{v} = \vec{0}$, as claimed.

9. These vectors are linearly dependent, since $\vec{v}_m = 0\vec{v}_1 + 0\vec{v}_2 + \cdots + 0\vec{v}_{m-1}$.

11. Linearly independent, since the two vectors are not parallel.

13. Linearly dependent, since $\begin{bmatrix} 1 \\ 2 \end{bmatrix} = 1\begin{bmatrix} 1 \\ 2 \end{bmatrix}$.

15. Linearly dependent, since $\ker \begin{bmatrix} 1 & 2 & 3 \\ 2 & 3 & 4 \end{bmatrix} \neq \{\vec{0}\}$ (by Fact 1.3.3).

17. Linearly independent, since $\mathrm{rref} \begin{bmatrix} 1 & 1 & 1 \\ 1 & 2 & 3 \\ 1 & 3 & 6 \end{bmatrix} = I_3$ (use Fact 3.2.6).

19. Linearly dependent, since $\ker \begin{bmatrix} 1 & 1 & 5 & 1 & 1 \\ 2 & 5 & 4 & 8 & 1 \\ 9 & 1 & 9 & 1 & 1 \\ 1 & 5 & 1 & 5 & 1 \end{bmatrix} \neq \{\vec{0}\}$ (by Fact 1.3.3).

21. Linearly dependent, since rref does not have a leading one in the fourth column.

23. The zero vector is in $V^\perp$, since $\vec{0} \cdot \vec{v} = 0$ for all $\vec{v}$ in V.

    If $\vec{w}_1$ and $\vec{w}_2$ are both in $V^\perp$, then $(\vec{w}_1 + \vec{w}_2) \cdot \vec{v} = \vec{w}_1 \cdot \vec{v} + \vec{w}_2 \cdot \vec{v} = 0 + 0 = 0$ for all $\vec{v}$ in V, so that $\vec{w}_1 + \vec{w}_2$ is in $V^\perp$ as well.

    If $\vec{w}$ is in $V^\perp$ and k is an arbitrary constant, then $(k\vec{w}) \cdot \vec{v} = k(\vec{w} \cdot \vec{v}) = k0 = 0$ for all $\vec{v}$ in V, so that $k\vec{w}$ is in $V^\perp$ as well.

25. We need to find all vectors $\vec{x}$ in $\mathbb{R}^5$ such that $\begin{bmatrix} x_1 \\ x_2 \\ x_3 \\ x_4 \\ x_5 \end{bmatrix} \cdot \begin{bmatrix} 1 \\ 2 \\ 3 \\ 4 \\ 5 \end{bmatrix} = x_1 + 2x_2 + 3x_3 + 4x_4 + 5x_5 = 0.$

    These vectors are of the form
    $$\begin{bmatrix} x_1 \\ x_2 \\ x_3 \\ x_4 \\ x_5 \end{bmatrix} = \begin{bmatrix} -2a - 3b - 4c - 5d \\ a \\ b \\ c \\ d \end{bmatrix} = a\begin{bmatrix} -2 \\ 1 \\ 0 \\ 0 \\ 0 \end{bmatrix} + b\begin{bmatrix} -3 \\ 0 \\ 1 \\ 0 \\ 0 \end{bmatrix} + c\begin{bmatrix} -4 \\ 0 \\ 0 \\ 1 \\ 0 \end{bmatrix} + d\begin{bmatrix} -5 \\ 0 \\ 0 \\ 0 \\ 1 \end{bmatrix}.$$

The four vectors to the right form a basis of $L^\perp$; they span $L^\perp$, by construction, and none of them is a linear combination of the three others (since each of them has a one as a component where the other three have a zero).

27. A basis of $\text{im}(A)$ is $\begin{bmatrix} 1 \\ 1 \\ 1 \end{bmatrix}, \begin{bmatrix} 1 \\ 2 \\ 3 \end{bmatrix}$, by Fact 3.1.3.

29. The three column vectors of A span all of $\mathbb{R}^2$, so that $\text{im}(A) = \mathbb{R}^2$. We can choose any two of the columns of A to form a basis of $\text{im}(A)$; another sensible choice is $\vec{e}_1, \vec{e}_2$.

31. The two column vectors of the given matrix A are linearly independent (they are not parallel), so that they form a basis of $\text{im}(A)$.

33. $\text{im}(A) = \text{span}(\vec{e}_1, \vec{e}_2, \vec{e}_3)$, so that $\vec{e}_1, \vec{e}_2, \vec{e}_3$ is a basis of $\text{im}(A)$.

35. Consider a nontrival relation $c_1\vec{v}_1 + c_2\vec{v}_2 + \cdots + c_m\vec{v}_m = \vec{0}$.
    Let i be the highest index such that $c_i \neq 0$; since $\vec{v}_1 \neq \vec{0}$ we know that $i > 1$. Now we have
    $c_1\vec{v}_1 + c_2\vec{v}_2 + \cdots + c_i\vec{v}_i = \vec{0}$.
    We can solve this relation for $\vec{v}_i$ and thus express $\vec{v}_i$ as a linear combination $\vec{v}_1, \vec{v}_2, \ldots, \vec{v}_{i-1}$:
    $\vec{v}_i = -\dfrac{c_1}{c_i}\vec{v}_1 - \dfrac{c_2}{c_i}\vec{v}_2 - \cdots - \dfrac{c_{i-1}}{c_i}\vec{v}_{i-1}$.

37. No; as a counterexample, consider the extreme case when T is the zero transformation, that is, $T(\vec{x}) = \vec{0}$ for all $\vec{x}$. Then the vectors $T(\vec{v}_1), \ldots, T(\vec{v}_m)$ will all be zero, so that they are linearly dependent.

39. Yes; we can use Exercise 35 here. None of the vectors in the sequence $\vec{v}_1, \ldots, \vec{v}_m, \vec{v}$ is a linear combination of the previous vectors in that sequence.

41. To show that the columns of B are linearly independent, we show that $\ker(B) = \{\vec{0}\}$. Indeed, if $B\vec{x} = \vec{0}$, then $AB\vec{x} = A\vec{0} = \vec{0}$, so that $\vec{x} = \vec{0}$ (since $AB = I_m$).
    By Fact 3.2.6, $\text{rank}(B) = \#$ columns $= m$, so that $m \leq n$ and in fact $m < n$ (we are told that $m \neq n$). This implies that the rank of the $m \times n$ matrix A is less than n, so that the columns of A are linearly dependent (by Fact 3.2.6).

43. Consider a linear relation $c_1\vec{v}_1 + c_2(\vec{v}_1 + \vec{v}_2) + c_3(\vec{v}_1 + \vec{v}_2 + \vec{v}_3) = \vec{0}$, or, $(c_1 + c_2 + c_3)\vec{v}_1 + (c_2 + c_3)\vec{v}_2 + c_3\vec{v}_3 = \vec{0}$. Since there is only the trivial relation among the vectors $\vec{v}_1, \vec{v}_2, \vec{v}_3$, we must have $c_1 + c_2 + c_3 = c_2 + c_3 = c_3 = 0$, so that $c_3 = 0$ and then $c_2 = 0$ and then $c_1 = 0$, as claimed.

45. Yes; if A is invertible, then $\text{rref}(A) = I_n$, so that the columns of A are linearly independent, by Fact 3.2.6.

47. By Fact 3.2.6, $\mathrm{rref}(A) = \begin{bmatrix} 1 & 0 & 0 \\ 0 & 1 & 0 \\ 0 & 0 & 1 \\ 0 & 0 & 0 \end{bmatrix}$.

49. $L = \mathrm{im} \begin{bmatrix} 1 \\ 1 \\ 1 \end{bmatrix}$

To write L as a kernel, think of L as the intersection of the planes $x = y$ and $y = z$, that is, as the solution set of the system $\begin{vmatrix} x & - & y & & = 0 \\ & & y & - & z & = 0 \end{vmatrix}$.

Therefore, $L = \ker \begin{bmatrix} 1 & -1 & 0 \\ 0 & 1 & -1 \end{bmatrix}$.

There are other solutions.

51. a. Consider a relation $c_1 \vec{v}_1 + \cdots + c_p \vec{v}_p + d_1 \vec{w}_1 + \cdots + d_q \vec{w}_q = \vec{0}$.

    Then the vector $c_1 \vec{v}_1 + \cdots + c_p \vec{v}_p = -d_1 \vec{w}_1 - \cdots - d_q \vec{w}_q$ is both in V and in W, so that this vector is $\vec{0}$: $c_1 \vec{v}_1 + \cdots + c_p \vec{v}_p = \vec{0}$ and $d_1 \vec{w}_1 + \cdots + d_q \vec{w}_q = \vec{0}$.

    Now the c_i are all zero (since the $\vec{v}_i$ are linearly independent) and the d_j are zero (since the $\vec{w}_j$ are linearly independent).

    Since there is only the trivial relation among the vectors $\vec{v}_1, \ldots, \vec{v}_p, \vec{w}_1, \ldots, \vec{w}_q$, they are linearly independent.

    b. In Exercise 50 we show that $V + W = \mathrm{span}(\vec{v}_1, \ldots, \vec{v}_p, \vec{w}_1, \ldots, \vec{w}_q)$, and in part (a) we show that these vectors are linearly independent.

3.3

1. $\mathrm{rref}(A) = \begin{bmatrix} 1 & 2 \\ 0 & 0 \end{bmatrix}$

   A basis of $\ker(A)$ is $\begin{bmatrix} -2 \\ 1 \end{bmatrix}$; $\dim(\ker(A)) = 1$.

3. $\mathrm{rref}(A) = \begin{bmatrix} 1 & 0 & 5 \\ 0 & 1 & -1 \\ 0 & 0 & 0 \end{bmatrix}$

   A basis of $\ker(A)$ is $\begin{bmatrix} -5 \\ 1 \\ 1 \end{bmatrix}$, so that $\dim(\ker(A)) = 1$.

5. $\mathrm{rref}(A) = \begin{bmatrix} 1 & -\frac{4}{5} & \frac{3}{5} \end{bmatrix}$

   A basis of $\ker A$ is $\begin{bmatrix} 4 \\ 5 \\ 0 \end{bmatrix}$, $\begin{bmatrix} -3 \\ 0 \\ 5 \end{bmatrix}$, so that $\dim(\ker(A)) = 2$.

7. $\text{rref}(A) = A$

A basis of $\ker(A)$ is $\begin{bmatrix} 1 \\ 0 \\ 0 \\ 0 \\ 0 \end{bmatrix}$, $\begin{bmatrix} 0 \\ -2 \\ 1 \\ 0 \\ 0 \end{bmatrix}$, $\begin{bmatrix} 0 \\ -3 \\ 0 \\ -4 \\ 1 \end{bmatrix}$, so that $\dim(\ker(A)) = 3$.

9. $\text{rref}(A) = A$

A basis of $\ker(A)$ is $\begin{bmatrix} 1 \\ 1 \\ 0 \\ 0 \\ 0 \end{bmatrix}$, $\begin{bmatrix} -1 \\ 0 \\ 1 \\ 0 \\ 0 \end{bmatrix}$, $\begin{bmatrix} 1 \\ 0 \\ 0 \\ 1 \\ 0 \end{bmatrix}$, $\begin{bmatrix} -1 \\ 0 \\ 0 \\ 0 \\ 1 \end{bmatrix}$, so that $\dim(\ker(A)) = 4$.

11. A basis of $\text{im}(A)$ is $\begin{bmatrix} 1 \\ 2 \end{bmatrix}$, so that $\dim(\text{im}(A)) = 1$ (see Exercise 1).

13. A basis of $\text{im}(A)$ is $\begin{bmatrix} 1 \\ 1 \\ 1 \end{bmatrix}$, $\begin{bmatrix} 3 \\ 2 \\ 1 \end{bmatrix}$, so that $\dim(\text{im}(A)) = 2$ (see Exercise 4).

15. A basis of $\text{im}(A)$ is $[5]$ (or $[k]$ for any nonzero k), so that $\dim(\text{im}(A)) = 1$.

17. $\text{rref}(A) = \begin{bmatrix} 1 & 2 & 0 \\ 0 & 0 & 1 \\ 0 & 0 & 0 \\ 0 & 0 & 0 \end{bmatrix}$, so that a basis of $\text{im}(A)$ is $\begin{bmatrix} 1 \\ 1 \\ 1 \\ 1 \end{bmatrix}$, $\begin{bmatrix} 1 \\ 2 \\ 3 \\ 4 \end{bmatrix}$, with $\dim(\text{im}(A)) = 2$.

19. $\text{rref}(A) = \begin{bmatrix} 1 & 0 & 2 & 0 \\ 0 & 1 & -3 & 0 \\ 0 & 0 & 0 & 1 \\ 0 & 0 & 0 & 0 \end{bmatrix}$, so that a basis of $\text{im}(A)$ is $\begin{bmatrix} 1 \\ 0 \\ 3 \\ 0 \end{bmatrix}$, $\begin{bmatrix} 0 \\ 1 \\ 4 \\ -1 \end{bmatrix}$, $\begin{bmatrix} 4 \\ -1 \\ 8 \\ 4 \end{bmatrix}$, with $\dim(\text{im}(A)) = 3$.

21. $\text{rref}(A) = \begin{bmatrix} 1 & -1 & 0 & 2 & 0 \\ 0 & 0 & 1 & 1 & 0 \\ 0 & 0 & 0 & 0 & 1 \\ 0 & 0 & 0 & 0 & 0 \end{bmatrix}$

A basis of $\text{im}(A)$ is $\begin{bmatrix} 1 \\ -1 \\ 1 \\ 2 \end{bmatrix}$, $\begin{bmatrix} -1 \\ 0 \\ -2 \\ -1 \end{bmatrix}$, $\begin{bmatrix} 1 \\ 2 \\ 3 \\ 4 \end{bmatrix}$, sot hat $\dim(\text{im}(A)) = 3$.

A basis of $\ker(A)$ is $\begin{bmatrix} 1 \\ 1 \\ 0 \\ 0 \\ 0 \end{bmatrix}$, $\begin{bmatrix} -2 \\ 0 \\ -1 \\ 1 \\ 0 \end{bmatrix}$, so that $\dim(\ker(A)) = 2$.

$\dim(\operatorname{im}(A)) + \dim(\ker(A)) = 5 = \#$ of columns, in accordance with Fact 3.3.9.

23. A basis of $\operatorname{im}(A)$ is $\begin{bmatrix} 1 \\ 1 \\ 1 \\ 1 \\ 1 \end{bmatrix}$ and for $\ker(A)$ we have $\begin{bmatrix} -1 \\ 1 \\ 0 \\ 0 \\ 0 \end{bmatrix}$, $\begin{bmatrix} -1 \\ 0 \\ 1 \\ 0 \\ 0 \end{bmatrix}$, $\begin{bmatrix} -1 \\ 0 \\ 0 \\ 1 \\ 0 \end{bmatrix}$, $\begin{bmatrix} -1 \\ 0 \\ 0 \\ 0 \\ 1 \end{bmatrix}$.

$\dim(\operatorname{im}(A)) + \dim(\ker(A)) = 1 + 4 = 5 = \#$ of columns, in accordance with Fact 3.3.9.

25. We form a 5×9 matrix A with the given vectors as its columns.

$$\operatorname{rref}(A) = \begin{bmatrix} 1 & 3 & 0 & -1 & 3 & 0 & 0 & -1 & 0 \\ 0 & 0 & 1 & 3 & -1 & 0 & 0 & 3 & 0 \\ 0 & 0 & 0 & 0 & 0 & 1 & 0 & -1 & 0 \\ 0 & 0 & 0 & 0 & 0 & 0 & 1 & 0 & 0 \\ 0 & 0 & 0 & 0 & 0 & 0 & 0 & 0 & 1 \end{bmatrix}$$

Since $\operatorname{rank}(A) = 5$ we have $\operatorname{im}(A) = \mathbb{R}^5$, and we can use Fact 3.3.7 to pick a basis of $\operatorname{im}(A) = \mathbb{R}^5$
from among the given vectors: $\begin{bmatrix} 1 \\ 2 \\ 3 \\ 2 \\ 1 \end{bmatrix}$, $\begin{bmatrix} 3 \\ 2 \\ 4 \\ 1 \\ 2 \end{bmatrix}$, $\begin{bmatrix} 4 \\ 3 \\ 2 \\ 1 \\ 4 \end{bmatrix}$, $\begin{bmatrix} 2 \\ 3 \\ 5 \\ 7 \\ 5 \end{bmatrix}$, $\begin{bmatrix} 1 \\ 2 \\ 9 \\ 1 \\ 8 \end{bmatrix}$.

27. Form a 4×4 matrix A with the given vectors as its columns. We find that $\operatorname{rref}(A) = I_4$, so that the vectors do indeed form a basis of $\mathbb{R}^4$, by Fact 3.3.10.

29. $x_1 = -\frac{3}{2}x_2 - \frac{1}{2}x_3$; let $x_2 = s$ and $x_3 = t$. Then the solutions are of the form

$$\begin{bmatrix} x_1 \\ x_2 \\ x_3 \end{bmatrix} = \begin{bmatrix} -\frac{3}{2}s - \frac{1}{2}t \\ s \\ t \end{bmatrix} = s\begin{bmatrix} -\frac{3}{2} \\ 1 \\ 0 \end{bmatrix} + t\begin{bmatrix} -\frac{1}{2} \\ 0 \\ 1 \end{bmatrix}.$$

Multiplying the two vectors by 2 to simplify, we obtain the basis $\begin{bmatrix} -3 \\ 2 \\ 0 \end{bmatrix}$, $\begin{bmatrix} -1 \\ 0 \\ 2 \end{bmatrix}$.

31. Proceeding as in Exercise 29, we can find the following basis of V: $\begin{bmatrix} 1 \\ 1 \\ 0 \\ 0 \end{bmatrix}$, $\begin{bmatrix} -2 \\ 0 \\ 1 \\ 0 \end{bmatrix}$, $\begin{bmatrix} -4 \\ 0 \\ 0 \\ 1 \end{bmatrix}$.

Now let A be the 4×3 matrix with these three vectors as its columns. Then $\operatorname{im}(A) = V$ by Fact 3.1.3, and $\ker(A) = \{\vec{0}\}$ by Fact 3.2.6, so that A does the job.

$$A = \begin{bmatrix} 1 & -2 & -4 \\ 1 & 0 & 0 \\ 0 & 1 & 0 \\ 0 & 0 & 1 \end{bmatrix}.$$

33. We can write $V = \ker(A)$, where A is the $1 \times n$ matrix $A = \begin{bmatrix} c_1 & c_2 & \cdots & c_n \end{bmatrix}$.
    Since at least one of the c_i is nonzero, the rank of A is 1, so that $\dim(V) = \dim(\ker(A)) = n - \operatorname{rank}(A) = n - 1$, by Fact 3.3.5.
    A "hyperplane" in $\mathbb{R}^2$ is a line, and a "hyperplane" in $\mathbb{R}^3$ is just a plane.

35. We need to find all vectors $\vec{x}$ in $\mathbb{R}^n$ such that $\vec{v} \cdot \vec{x} = 0$, or $v_1 x_1 + v_2 x_2 + \cdots + v_n x_n = 0$, where the v_i are the components of the vector $\vec{v}$. These vectors form a hyperplane in $\mathbb{R}^n$ (see Exercise 33), so that the dimension of the space is $n - 1$.

37. Since $\dim(\ker(A)) = 5 - \operatorname{rank}(A)$, any 4×5 matrix with rank 2 will do; for example,

$$A = \begin{bmatrix} 1 & 0 & 0 & 0 & 0 \\ 0 & 1 & 0 & 0 & 0 \\ 0 & 0 & 0 & 0 & 0 \\ 0 & 0 & 0 & 0 & 0 \end{bmatrix}.$$

39. Note that $\ker(C) \neq \{\vec{0}\}$, by Fact 1.3.3, and $\ker(C) \subseteq \ker(A)$. Therefore, $\ker(A) \neq \{\vec{0}\}$, so that A is not invertible.

41. We can choose a basis $\vec{v}_1, \ldots, \vec{v}_p$ in V, where $p = \dim(V) = \dim(W)$. Then $\vec{v}_1, \ldots, \vec{v}_p$ is a basis of W as well, by Fact 3.3.4c, so that $V = W = \operatorname{span}(\vec{v}_1, \ldots, \vec{v}_p)$, as claimed.

43. $\dim(V + W) = \dim(V) + \dim(W)$, by Exercise 3.2.51b.

45. Note that $\operatorname{im}(A) = \operatorname{span}(\vec{v}_1, \ldots, \vec{v}_p, \vec{w}_1, \ldots, \vec{w}_q) = V$, since the $\vec{w}_j$ alone span V.
    Note further that the first p columns of $\operatorname{rref}(A)$ will contain leading ones (since the $\vec{v}_i$ are linearly independent); therefore the $\vec{v}_i$ are pivot columns of A.
    If we use Fact 3.3.7 to find a basis of $V = \operatorname{im}(A)$, this basis will contain all of the $\vec{v}_i$ (since they are pivot columns) and possibly some of the $\vec{w}_j$.

47. Using the terminology suggested in the hint, we need to show that $\vec{u}_1, \ldots, \vec{u}_m, \vec{v}_1, \ldots, \vec{v}_p, \vec{w}_1, \ldots, \vec{w}_q$ is a basis of $V + W$. Then $\dim(V + W) + \dim(V \cap W) = (m + p + q) + m = (m + p) + (m + q) = \dim(V) + \dim(W)$, as claimed. Any vector $\vec{x}$ in $V + W$ can be written as $\vec{x} = \vec{v} + \vec{w}$, where $\vec{v}$ is in V and $\vec{w}$ is in W. Since $\vec{v}$ is a linear combination of the $\vec{u}_i$ and the $\vec{v}_j$, and $\vec{w}$ is a linear combination of the $\vec{u}_i$ and $\vec{w}_j$, $\vec{x}$ will be a linear combination of the $\vec{u}_i, \vec{v}_j$, and $\vec{w}_k$; this shows that the vectors $\vec{u}_1, \ldots, \vec{u}_m, \vec{v}_1, \ldots, \vec{v}_p, \vec{w}_1, \ldots, \vec{w}_q$ span $V + W$.

    To show linear independence, consider the relation $a_1 \vec{u}_1 + \cdots + a_m \vec{u}_m + b_1 \vec{v}_1 + \cdots + b_p \vec{v}_p + c_1 \vec{w}_1 + \cdots + c_q \vec{w}_q = \vec{0}$. Then the vector $a_1 \vec{u}_1 + \cdots + a_m \vec{u}_m + b_1 \vec{v}_1 + \cdots + b_p \vec{v}_p = -c_1 \vec{w}_1 - \cdots - c_q \vec{w}_q$ is in

$V \cap W$, so that it can be expressed uniquely as a linear combination of $\vec{u}_1, \ldots, \vec{u}_m$ alone; this implies that the b_i are all zero. Now our relation simplifies to $a_1 \vec{u}_1 + \cdots + a_m \vec{u}_m + c_1 \vec{w}_1 + \cdots + c_q \vec{w}_q = \vec{0}$, which implies that the a_i and the c_j are zero as well (since the vectors $\vec{u}_1, \ldots, \vec{u}_m, \vec{w}_1, \ldots, \vec{w}_q$ are linearly independent).

49. The nonzero rows of E span the row space, and they are linearly independent (consider the leading ones), so that they form a basis of the row space: $[0\ 1\ 0\ 2\ 0]$, $[0\ 0\ 1\ 3\ 0]$, $[0\ 0\ 0\ 0\ 1]$.

51. a. All elementary row operations leave the row space unchanged, so that A and rref(A) have the same row space.

    b. By part (a) and Exercise 50, dim(row space of A) = dim(row space of rref(A)) = rank(rref(A)) = rank(A).

53. Using the terminology suggested in the hint, we observe that the vectors $\vec{v}, A\vec{v}, \ldots, A^n \vec{v}$ are linearly dependent (by Fact 3.3.4a), so that there is a nontrivial relation $c_0 \vec{v} + c_1 A\vec{v} + \cdots + c_n A^n \vec{v} = \vec{0}$. We can rewrite this relation in the form $(c_0 I_n + c_1 A + \cdots + c_n A^n)\vec{v} = \vec{0}$. The nonzero vector $\vec{v}$ is in the kernel of the matrix $c_0 I_n + c_1 A + \cdots + c_n A^n$, so that this matrix is not invertible.

55. If rank(A) = m, then the m pivot columns of A form a basis of im(A) = $\mathbb{R}^m$, so that the matrix formed by the pivot columns is invertible (by Fact 3.3.10).
    Conversely, if A has an invertible $m \times m$ submatrix B, then the columns of B form a basis of $\mathbb{R}^m$ (again by Fact 3.3.10), so that im(A) = $\mathbb{R}^m$ and therefore rank(A) = dim(im(A)) = m.

57. As in Exercise 56, let m be the smallest positive integer such that $A^m = 0$. In Exercise 56 we construct m linearly independent vectors $\vec{v}, A\vec{v}, \ldots, A^{m-1}\vec{v}$ in $\mathbb{R}^n$; now $m \leq n$ by Fact 3.3.4a. Therefore $A^n = A^m A^{n-m} = 0 A^{n-m} = 0$, as claimed.

59. Prove Fact 3.3.4d: If m vectors $\vec{v}_1, \ldots, \vec{v}_m$ span an m-dimensional space V, then they form a basis of V. We need to show that $\vec{v}_i$ are linearly independent. We will argue indirectly, assuming that the vectors are linearly dependent; this means that one of the vectors is a linear combination of the others, say $\vec{v}_m = c_1 \vec{v}_1 + c_2 \vec{v}_2 + \cdots + c_{m-1} \vec{v}_{m-1}$.
    But then $V = \text{span}(\vec{v}_1, \ldots, \vec{v}_m) = \text{span}(\vec{v}_1, \ldots, \vec{v}_{m-1})$, contradicting Fact 3.3.4b (see Exercise 58).

61. a. Note that rank(B) ≤ 2, so that dim(ker(B)) = $5 - $ rank(B) ≥ 3 and dim(ker(AB)) ≥ 3 since ker(B) $\subseteq$ ker(AB). Since ker(AB) is an subspace of $\mathbb{R}^5$, dim(ker(AB)) could be 3,4, or 5. It is easy to give an example for each case; for example, if $A = \begin{bmatrix} 1 & 0 \\ 0 & 1 \\ 0 & 0 \\ 0 & 0 \end{bmatrix}$ and $B = \begin{bmatrix} 1 & 0 & 0 & 0 & 0 \\ 0 & 1 & 0 & 0 & 0 \end{bmatrix}$,

    then $AB = \begin{bmatrix} 1 & 0 & 0 & 0 & 0 \\ 0 & 1 & 0 & 0 & 0 \\ 0 & 0 & 0 & 0 & 0 \\ 0 & 0 & 0 & 0 & 0 \end{bmatrix}$ and dim(ker(AB)) = 3.

b. Since $\dim(\text{im}(AB)) = 5 - \dim(\ker(AB))$, the possible values of $\dim(\text{im}(AB))$ are 0,1, and 2, by part a.

63. a. By Exercise 3.1.39b, $\text{im}(AB) \subseteq \text{im}(A)$, and therefore $\text{rank}(AB) \leq \text{rank}(A)$.

    b. Write $B = [\vec{v}_1 \cdots \vec{v}_n]$ and $AB = [A\vec{v}_1 \cdots A\vec{v}_n]$. If $r = \text{rank}(B)$, then the r pivot columns of B will span $\text{im}(B)$, and the corresponding r columns of AB will span $\text{im}(AB)$, by linearity of A. By Fact 3.3.4b, $\text{rank}(AB) = \dim(\text{im}(AB)) \leq r = \text{rank}(B)$.
    Summary: $\text{rank}(AB) \leq \text{rank}(A)$, and $\text{rank}(AB) \leq \text{rank}(B)$.

65. Let $\vec{v}_1, \ldots, \vec{v}_6$ be the columns of matrix A. Following the hint, we observe that $\vec{v}_5 = 4\vec{v}_1 + 5\vec{v}_2 + 6\vec{v}_4$, which gives the relation $4\vec{v}_1 + 5\vec{v}_2 + 6\vec{v}_4 - \vec{v}_5 = \vec{0}$. Thus the vector

$$\vec{x} = \begin{bmatrix} 4 \\ 5 \\ 0 \\ 6 \\ -1 \\ 0 \end{bmatrix}$$

is in the kernel of matrix A. Since $\vec{x}$ fails to be in the kernel of matrix B, the two kernels are different, as claimed.

67. Exercise 66 shows that if two matrices A and B of the same size are both in rref and have the same kernel, then $A = B$. Apply this fact to A and $B = \text{rref}(M)$.

3.4

1. We need to find the scalars c_1 and c_2 such that $\begin{bmatrix} 3 \\ 1 \\ -4 \end{bmatrix} = c_1 \begin{bmatrix} 1 \\ -1 \\ 0 \end{bmatrix} + c_2 \begin{bmatrix} 0 \\ 1 \\ -1 \end{bmatrix}$. Solving a linear system gives $c_1 = 3$, $c_2 = 4$. Thus $[\vec{x}]_\mathcal{B} = \begin{bmatrix} c_1 \\ c_2 \end{bmatrix} = \begin{bmatrix} 3 \\ 4 \end{bmatrix}$.

3. Proceeding as in Example 1, we find $[\vec{x}]_\mathcal{B} = \begin{bmatrix} \frac{1}{2} \\ \frac{1}{2} \end{bmatrix}$.

5. By definition of coordinates (Definition 3.4.1), $\vec{x} = 2 \begin{bmatrix} -1 \\ 0 \\ 1 \end{bmatrix} + (-3) \begin{bmatrix} -2 \\ 1 \\ 0 \end{bmatrix} = \begin{bmatrix} 4 \\ -3 \\ 2 \end{bmatrix}$.

7. If $\vec{v}_1, \vec{v}_2$ is a basis with the desired property, then $\vec{x} = 2\vec{v}_1 + 3\vec{v}_2$, or $\vec{v}_2 = \frac{1}{3}\vec{x} - \frac{2}{3}\vec{v}_1$. Thus we can make $\vec{v}_1$ any vector in the plane that is not parallel to $\vec{x}$, and then let $\vec{v}_2 = \frac{1}{3}\vec{x} - \frac{2}{3}\vec{v}_1$. For example, if we choose $\vec{v}_1 = \begin{bmatrix} 3 \\ 2 \\ 0 \end{bmatrix}$, then $\vec{v}_2 = \frac{1}{3}\begin{bmatrix} -4 \\ -4 \\ -1 \end{bmatrix}$.

9. The equation $\begin{bmatrix} 7 \\ 16 \end{bmatrix} = c_1 \begin{bmatrix} 2 \\ 5 \end{bmatrix} + c_2 \begin{bmatrix} 5 \\ 12 \end{bmatrix}$ has the solution $c_1 = -4$, and $c_2 = 3$. Thus the coordinate vector is $\begin{bmatrix} -4 \\ 3 \end{bmatrix}$.

11. The equation $\begin{bmatrix} 1 \\ 1 \\ 1 \end{bmatrix} = c_1 \begin{bmatrix} 1 \\ 2 \\ 3 \end{bmatrix} + c_2 \begin{bmatrix} 0 \\ 1 \\ 2 \end{bmatrix} + c_3 \begin{bmatrix} 0 \\ 0 \\ 1 \end{bmatrix}$ has the solution $c_1 = 1$, $c_2 = -1$, and $c_3 = 0$.

    Thus the coordinate vector is $\begin{bmatrix} 1 \\ -1 \\ 0 \end{bmatrix}$.

13. $A = \begin{bmatrix} 1 & 2 \\ 3 & 4 \end{bmatrix}$, $S = \begin{bmatrix} 1 & 1 \\ 1 & 2 \end{bmatrix}$, $S^{-1} = \begin{bmatrix} 2 & -1 \\ -1 & 1 \end{bmatrix}$.

    By Fact 3.4.4 the new matrix of T, namely B, is given by $B = S^{-1}AS = \begin{bmatrix} -1 & -1 \\ 4 & 6 \end{bmatrix}$.

15. a. Let B be the matrix of T with respect to the basis $\vec{v}_1 = \begin{bmatrix} 1 \\ 3 \end{bmatrix}$, $\vec{v}_2 = \begin{bmatrix} -3 \\ 1 \end{bmatrix}$. By Fact 3.4.3, $B =$

    $[[T(\vec{v}_1)]_\mathcal{B} \quad [T(\vec{v}_2)]_\mathcal{B}] = [[\vec{v}_1]_\mathcal{B} \quad [\vec{0}]_\mathcal{B}] = \begin{bmatrix} 1 & 0 \\ 0 & 0 \end{bmatrix}$.

    b. $A = SBS^{-1}$, with the matrix $B = \begin{bmatrix} 1 & 0 \\ 0 & 0 \end{bmatrix}$ from part a, and $S = [\vec{v}_1 \ \vec{v}_2] = \begin{bmatrix} 1 & -3 \\ 3 & 1 \end{bmatrix}$. A straight-

    forward computation gives $A = \begin{bmatrix} 0.1 & 0.3 \\ 0.3 & 0.9 \end{bmatrix}$.

17. By Fact 3.4.4, $B = S^{-1}AS = \begin{bmatrix} 3 & 5 \\ 5 & 8 \end{bmatrix}^{-1} \begin{bmatrix} 1 & 9 \\ 9 & 4 \end{bmatrix} \begin{bmatrix} 3 & 5 \\ 5 & 8 \end{bmatrix} = \begin{bmatrix} -149 & -231 \\ 99 & 154 \end{bmatrix}$.

19. By Fact 3.4.4, $A = SBS^{-1} = \begin{bmatrix} 0 & 1 \\ 1 & 0 \end{bmatrix} \begin{bmatrix} a & b \\ c & d \end{bmatrix} \begin{bmatrix} 0 & 1 \\ 1 & 0 \end{bmatrix}^{-1} = \begin{bmatrix} d & c \\ b & a \end{bmatrix}$.

21. By Fact 3.4.1, $\begin{bmatrix} 2 \\ 0 \end{bmatrix}_\mathcal{B} = \begin{bmatrix} 3 & -1 \\ 1 & 1 \end{bmatrix}^{-1} \begin{bmatrix} 2 \\ 0 \end{bmatrix} = \begin{bmatrix} \frac{1}{2} \\ -\frac{1}{2} \end{bmatrix}$.

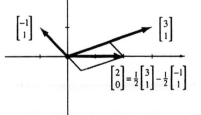

23. From the picture, $\vec{u} + \vec{v} = -\vec{w}$ so that $\vec{w} = -\vec{u} - \vec{v}$, i.e. $[\vec{w}]_B = \begin{bmatrix} -1 \\ -1 \end{bmatrix}$.

25. Let $\mathcal{B}$ be the basis consisting of vectors $\vec{v}_1, \ldots, \vec{v}_m$. If $\vec{x} = c_1\vec{v}_1 + \cdots + c_m\vec{v}_m$ and $\vec{y} = d_1\vec{v}_1 + \cdots + d_m\vec{v}_m$, then $\vec{x} + \vec{y} = (c_1 + d_1)\vec{v}_1 + \cdots + (c_m + d_m)\vec{v}_m$ and $k\vec{x} = (kc_1)\vec{v}_1 + \cdots + (kc_m)\vec{v}_m$, so that

$$[\vec{x} + \vec{y}]_B = \begin{bmatrix} c_1 + d_1 \\ \cdots \\ c_m + d_m \end{bmatrix} = \begin{bmatrix} c_1 \\ \cdots \\ d_m \end{bmatrix} + \begin{bmatrix} d_1 \\ \cdot \\ d_m \end{bmatrix} = [\vec{x}]_B + [\vec{y}]_B \text{ and}$$

$$[k\vec{x}]_B = \begin{bmatrix} kc_1 \\ \cdot \\ kc_m \end{bmatrix} = k \begin{bmatrix} c_1 \\ \cdot \\ c_m \end{bmatrix} = k[\vec{x}]_B, \text{ as claimed.}$$

27. By Fact 3.4.1, $\vec{x} = S[\vec{x}]_B = \begin{bmatrix} 1 & 3 \\ 2 & 4 \end{bmatrix} \begin{bmatrix} 7 \\ 11 \end{bmatrix} = \begin{bmatrix} 40 \\ 58 \end{bmatrix}$.

29. By Fact 3.4.1, $\vec{x} = \begin{bmatrix} 1 & 1 \\ 1 & 2 \end{bmatrix} [\vec{x}]_B$ and $\vec{x} = \begin{bmatrix} 1 & 3 \\ 2 & 4 \end{bmatrix} [\vec{x}]_\mathcal{R}$, so that $\begin{bmatrix} 1 & 1 \\ 1 & 2 \end{bmatrix} [\vec{x}]_B = \begin{bmatrix} 1 & 3 \\ 2 & 4 \end{bmatrix} [\vec{x}]_\mathcal{R}$ and

$$[\vec{x}]_\mathcal{R} = \underbrace{\begin{bmatrix} 1 & 3 \\ 2 & 4 \end{bmatrix}^{-1} \begin{bmatrix} 1 & 1 \\ 1 & 2 \end{bmatrix}}_{P} [\vec{x}]_B, \text{ i.e. } P = \begin{bmatrix} -\frac{1}{2} & 1 \\ \frac{1}{2} & 0 \end{bmatrix}.$$

31. $T(\vec{v}_1) = \vec{v}_1 \times \vec{v}_2 = \vec{v}_3$ so $[T(\vec{v}_1)]_B = \begin{bmatrix} 0 \\ 0 \\ 1 \end{bmatrix}$.

    $T(\vec{v}_2) = \vec{v}_2 \times \vec{v}_2 = \vec{0}$ so $[T(\vec{v}_2)]_B = \begin{bmatrix} 0 \\ 0 \\ 0 \end{bmatrix}$.

    $T(\vec{v}_3) = \vec{v}_3 \times \vec{v}_2 = -\vec{v}_1$ so $[T(\vec{v}_3)]_B = \begin{bmatrix} -1 \\ 0 \\ 0 \end{bmatrix}$.

    Hence, by Fact 3.4.3, the desired matrix is $\begin{bmatrix} 0 & 0 & -1 \\ 0 & 0 & 0 \\ 1 & 0 & 0 \end{bmatrix}$.

33. First we find the matrices $S = \begin{bmatrix} x & y \\ z & t \end{bmatrix}$ such that $\begin{bmatrix} 2 & 0 \\ 0 & 3 \end{bmatrix} \begin{bmatrix} x & y \\ z & t \end{bmatrix} = \begin{bmatrix} x & y \\ z & t \end{bmatrix} \begin{bmatrix} 2 & 1 \\ 0 & 3 \end{bmatrix}$, or

    $\begin{bmatrix} 2x & 2y \\ 3z & 3t \end{bmatrix} = \begin{bmatrix} 2x & x + 3y \\ 2z & z + 3t \end{bmatrix}$. The solutions are of the form $S = \begin{bmatrix} -y & y \\ 0 & t \end{bmatrix}$, where y and t are arbitrary constants. Since there are *invertible* solutions S (for example, let $y = t = 1$), the matrices $\begin{bmatrix} 2 & 0 \\ 0 & 3 \end{bmatrix}$ and $\begin{bmatrix} 2 & 1 \\ 0 & 3 \end{bmatrix}$ are indeed similar.

35. We seek a basis $\vec{v}_1 = \begin{bmatrix} x \\ z \end{bmatrix}, \vec{v}_2 = \begin{bmatrix} y \\ t \end{bmatrix}$ such that the matrix $S = [\vec{v}_1 \ \vec{v}_2] = \begin{bmatrix} x & y \\ z & t \end{bmatrix}$ satisfies the

    equation $\begin{bmatrix} -5 & -9 \\ 4 & 7 \end{bmatrix} \begin{bmatrix} x & y \\ z & t \end{bmatrix} = \begin{bmatrix} x & y \\ z & t \end{bmatrix} \begin{bmatrix} 1 & 1 \\ 0 & 1 \end{bmatrix}$. Solving the ensuing linear system gives $S = \begin{bmatrix} -\frac{3z}{2} & \frac{z}{4} - \frac{3t}{2} \\ z & t \end{bmatrix}$.

    We need to choose z and t so that S will be invertible. For example, if we let $z = 6$ and $t = 1$, then $S = \begin{bmatrix} -9 & 0 \\ 6 & 1 \end{bmatrix}$, so that $\vec{v}_1 = \begin{bmatrix} -9 \\ 6 \end{bmatrix}, \vec{v}_2 = \begin{bmatrix} 0 \\ 1 \end{bmatrix}$.

37. First we find the matrices $S = \begin{bmatrix} x & y \\ z & t \end{bmatrix}$ such that $\begin{bmatrix} p & -q \\ q & p \end{bmatrix} \begin{bmatrix} x & y \\ z & t \end{bmatrix} = \begin{bmatrix} x & y \\ z & t \end{bmatrix} \begin{bmatrix} p & q \\ -q & p \end{bmatrix}$, or,

    $\begin{bmatrix} px - qz & py - qt \\ qx + pz & qy + pt \end{bmatrix} = \begin{bmatrix} px - qy & qx + py \\ pz - qt & qz + pt \end{bmatrix}$. If $q \neq 0$, then the solutions are of the form

    $S = \begin{bmatrix} -t & z \\ z & t \end{bmatrix}$, where z and t are arbitrary constants. Since there are *invertible* solutions S (for

    example, let $z = t = 1$), the matrices $\begin{bmatrix} p & -q \\ q & p \end{bmatrix}$ and $\begin{bmatrix} p & q \\ -q & p \end{bmatrix}$ are indeed similar. (If $q = 0$, then

    the two matrices are equal.)

39. a. If $S = I_n$, then $S^{-1}AS = A$.

    b. If $S^{-1}AS = B$, then $SBS^{-1} = A$. If we let $R = S^{-1}$, then $R^{-1}BR = A$, showing that B is similar to A.

41. The matrix we seek is $\left[\left[T \begin{bmatrix} 1 \\ 0 \end{bmatrix} \right]_\mathcal{B}, \left[T \begin{bmatrix} a \\ c \end{bmatrix} \right]_\mathcal{B} \right] = \left[\begin{bmatrix} a \\ c \end{bmatrix}_\mathcal{B} \begin{bmatrix} a^2 + bc \\ ac + cd \end{bmatrix}_\mathcal{B} \right] = \begin{bmatrix} 0 & bc - ad \\ 1 & a + d \end{bmatrix}$.

43. The matrix of the transformation $T(\vec{x}) = A\vec{x}$ with respect to the basis $\begin{bmatrix} 1 \\ 2 \end{bmatrix}, \begin{bmatrix} 2 \\ 1 \end{bmatrix}$ is $D = \left[\begin{bmatrix} 3 \\ 6 \end{bmatrix}_\mathcal{B} \begin{bmatrix} -2 \\ -1 \end{bmatrix}_\mathcal{B} \right] = \begin{bmatrix} 3 & 0 \\ 0 & -1 \end{bmatrix}$. Thus $S^{-1}AS = D$ for $S = \begin{bmatrix} 1 & 2 \\ 2 & 1 \end{bmatrix}$.

45. a. Note that $AS = SB$. If $\vec{x}$ is in $\ker(B)$, then $A(S\vec{x}) = SB\vec{x} = S\vec{0} = \vec{0}$, so that $S\vec{x}$ is in $\ker(A)$, as claimed.

    b. We use the hint and observe that nullity $(B) = \dim(\ker B) = p \leq \dim(\ker A) = \text{nullity}(A)$, since $S\vec{v}_1, \ldots, S\vec{v}_p$ are p linearly independent vectors in $\ker(A)$. Reversing the roles of A and B shows that, conversely, $\text{nullity}(A) \leq \text{nullity}(B)$, so that the equation $\text{nullity}(A) = \text{nullity}(B)$ holds, as claimed.

47. a. By inspection, we can find an orthonormal basis $\vec{v}_1 = \vec{v}, \vec{v}_2, \vec{v}_3$ of $\mathbb{R}^3$:

    $\vec{v}_1 = \vec{v} = \begin{bmatrix} 0.6 \\ 0.8 \\ 0 \end{bmatrix}, \vec{v}_2 = \begin{bmatrix} 0 \\ 0 \\ 1 \end{bmatrix}, \vec{v}_3 = \begin{bmatrix} 0.8 \\ -0.6 \\ 0 \end{bmatrix}$

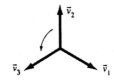

b. Now $T(\vec{v}_1) = \vec{v}_1, T(\vec{v}_2) = \vec{v}_3$ and $T(\vec{v}_3) = -\vec{v}_2$, so that the matrix B of T with respect to the basis $\vec{v}_1, \vec{v}_2, \vec{v}_3$ is

$$B = \begin{bmatrix} 1 & 0 & 0 \\ 0 & 0 & -1 \\ 0 & 1 & 0 \end{bmatrix}. \text{ Then } A = SBS^{-1} = \begin{bmatrix} 0.36 & 0.48 & 0.8 \\ 0.48 & 0.64 & -0.6 \\ -0.8 & 0.6 & 0 \end{bmatrix}.$$

49. $B = S^{-1}AS$, where $S = A = \begin{bmatrix} 0 & -1 \\ 1 & 0 \end{bmatrix}$. Thus $B = A = \begin{bmatrix} 0 & -1 \\ 1 & 0 \end{bmatrix}$

51. Let S be the $n \times n$ matrix whose columns are $\vec{e}_n, \vec{e}_{n-1}, \ldots, \vec{e}_1$. Note that S has all 1's on "the other diagonal" and 0's elsewhere:

$$s_{ij} = \begin{cases} 1 & \text{if } i + j = n + 1 \\ 0 & \text{otherwise} \end{cases}$$

Also, $S^{-1} = S$.
Now, $B = S^{-1}AS = SAS$; the entries of B are $b_{ij} = s_{i,n+1-i}a_{n+1-i,n+1-j}s_{n+1-j,j} = a_{n+1-i,n+1-j}$.
Answer: $b_{ij} = a_{n+1-i,n+1-j}$
B is obtained from A by reversing the order of the rows and of the columns.

True or False

1. F; It's a subspace of $\mathbb{R}^3$.

3. T, by Summary 3.3.11.

5. T, by Summary 3.3.11.

7. T; We have the nontrivial relation $3\vec{u} + 3\vec{v} + 3\vec{w} = \vec{0}$.

9. T, by Fact 3.3.2.

11. T, by Fact 3.2.6.

13. F; The number n may exceed 4.

15. T, by Fact 3.4.6, parts b and c.

17. T, by Definition 3.2.3.

19. T; Check that $\begin{bmatrix} 1 & 0 \\ 0 & -1 \end{bmatrix} \begin{bmatrix} 1 & 1 \\ -1 & 1 \end{bmatrix} = \begin{bmatrix} 1 & 1 \\ -1 & 1 \end{bmatrix} \begin{bmatrix} 0 & 1 \\ 1 & 0 \end{bmatrix}$.

21. F; We are unable to find an invertible matrix S as required in the definition of similarity.

23. T, by Definition 3.2.1 (all vectors in $\mathbb{R}^3$ are linear combinations of $\vec{e}_1, \vec{e}_2, \vec{e}_3$).

25. T, since $AB\vec{v} = A\vec{0} = \vec{0}$.

27. F; Suppose $\vec{v}_2 = 2\vec{v}_1$. Then $T(\vec{v}_2) = 2T(\vec{v}_1) = 2\vec{e}_1$ cannot be $\vec{e}_2$.

29. T, since $A^{-1}(AB)A = BA$.

31. T; Consider any basis $\vec{v}_1, \vec{v}_2, \vec{v}_3$ of V. Then $k\vec{v}_1, \vec{v}_2, \vec{v}_3$ is a basis as well, for any nonzero scalar k.

33. F; Consider $\begin{bmatrix} 0 & 1 \\ 0 & 1 \end{bmatrix} \begin{bmatrix} 1 & 1 \\ 0 & 0 \end{bmatrix} = \begin{bmatrix} 0 & 0 \\ 0 & 0 \end{bmatrix}$.

35. F; Let $V = \text{span}(\vec{e}_1)$ and $W = \text{span}(\vec{e}_2)$ in $\mathbb{R}^2$, for example.

37. T; Consider the linear transformation with matrix $[\vec{w}_1 \ \dots \ \vec{w}_n][\vec{v}_1 \ \dots \ \vec{v}_n]^{-1}$.

39. F; Note that $\mathbb{R}^2$ isn't even a subset of $\mathbb{R}^3$. A vector in $\mathbb{R}^2$, with two components, does not belong to $\mathbb{R}^3$.

41. T; Let $A = \begin{bmatrix} 0 & 1 \\ 0 & 0 \end{bmatrix}$, for example.

43. T; Matrix $B = S^{-1}AS$ is invertible, being the product of invertible matrices.

45. T; Pick three vectors $\vec{v}_1, \vec{v}_2, \vec{v}_3$ that span V. Then $V = \text{im}[\vec{v}_1 \ \vec{v}_2 \ \vec{v}_3]$.

47. T; Pick a vector $\vec{v}$ that is neither on the line nor perpendicular to it. Then the matrix of the linear transformation $T(\vec{x}) = R\vec{x}$ with respect to the basis $\vec{v}, R\vec{v}$ is $\begin{bmatrix} 0 & 1 \\ 1 & 0 \end{bmatrix}$, since $R(R\vec{v}) = \vec{v}$.

49. T; Note that $A(B - C) = 0$, so that all the columns of matrix $B - C$ are in the kernel of A. Thus $B - C = 0$ and $B = C$, as claimed.

51. F; Suppose such a matrix A exists. Then there is a vector $\vec{v}$ in $\mathbb{R}^2$ such that $A^2\vec{v} \neq \vec{0}$ but $A^3\vec{v} = \vec{0}$. As in Exercise 3.4.32a we can show that vectors $\vec{v}, A\vec{v}, A^2\vec{v}$ are linearly independent, a contradiction (we are looking at three vectors in $\mathbb{R}^2$).

Chapter 4

1. Not a subspace since it does not contain the neutral element, that is, the function $f(t) = 0$, for all t.

3. This subset V is a subspace of P_2:

    • The neutral element $f(t) = 0$ (for all t) is in V since $f'(1) = f(2) = 0$.

    • If f and g are in V (so that $f'(1) = f(2)$ and $g'(1) = g(2)$), then
    $(f + g)'(1) = (f' + g')(1) = f'(1) + g'(1) = f(2) + g(2) = (f + g)(2)$, so that $f + g$ is in V.

    • If f is in V (so that $f'(1) = f(2)$) and k is any constant, then $(kf)'(1) = (kf')(1) = kf'(1) = kf(2) = (kf)(2)$, so that kf is in V.

    If $f(t) = a + bt + ct^2$ then $f'(t) = b + 2ct$, and f is in V if
    $f'(1) = b + 2c = a + 2b + 4c = f(2)$, or $a + b + 2c = 0$. The general element of V is of the form $f(t) = (-b - 2c) + bt + ct^2 = b(t - 1) + c(t^2 - 2)$, so that $t - 1, t^2 - 2$ is a basis of V.

5. If $p(t) = a + bt + ct^2$ then $p(-t) = a - bt + ct^2$ and $-p(-t) = -a + bt - ct^2$.
    Comparing coefficients we see that $p(t) = -p(-t)$ for all t if (and only if) $a = c = 0$.
    The general element of the subset is of the form $p(t) = bt$.
    These polynomials form a subspace of P_2, with basis t.

7. The set V of diagonal 3×3 matrices is a subspace of $\mathbb{R}^{3 \times 3}$:

    a. The zero matrix $\begin{bmatrix} 0 & 0 & 0 \\ 0 & 0 & 0 \\ 0 & 0 & 0 \end{bmatrix}$ is in V,

    b. If $A = \begin{bmatrix} a & 0 & 0 \\ 0 & b & 0 \\ 0 & 0 & c \end{bmatrix}$ and $B = \begin{bmatrix} p & 0 & 0 \\ 0 & q & 0 \\ 0 & 0 & r \end{bmatrix}$ are in V, then so is their sum

    $A + B = \begin{bmatrix} a + p & 0 & 0 \\ 0 & b + q & 0 \\ 0 & 0 & c + r \end{bmatrix}$.

    c. If $A = \begin{bmatrix} a & 0 & 0 \\ 0 & b & 0 \\ 0 & 0 & c \end{bmatrix}$ is in V, then so is $kA = \begin{bmatrix} ka & 0 & 0 \\ 0 & kb & 0 \\ 0 & 0 & kc \end{bmatrix}$, for all constants k.

9. Not a subspace; consider multiplication with a negative scalar. I_3 belongs to the set, but $-I_3$ doesn't.

11. Not a subspace: I_3 is in rref, but $2I_3$ isn't.

13. Not a subspace: $(1, 2, 4, 8, \ldots)$ and $(1, 1, 1, 1, \ldots)$ are both geometric sequences, but their sum $(2, 3, 5, 9, \ldots)$ is not.

15. The set W of all square-summable sequences is a subspace of V:

- The sequence $(0, 0, 0, \ldots)$ is in W.

- Suppose (x_n) and (y_n) are in W. Note that the inequality $(x_n + y_n)^2 \leq 2x_n^2 + 2y_n^2$ holds for all n, since $2x_n^2 + 2y_n^2 - (x_n + y_n)^2 = x_n^2 + y_n^2 - 2x_n y_n = (x_n - y_n)^2 \geq 0$. Thus $\sum_{n=1}^{\infty}(x_n + y_n)^2 \leq 2\sum_{n=1}^{\infty} x_n^2 + 2\sum_{n=1}^{\infty} y_n^2$ converges, so that the sequence $(x_n + y_n)$ is in W as well.

- If (x_n) is in W $\left(\text{so that } \sum_{n=1}^{\infty} x_n^2 \text{ converges}\right)$, then (kx_n) is in W as well, for any constant k, since $\sum_{n=1}^{\infty}(kx_n)^2 = k^2 \sum_{n=1}^{\infty} x_n^2$ will converge.

17. Let E_{ij} be the $m \times n$ matrix with a 1 as its ijth entry, and zeros everywhere else. Any A in $\mathbb{R}^{m \times n}$ can be written as the sum of all $a_{ij}E_{ij}$, and the E_{ij} are linearly independent, so that they form a basis of $\mathbb{R}^{m \times n}$. Thus $\dim(\mathbb{R}^{m \times n}) = mn$.

19. $\begin{bmatrix} a + bi \\ c + di \end{bmatrix} = a\begin{bmatrix} 1 \\ 0 \end{bmatrix} + b\begin{bmatrix} i \\ 0 \end{bmatrix} + c\begin{bmatrix} 0 \\ 1 \end{bmatrix} + d\begin{bmatrix} 0 \\ i \end{bmatrix}$

The vectors $\begin{bmatrix} 1 \\ 0 \end{bmatrix}, \begin{bmatrix} i \\ 0 \end{bmatrix}, \begin{bmatrix} 0 \\ 1 \end{bmatrix}, \begin{bmatrix} 0 \\ i \end{bmatrix}$ form a basis of $\mathbb{C}^2$ as a *real* linear space, so that $\dim(\mathbb{C}^2) = 4$.

21. Use the strategy outlined on Page 155. The general element of the subspace is

$\begin{bmatrix} a & 0 \\ 0 & d \end{bmatrix} = a\begin{bmatrix} 1 & 0 \\ 0 & 0 \end{bmatrix} + d\begin{bmatrix} 0 & 0 \\ 0 & 1 \end{bmatrix}$. Thus $\begin{bmatrix} 1 & 0 \\ 0 & 0 \end{bmatrix}, \begin{bmatrix} 0 & 0 \\ 0 & 1 \end{bmatrix}$ is a basis of the subspace; the dimension is 2.

23. Proceeding as in Exercise 21, we find the basis $\begin{bmatrix} 1 & 0 \\ 0 & 0 \end{bmatrix}, \begin{bmatrix} 0 & 0 \\ 1 & 0 \end{bmatrix}, \begin{bmatrix} 0 & 0 \\ 0 & 1 \end{bmatrix}$; the dimension is 3.

25. A polynomial $f(t) = a + bt + ct^2$ is in this subspace if $f(1) = a + b + c = 0$, or $a = -b - c$.
    The polynomials in the subspace are of the form $f(t) = (-b - c) + bt + ct^2 = b(t - 1) + c(t^2 - 1)$, so that $t - 1$, $t^2 - 1$ is a basis of the subspace, whose dimension is 2.

27. $\begin{bmatrix} a & b \\ c & d \end{bmatrix}$ is in the subspace if $\begin{bmatrix} a & b \\ c & d \end{bmatrix}\begin{bmatrix} 1 & 0 \\ 0 & 2 \end{bmatrix} = \begin{bmatrix} a & 2b \\ c & 2d \end{bmatrix}$ equals $\begin{bmatrix} 1 & 0 \\ 0 & 2 \end{bmatrix}\begin{bmatrix} a & b \\ c & d \end{bmatrix} = \begin{bmatrix} a & b \\ 2c & 2d \end{bmatrix}$,

    which is the case if $b = c = 0$. The matrices in the subspace are of the form $\begin{bmatrix} a & 0 \\ 0 & d \end{bmatrix} = a\begin{bmatrix} 1 & 0 \\ 0 & 0 \end{bmatrix} + d\begin{bmatrix} 0 & 0 \\ 0 & 1 \end{bmatrix}$, so that $\begin{bmatrix} 1 & 0 \\ 0 & 0 \end{bmatrix}, \begin{bmatrix} 0 & 0 \\ 0 & 1 \end{bmatrix}$ is a basis, and the dimension is 2.

29. We are looking for the matrices $\begin{bmatrix} a & b \\ c & d \end{bmatrix}$ such that $\begin{bmatrix} a & b \\ c & d \end{bmatrix}\begin{bmatrix} 1 & 1 \\ 1 & 1 \end{bmatrix} = \begin{bmatrix} a+b & a+b \\ c+d & c+d \end{bmatrix} = \begin{bmatrix} 0 & 0 \\ 0 & 0 \end{bmatrix}$.

    It is required that $a = -b$ and $c = -d$. Thus the general element is $\begin{bmatrix} -b & b \\ -d & d \end{bmatrix} = b\begin{bmatrix} -1 & 1 \\ 0 & 0 \end{bmatrix} + d\begin{bmatrix} 0 & 0 \\ -1 & 1 \end{bmatrix}$. Thus $\begin{bmatrix} -1 & 1 \\ 0 & 0 \end{bmatrix}, \begin{bmatrix} 0 & 0 \\ -1 & 1 \end{bmatrix}$ is a basis, and the dimension is 2.

31. We are looking for the matrices $\begin{bmatrix} a & b \\ c & d \end{bmatrix}$ such that $\begin{bmatrix} 0 & 1 \\ 1 & 0 \end{bmatrix}\begin{bmatrix} a & b \\ c & d \end{bmatrix} = \begin{bmatrix} a & b \\ c & d \end{bmatrix}\begin{bmatrix} 1 & 0 \\ 0 & -1 \end{bmatrix}$,

    or, $\begin{bmatrix} c & d \\ a & b \end{bmatrix} = \begin{bmatrix} a & -b \\ c & -d \end{bmatrix}$. It is required that $a = c$ and $b = -d$.

    Thus the general element is $\begin{bmatrix} c & -d \\ c & d \end{bmatrix} = c\begin{bmatrix} 1 & 0 \\ 1 & 0 \end{bmatrix} + d\begin{bmatrix} 0 & -1 \\ 0 & 1 \end{bmatrix}$. Thus $\begin{bmatrix} 1 & 0 \\ 1 & 0 \end{bmatrix}, \begin{bmatrix} 0 & -1 \\ 0 & 1 \end{bmatrix}$ is a basis, and the dimension is 2.

33. We show that the set of all even functions is a subspace of $F(\mathbb{R}, \mathbb{R})$:

    - If $f(t) = 0$ for all t, then $f(-t) = f(t) = 0$ for all t.

    - If f and g are even (that is, $f(-t) = f(t)$ and $g(-t) = g(t)$ for all t), then $(f + g)(-t) = f(-t) + g(-t) = f(t) + g(t) = (f + g)(t)$, so that $f + g$ is even as well.

    - If f is even and k is any constant, then $(kf)(-t) = kf(-t) = kf(t) = (kf)(t)$, so that kf is even as well.

    An analogous proof shows that the odd functions form a subspace of $F(\mathbb{R}, \mathbb{R})$.

35. We show that $L(\mathbb{R}^n, \mathbb{R}^m)$ is a subspace of $F(\mathbb{R}^n, \mathbb{R}^m)$:

    - The zero transformation $T(\vec{x}) = \vec{0}$ (for all $\vec{x}$) is linear, represented by the zero matrix.

    - If T and S are linear transformations from $\mathbb{R}^n$ to $\mathbb{R}^m$ (with $T(\vec{x}) = A\vec{x}$ and $S(\vec{x}) = B\vec{x}$ for some $m \times n$ matrices A and B), then $(T + S)(\vec{x}) = T(\vec{x}) + S(\vec{x}) = A\vec{x} + B\vec{x} = (A + B)\vec{x}$, so that $T + S$ is linear as well, given by the matrix $A + B$.

    - If T is a linear transformation from $\mathbb{R}^n$ to $\mathbb{R}^m$ (with $T(\vec{x}) = A\vec{x}$) and k is any constant, then $(kT)(\vec{x}) = kT(\vec{x}) = kA\vec{x} = (kA)\vec{x}$, so that kT is linear as well, with matrix kA.

37. Using Example 18 as a guide, we first look for solutions of the form $f(x) = e^{kx}$. It is required that $f''(x) - 7f'(x) + 12f(x) = k^2 e^{kx} - 7ke^{kx} + 12e^{kx} = 0$ for all x, or $k^2 - 7k + 12 = (k-3)(k-4) = 0$. Thus $k = 3$ or $k = 4$. By Fact 4.1.5, the solutions of the differential equation are of the form $f(x) = c_1 e^{3x} + c_2 e^{4x}$, where c_1 and c_2 are arbitrary constants.

39. The claim is equivalent to the following: If a linear space V is finite-dimensional, then all its subspaces W are finite-dimensional as well (in fact, if $\dim(V) = n$, then $\dim(W) \le n$). This is a generalization of Exercise 38 of Section 3.2. The key step is to show that there are at most n linearly independent elements in an n-dimensional space V. Now let $f_1, \ldots, f_n$ be a basis of V. Every element f of V can be written uniquely as $f = c_1 f_1 + \cdots + c_n f_n$; it will be convenient to introduce the notation $[f] = \begin{bmatrix} c_1 \\ \cdots \\ c_n \end{bmatrix}$, a vector in $\mathbb{R}^n$ (in Section 4.2 we will call $[f]$ the coordinate vector of f with respect to basis $f_1, \ldots, f_n$). Now suppose the elements $g_1, \ldots, g_m$ in V are linearly independent. Then the coordinate vectors $[g_1], \ldots, [g_m]$ in $\mathbb{R}^n$ are independent as well (verify this!), so that $m \le n$, by Fact 3.2.6. (This way of reasoning will become clearer after you have studied Section 4.2).

41. Argue indirectly and assume that the space V of infinite sequences is finite-dimensional, with $\dim(V) = n$. According to the solution to Exercise 39, there can be at most n linearly independent elements in V. But here is our contradiction: It is easy to give $n + 1$ linearly independent infinite sequences, namely, $(1, 0, 0, 0, \ldots), (0, 1, 0, 0, \ldots), (0, 0, 1, 0, \ldots), \ldots, (0, 0, 0, \ldots, 0, 1, 0, \ldots)$; in the last sequence the 1 is in the $(n+1)$th place.

4.2

1. Fails to be linear, since $T(A + B) = A + B + I_2$ doesn't equal

   $T(A) + T(B) = A + I_2 + B + I_2 = A + B + 2I_2$.

3. Linear, since $T\left(\begin{bmatrix} a & b \\ c & d \end{bmatrix} + \begin{bmatrix} p & q \\ r & s \end{bmatrix} \right) = T\begin{bmatrix} a+p & b+q \\ c+r & d+s \end{bmatrix} = a + p + d + s$

   equals $T\begin{bmatrix} a & b \\ c & d \end{bmatrix} + T\begin{bmatrix} p & q \\ r & s \end{bmatrix} = a + d + p + s$, and $T\left(k\begin{bmatrix} a & b \\ c & d \end{bmatrix} \right) = T\begin{bmatrix} ka & kb \\ kc & kd \end{bmatrix} = ka + kd$

   equals $kT\begin{bmatrix} a & b \\ c & d \end{bmatrix} = k(a + d) = ka + kd$.

   No, T fails to be an isomorphism, since $4 = \dim(\mathbb{R}^{2 \times 2}) \ne \dim(\mathbb{R}) = 1$; see Fact 4.2.3d.

5. Fails to be linear, since $T(2I_2) = 4I_2$ does not equal $2T(I_2) = 2I_2$.

7. Linear, since $T(A + B) = S^{-1}(A + B)S = S^{-1}AS + S^{-1}BS$ equals

   $T(A) + T(B) = S^{-1}AS + S^{-1}BS$, and $T(kA) = S^{-1}(kA)S = kS^{-1}AS$ equals

   $kT(A) = kS^{-1}AS$.

Yes, T is an isomorphism. Solve the equation $B = S^{-1}AS$ for A to find the inverse $A = SBS^{-1}$.

9. Let $M = \begin{bmatrix} 1 & 2 \\ 0 & 1 \end{bmatrix}$. Transformation T is linear, since

$T(A + B) = (A + B)M - M(A + B) = AM + BM - MA - MB$ equals
$T(A) + T(B) = AM - MA + BM - MB$, and $T(kA) = (kA)M - M(kA) = kAM - kMA$
equals $kT(A) = k(AM - MA) = kAM - kMA$.
No, T isn't an isomorphism, since $A = I_2$ is in $\ker(T)$; see Fact 4.2.3b.

11. Linear, since $T((x + iy) + (z + it)) = T(x + z + i(y + t)) = y + t + i(x + z)$ equals
$T(x + iy) + T(z + it) = y + ix + t + iz = y + t + i(x + z)$, and
$T(k(x + iy)) = T(kx + iky) = ky + ikx$ equals $kT(x + iy) = k(y + ix) = ky + ikx$.
Yes, T is an isomorphism; it's its own inverse, since $T(T(x + iy)) = T(y + ix) = x + iy$.

13. Linear, since $T(f + g) = (f + g)'' + 4(f + g)' = f'' + 4f' + g'' + 4g'$ equals
$T(f) + T(g) = f'' + 4f' + g'' + 4g'$, and $T(kf) = (kf)'' + 4(kf)' = kf'' + 4kf'$ equals
$kT(f) = k(f'' + 4f') = kf'' + 4kf'$. No, it isn't an isomorphism, since the constant function
$f(x) = 1$ is in $\ker(T)$.

15. Linear, since $T(f(t) + g(t)) = f(2t) + g(2t)$ equals
$T(f(t)) + T(g(t)) = f(2t) + g(2t)$, and $T(kf(t)) = kf(2t)$ equals $kT(f(t)) = kf(2t)$.
Yes, T is an isomorphism; the inverse is $T^{-1}(f(t)) = f\left(\frac{t}{2}\right)$.

17. Linear, since $T((x_0, x_1, x_2, \ldots) + (y_0, y_1, y_2, \ldots)) = T(x_0 + y_0, x_1 + y_1, x_2 + y_2, \ldots) = (x_0 + y_0, x_2 + y_2, \ldots)$ equals $T(x_0, x_1, x_2, \ldots) + T(y_0, y_1, y_2, \ldots) = (x_0, x_2, \ldots) + (y_0, y_2, \ldots) = (x_0 + y_0, x_2 + y_2, \ldots)$, and $T(k(x_0, x_1, x_2, \ldots)) = T(kx_0, kx_1, kx_2, \ldots) = (kx_0, kx_2, \ldots)$ equals
$kT(x_0, x_1, x_2, \ldots) = k(x_0, x_2, \ldots) = (kx_0, kx_2, \ldots)$.
No, T isn't an isomorphism, since $(0, 1, 0, 0, 0, \ldots)$ is in $\ker(T)$.

19. Linear; the proof is analogous to Exercise 13.
No, T isn't an isomorphism, since the kernel of T is two-dimensional, by Fact 4.1.5.

21. Linear, since $T(f(t) + g(t)) = f(7) + g(7)$ equals
$T(f(t)) + T(g(t)) = f(7) + g(7)$, and $T(kf(t)) = kf(7)$ equals
$kT(f(t)) = kf(7)$.
Not an isomorphism, since domain and codomain have different dimensions.

23. Linear, as in Exercise 16. Not an isomorphism, since the constant function $f(t) = 1$ isn't in the image.

25. We need to find the matrices $A = \begin{bmatrix} x & y \\ z & t \end{bmatrix}$ that commute with $\begin{bmatrix} 1 & 2 \\ 0 & 1 \end{bmatrix}$, that is,

$$\begin{bmatrix} x & y \\ z & t \end{bmatrix} \begin{bmatrix} 1 & 2 \\ 0 & 1 \end{bmatrix} = \begin{bmatrix} 1 & 2 \\ 0 & 1 \end{bmatrix} \begin{bmatrix} x & y \\ z & t \end{bmatrix}, \text{ or, } \begin{bmatrix} x & 2x + y \\ z & 2z + t \end{bmatrix} = \begin{bmatrix} x + 2z & y + 2t \\ z & t \end{bmatrix}. \text{ It follows that}$$

$z = 0$ and $x = t$, so that the kernel of T consists of all matrices of the form $\begin{bmatrix} t & y \\ 0 & t \end{bmatrix}$. The nullity (i.e., the dimension of the kernel of T) is 2.

27. Note that $T(a + bt + ct^2) = 2c + 4b + 8ct$. Thus the kernel consists of all constant polynomials $f(t) = a$(when $b = c = 0$), and the nullity is 1. The image consists of all linear polynomials $f(t) = p + qt$, and the rank is 2.

29. The kernel consists of all infinite sequences such that
$T(x_0, x_1, x_2, x_3, x_4, \ldots) = (x_0, x_2, x_4, \ldots) = (0, 0, 0, \ldots)$, that is, all terms x_k with even k must be 0. Thus the kernel consists of all sequences of the form $(0, x_1, 0, x_3, 0, \ldots)$. The image consists of all infinite sequences $(y_0, y_1, y_2, \ldots)$, since
$(y_0, y_1, y_2, \ldots) = T(y_0, 0, y_1, 0, y_2, 0, \ldots)$.

31. The kernel consists of the solutions of the differential equation $f''(t) - 5f'(t) + 6f(t) = 0$. Using the approach outlined in Example 18 of Section 4.1 (involving a trial solution $f(t) = e^{kt}$), we find the general solution $f(t) = c_1 e^{2t} + c_2 e^{3t}$; thus the nullity is 2.

33. Note that $T(a + bt + ct^2) = a + 7b + 49c$. The image of T is all of $\mathbb{R}$, and the rank is 1. The kernel of T consists of all polynomials of the form $f(t) = -7b - 49c + bt + ct^2 = b(t - 7) + c(t^2 - 49)$. The nullity is 2.

35. The kernel consists of all polynomials $f(t)$ such that $t(f(t)) = 0$, that is, the zero polynomial $f(t) = 0$ alone. The image consists of all polynomials $g(t)$ that can be written as $g(t) = t(f(t))$, meaning that we can factor out a t. These are the polynomials with constant term 0, of the form $g(t) = a_1 t + a_2 t^2 + \cdots + a_n t^n$.

37. This is impossible, since $\dim(P_3) = 4$ and $\dim(\mathbb{R}^3) = 3$. See Fact 4.2.3d.

39. a. First, we need to show that $T(A + B) = T(A) + T(B)$ for all $m \times n$ matrices A and B, that is $(T(A + B))(\vec{v}) = (T(A) + T(B))(\vec{v})$ for all $\vec{v}$ in $\mathbb{R}^n$. Indeed
$(T(A + B))(\vec{v}) = (A + B)\vec{v} = A\vec{v} + B\vec{v}$ equals
$(T(A) + T(B))(\vec{v}) = T(A)(\vec{v}) + T(B)(\vec{v}) = A\vec{v} + B\vec{v}$. Also
$(T(kA))(\vec{v}) = (kA)\vec{v} = kA\vec{v}$ equals $(kT(A))(\vec{v}) = k(T(A))(\vec{v}) = kA\vec{v}$.

   b. The kernel of T consists of all $m \times n$ matrices A such that $T(A) = 0$, that is $(T(A))(\vec{v}) = A\vec{v} = \vec{0}$ for all $\vec{v}$ in $\mathbb{R}^n$. This holds for the zero matrix only. Thus $\ker(T) = \{0\}$.

   c. This is true by definition of a linear transformation (Definition 2.1.1).

   d. Note that T gives an isomorphism from $\mathbb{R}^{m \times n}$ to $L(\mathbb{R}^n, \mathbb{R}^m)$, by parts a, b, and c. Since $\dim(\mathbb{R}^{m \times n}) = mn$, by Exercise 17 of Seciton 4.1, we have $\dim(L(\mathbb{R}^n, \mathbb{R}^m)) = mn$, by Fact 4.2.3d.

41. To see that $0 + 0 = 0$, apply the formula $f + 0 = f$ to $f = 0$ (see Definition 4.1.1). Then $0 = k0 - k0 = k(0 + 0) - k0 = k0 + k0 - k0 = k0$.

43.

If T and L are linear, then

$(L \circ T)(f + g) = L(T(f + g)) = L(T(f) + T(g)) = L(T(f)) + L(T(g)) = (L \circ T)(f) + (L \circ T)(g)$,

and $(L \circ T)(kf) = L(T(kf)) = L(kT(f)) = kL(T(f)) = k(L \circ T)(f)$, so that $L \circ T$ is linear as well.

If T and L are isomorphism, then $L \circ T$ is an isomorphism as well, since the composite of invertible functions is invertible.

45. Yes; let T be an invertible function from $\mathbb{R}^2$ to $\mathbb{R}$ (see page 67). On $\mathbb{R}^2$ we can define the "exotic" operations $\vec{v} \oplus \vec{w} = T^{-1}(T(\vec{v}) + T(\vec{w}))$ and $k \odot \vec{v} = T^{-1}(kT(\vec{v}))$ (check that the conditions of Definition 4.1.1 hold). Then T is a linear transformation from $\mathbb{R}^2$ (with these exotic operations) to $\mathbb{R}$ (with the usual operations): $T(\vec{v} \oplus \vec{w}) = T(T^{-1}(T(\vec{v}) + T(\vec{w}))) = T(\vec{v}) + T(\vec{w})$, and $T(k \odot v) = kT(\vec{v})$. Now T is an isomorphism, so that the dimension of $\mathbb{R}^2$ (with our exotic operations) equals the dimension of the "usual" $\mathbb{R}$, which is 1.

4.3

1. Let $\mathcal{B}$ be the standard basis of $P_2 : 1, t, t^2$. Then the coordinates of the given polynomials with respect to $\mathcal{B}$ are $[f]_\mathcal{B} = \begin{bmatrix} 7 \\ 3 \\ 1 \end{bmatrix}, [g]_\mathcal{B} = \begin{bmatrix} 9 \\ 9 \\ 4 \end{bmatrix}, [h]_\mathcal{B} = \begin{bmatrix} 3 \\ 2 \\ 1 \end{bmatrix}$. Finding rref $\begin{bmatrix} 7 & 9 & 3 \\ 3 & 9 & 2 \\ 1 & 4 & 1 \end{bmatrix} = I_3$, we conclude

that $[f]_\mathcal{B}, [g]_\mathcal{B}, [h]_\mathcal{B}$ are linearly independent, hence so are f, g, h, since the coordinate transformation is an isomorphism.

3. We proceed as in Exercise 1. Since rref $\begin{bmatrix} 1 & 1 & 1 & 1 \\ 2 & 7 & 8 & 8 \\ 9 & 0 & 1 & 4 \\ 1 & 7 & 5 & 8 \end{bmatrix} = I_4$, the four given polynomials do form a

basis of P_3.

5. Use a diagram as in Definition 4.3.2:

$$\begin{bmatrix} a & b \\ 0 & c \end{bmatrix} \xrightarrow{\;T\;} \begin{bmatrix} 1 & 2 \\ 0 & 3 \end{bmatrix} \begin{bmatrix} a & b \\ 0 & c \end{bmatrix} = \begin{bmatrix} a & b + 2c \\ 0 & 3c \end{bmatrix}$$

$$\begin{bmatrix} a \\ b \\ c \end{bmatrix} \xrightarrow{\;B\;} \begin{bmatrix} a \\ b + 2c \\ 3c \end{bmatrix}$$

The matrix B that transforms $\begin{bmatrix} a \\ b \\ c \end{bmatrix}$ into $\begin{bmatrix} a \\ b + 2c \\ 3c \end{bmatrix}$ is $B = \begin{bmatrix} 1 & 0 & 0 \\ 0 & 1 & 2 \\ 0 & 0 & 3 \end{bmatrix}$.

7. Use Fact 4.3.3 to construct B column by column:

$$B = \left[\left[T \begin{bmatrix} 1 & 0 \\ 0 & 1 \end{bmatrix} \right]_{\mathcal{B}} \left[T \begin{bmatrix} 0 & 1 \\ 0 & 0 \end{bmatrix} \right]_{\mathcal{B}} \left[T \begin{bmatrix} 1 & 0 \\ 0 & -1 \end{bmatrix} \right]_{\mathcal{B}} \right] = \left[\begin{bmatrix} 0 & 0 \\ 0 & 0 \end{bmatrix}_{\mathcal{B}} \begin{bmatrix} 0 & 0 \\ 0 & 0 \end{bmatrix}_{\mathcal{B}} \begin{bmatrix} 0 & 4 \\ 0 & 0 \end{bmatrix}_{\mathcal{B}} \right]$$

$$= \begin{bmatrix} 0 & 0 & 0 \\ 0 & 0 & 4 \\ 0 & 0 & 0 \end{bmatrix}.$$

9. Use a diagram as in Definition 4.3.2:

$$\begin{bmatrix} a & b \\ 0 & c \end{bmatrix} \xrightarrow{\;T\;} \begin{bmatrix} a & 2b \\ 0 & c \end{bmatrix}$$

$$\downarrow \qquad\qquad \downarrow$$

$$\begin{bmatrix} a \\ b \\ c \end{bmatrix} \xrightarrow{\;B\;} \begin{bmatrix} a \\ 2b \\ c \end{bmatrix}$$

The matrix B that transforms $\begin{bmatrix} a \\ b \\ c \end{bmatrix}$ into $\begin{bmatrix} a \\ 2b \\ c \end{bmatrix}$ is $B = \begin{bmatrix} 1 & 0 & 0 \\ 0 & 2 & 0 \\ 0 & 0 & 1 \end{bmatrix}$.

11. Use Fact 4.3.3. to construct matrix B column by column:

$$B = \left[\left[T \begin{bmatrix} 1 & -1 \\ 0 & 0 \end{bmatrix} \right]_{\mathcal{B}} \left[T \begin{bmatrix} 0 & 1 \\ 0 & 1 \end{bmatrix} \right]_{\mathcal{B}} \left[T \begin{bmatrix} 0 & 1 \\ 0 & 0 \end{bmatrix} \right]_{\mathcal{B}} \right] = \left[\begin{bmatrix} 1 & -1 \\ 0 & 0 \end{bmatrix}_{\mathcal{B}} \begin{bmatrix} 0 & 1 \\ 0 & 1 \end{bmatrix}_{\mathcal{B}} \begin{bmatrix} 0 & 3 \\ 0 & 0 \end{bmatrix}_{\mathcal{B}} \right]$$

$$= \begin{bmatrix} 1 & 0 & 0 \\ 0 & 1 & 0 \\ 0 & 0 & 3 \end{bmatrix}.$$

13. Use a diagram as in Definition 4.3.2:

$$\begin{bmatrix} a & b \\ c & d \end{bmatrix} \xrightarrow{\;T\;} \begin{bmatrix} a+c & b+d \\ 2a+2c & 2b+2d \end{bmatrix}$$

$$\downarrow \qquad\qquad\qquad \downarrow$$

$$\begin{bmatrix} a \\ b \\ c \\ d \end{bmatrix} \xrightarrow{\;B\;} \begin{bmatrix} a+c \\ b+d \\ 2a+2c \\ 2b+2d \end{bmatrix}$$

The matrix is $B = \begin{bmatrix} 1 & 0 & 1 & 0 \\ 0 & 1 & 0 & 1 \\ 2 & 0 & 2 & 0 \\ 0 & 2 & 0 & 2 \end{bmatrix}$.

15.

$$x + iy \xrightarrow{\ T\ } x - iy$$

$$\downarrow \qquad\qquad \downarrow$$

$$\begin{bmatrix} x \\ y \end{bmatrix} \xrightarrow{\ B\ } \begin{bmatrix} x \\ -y \end{bmatrix}$$

Thus $B = \begin{bmatrix} 1 & 0 \\ 0 & -1 \end{bmatrix}$.

17.

$$x + iy \xrightarrow{\ T\ } -y + ix$$

$$\downarrow \qquad\qquad \downarrow$$

$$\begin{bmatrix} x \\ y \end{bmatrix} \xrightarrow{\ B\ } \begin{bmatrix} -y \\ x \end{bmatrix}$$

$B = \begin{bmatrix} 0 & -1 \\ 1 & 0 \end{bmatrix}$.

19.

$$x + iy \xrightarrow{\ T\ } px - qy + i(qx + py)$$

$$\downarrow \qquad\qquad\qquad \downarrow$$

$$\begin{bmatrix} x \\ y \end{bmatrix} \xrightarrow{\ B\ } \begin{bmatrix} px - qy \\ qx + py \end{bmatrix}$$

$B = \begin{bmatrix} p & -q \\ q & p \end{bmatrix}$.

21.

$$a + bt + ct^2 \xrightarrow{\ T\ } b - 3a + (2c - 3b)t - 3ct^2$$

$$\downarrow \qquad\qquad\qquad \downarrow$$

$$\begin{bmatrix} a \\ b \\ c \end{bmatrix} \xrightarrow{\ B\ } \begin{bmatrix} b - 3a \\ 2c - 3b \\ -3c \end{bmatrix}$$

Thus $B = \begin{bmatrix} -3 & 1 & 0 \\ 0 & -3 & 2 \\ 0 & 0 & -3 \end{bmatrix}$.

23.

$$a + bt + ct^2 \xrightarrow{\;T\;} a + 3b + 9c$$

$$\begin{bmatrix} a \\ b \\ c \end{bmatrix} \xrightarrow{\;B\;} \begin{bmatrix} a + 3b + 9c \\ 0 \\ 0 \end{bmatrix}$$

Thus $B = \begin{bmatrix} 1 & 3 & 9 \\ 0 & 0 & 0 \\ 0 & 0 & 0 \end{bmatrix}$.

25.

$$a + bt + ct^2 \xrightarrow{\;T\;} a - bt + ct^2$$

$$\begin{bmatrix} a \\ b \\ c \end{bmatrix} \xrightarrow{\;B\;} \begin{bmatrix} a \\ -b \\ c \end{bmatrix}$$

Thus $B = \begin{bmatrix} 1 & 0 & 0 \\ 0 & -1 & 0 \\ 0 & 0 & 1 \end{bmatrix}$.

27.

$$a + bt + ct^2 \xrightarrow{\;T\;} \begin{array}{l} a + b(2t-1) + c(2t-1)^2 \\ = a - b + c + (2b - 4c)t + 4ct^2 \end{array}$$

$$\begin{bmatrix} a \\ b \\ c \end{bmatrix} \xrightarrow{\;B\;} \begin{bmatrix} a - b + c \\ 2b - 4c \\ 4c \end{bmatrix}$$

Thus $B = \begin{bmatrix} 1 & -1 & 1 \\ 0 & 2 & -4 \\ 0 & 0 & 4 \end{bmatrix}$.

29.

$$a + bt + ct^2 \xrightarrow{\;T\;} 2a + 2b + 8c/3$$

$$\begin{bmatrix} a \\ b \\ c \end{bmatrix} \xrightarrow{\;B\;} \begin{bmatrix} 2a + 2b + 8c/3 \\ 0 \\ 0 \end{bmatrix}$$

Thus $B = \begin{bmatrix} 2 & 2 & 8/3 \\ 0 & 0 & 0 \\ 0 & 0 & 0 \end{bmatrix}$.

31.

$a + bt + ct^2 \quad \xrightarrow{\quad T \quad} \quad \dfrac{a + b(t+h) + c(t+h)^2 - a - b(t-h) - c(t-h)^2}{2h}$

$= b + 2ct$

$\downarrow \qquad\qquad\qquad\qquad\qquad\qquad\qquad\qquad\qquad \downarrow$

$\begin{bmatrix} a \\ b \\ c \end{bmatrix} \quad \xrightarrow{\quad B \quad} \qquad\qquad\qquad\qquad \begin{bmatrix} b \\ 2c \\ 0 \end{bmatrix}$

Thus $B = \begin{bmatrix} 0 & 1 & 0 \\ 0 & 0 & 2 \\ 0 & 0 & 0 \end{bmatrix}$.

Geometrically, $\dfrac{f(t+h) - f(t-h)}{2h}$ is the slope of the secant through points $(t-h, f(t-h))$ and $(t+h, f(t+h))$. This exercise shows that for a quadratic polynomial $f(t)$ this secant is parallel to the tangent at the midpoint $(t, f(t))$, a fact that was known to Archimedes. Draw a sketch! Thus $T(f(t)) = \dfrac{f(t+h) - f(t-h)}{2h} = f'(t)$ in this case. Compare with Exercise 20.

33. $B = [[1]_{\mathcal{B}} \ [t-1]_{\mathcal{B}} \ [0]_{\mathcal{B}}] = \begin{bmatrix} 1 & 0 & 0 \\ 0 & 1 & 0 \\ 0 & 0 & 0 \end{bmatrix}$.

35. In Exercise 13 we found $B = \begin{bmatrix} 1 & 0 & 1 & 0 \\ 0 & 1 & 0 & 1 \\ 2 & 0 & 2 & 0 \\ 0 & 2 & 0 & 2 \end{bmatrix}$, with rref $B = \begin{bmatrix} 1 & 0 & 1 & 0 \\ 0 & 1 & 0 & 1 \\ 0 & 0 & 0 & 0 \\ 0 & 0 & 0 & 0 \end{bmatrix}$.

Now $\text{im}(B) = \text{span}\left(\begin{bmatrix} 1 \\ 0 \\ 2 \\ 0 \end{bmatrix}, \begin{bmatrix} 0 \\ 1 \\ 0 \\ 2 \end{bmatrix} \right)$, and $\ker(B) = \text{span}\left(\begin{bmatrix} -1 \\ 0 \\ 1 \\ 0 \end{bmatrix}, \begin{bmatrix} 0 \\ -1 \\ 0 \\ 1 \end{bmatrix} \right)$. Thus

$\text{im}(T) = \text{span}\left(\begin{bmatrix} 1 & 0 \\ 2 & 0 \end{bmatrix}, \begin{bmatrix} 0 & 1 \\ 0 & 2 \end{bmatrix} \right)$, $\text{rank}(T) = 2$, and $\ker(T) = \text{span}\left(\begin{bmatrix} -1 & 0 \\ 1 & 0 \end{bmatrix}, \begin{bmatrix} 0 & -1 \\ 0 & 1 \end{bmatrix} \right)$.

37. In Exercise 21, we found the invertible matrix $B = \begin{bmatrix} -3 & 1 & 0 \\ 0 & -3 & 2 \\ 0 & 0 & -3 \end{bmatrix}$. Thus T is an isomorphism, $\text{im}(T) = P_2$, $\text{rank}(T) = 3$, and $\ker(T) = \{0\}$.

39. In Exercise 23, we found $B = \begin{bmatrix} 1 & 3 & 9 \\ 0 & 0 & 0 \\ 0 & 0 & 0 \end{bmatrix}$. Now $\text{im}(B) = \text{span}(\vec{e}_1)$, and

    $\ker(B) = \text{span} \left(\begin{bmatrix} -3 \\ 1 \\ 0 \end{bmatrix}, \begin{bmatrix} -9 \\ 0 \\ 1 \end{bmatrix} \right)$. Thus $\text{im}(T) = \text{span}(1)$, $\text{rank}(T) = 1$, and

    $\ker(T) = \text{span}(t - 3, t^2 - 9)$.

41. Apply the method outlined in the proof of Fact 4.3.4a. In Exercise 5 we consider the standard basis $\mathcal{A}$ of $U^{2 \times 2}$, and in Exercise 6 we work with the alternative basis $\mathcal{B}$

    consisting of $\begin{bmatrix} 1 & 0 \\ 0 & 0 \end{bmatrix}, \begin{bmatrix} 0 & 1 \\ 0 & 0 \end{bmatrix}, \begin{bmatrix} 0 & 1 \\ 0 & 1 \end{bmatrix}$. Now $S = \left[\begin{bmatrix} 1 & 0 \\ 0 & 0 \end{bmatrix}_{\mathcal{A}} \begin{bmatrix} 0 & 1 \\ 0 & 0 \end{bmatrix}_{\mathcal{A}} \begin{bmatrix} 0 & 1 \\ 0 & 1 \end{bmatrix}_{\mathcal{A}} \right] = \begin{bmatrix} 1 & 0 & 0 \\ 0 & 1 & 1 \\ 0 & 0 & 1 \end{bmatrix}$.

    Check that $AS = SB = \begin{bmatrix} 1 & 0 & 0 \\ 0 & 1 & 3 \\ 0 & 0 & 3 \end{bmatrix}$.

43. Apply the method outlined in the proof of Fact 4.3.4a. If $\mathcal{A}$ is the standard basis considered in Exercise 10 and $\mathcal{B}$ is the basis in Exercise 11, then

    $S = \left[\begin{bmatrix} 1 & -1 \\ 0 & 0 \end{bmatrix}_{\mathcal{A}} \begin{bmatrix} 0 & 1 \\ 0 & 1 \end{bmatrix}_{\mathcal{A}} \begin{bmatrix} 0 & 1 \\ 0 & 0 \end{bmatrix}_{\mathcal{A}} \right] = \begin{bmatrix} 1 & 0 & 0 \\ -1 & 1 & 1 \\ 0 & 1 & 0 \end{bmatrix}$.

    Check that $AS = SB = \begin{bmatrix} 1 & 0 & 0 \\ -1 & 1 & 3 \\ 0 & 1 & 0 \end{bmatrix}$.

45. Apply the method outlined in the proof of Fact 4.3.4a. If $\mathcal{A}$ is the standard basis considered in Exercise 15 and $\mathcal{B}$ is the basis in Exercise 16, then

    $S = \left[[1+i]_{\mathcal{A}} \ [1-i]_{\mathcal{A}} \right] = \begin{bmatrix} 1 & 1 \\ 1 & -1 \end{bmatrix}$.

    Check that $AS = SB = \begin{bmatrix} 1 & 1 \\ -1 & 1 \end{bmatrix}$.

47. Apply the method outlined in the proof of Fact 4.3.4a. If $\mathcal{A}$ is the standard basis considered in Exercise 27 and $\mathcal{B}$ is the basis in Exercise 28, then

    $S = \left[[1]_{\mathcal{A}} \ [-1+t]_{\mathcal{A}} \ [1-2t+t^2]_{\mathcal{A}} \right] = \begin{bmatrix} 1 & -1 & 1 \\ 0 & 1 & -2 \\ 0 & 0 & 1 \end{bmatrix}$. Check that

    $AS = SB = \begin{bmatrix} 1 & -2 & 4 \\ 0 & 2 & -8 \\ 0 & 0 & 4 \end{bmatrix}$.

49. $B = [[2\cos(t) - 2\sin(t)]_{\mathcal{B}} \ \ [2\cos(t) + 2\sin(t)]_{\mathcal{B}}] = \begin{bmatrix} 2 & 2 \\ -2 & 2 \end{bmatrix}.$

51. Note that $\cos(t - \pi/2) = \sin(t)$ and $\sin(t - \pi/2) = -\cos(t)$. Thus

$$B = [[\cos(t - \pi/2)]_{\mathcal{B}} \ \ [\sin(t - \pi/2)]_{\mathcal{B}}] = [[\sin(t)]_{\mathcal{B}} \ \ [-\cos(t)]_{\mathcal{B}}] = \begin{bmatrix} 0 & -1 \\ 1 & 0 \end{bmatrix}.$$

53. Recall that $\cos(t - \delta) = \cos(\delta)\cos(t) + \sin(\delta)\sin(t)$ and $\sin(t - \delta) = \cos(\delta)\sin(t) - \sin(\delta)\cos(t)$.
Thus $B = [[\cos(t - \delta)]_{\mathcal{B}} \ \ [\sin(t - \delta)]_{\mathcal{B}}]$

$$= [[\cos(\delta)\cos(t) + \sin(\delta)\sin(t)]_{\mathcal{B}} \ \ [-\sin(\delta)\cos(t) + \cos(\delta)\sin(t)]_{\mathcal{B}}] = \begin{bmatrix} \cos(\delta) & -\sin(\delta) \\ \sin(\delta) & \cos(\delta) \end{bmatrix}.$$

Note that B is a rotation matrix.

55. Let $\vec{u} = \dfrac{1}{\sqrt{6}} \begin{bmatrix} 1 \\ -2 \\ 1 \end{bmatrix}$ be the unit vector in the direction of $\begin{bmatrix} 1 \\ -2 \\ 1 \end{bmatrix}.$

Now $T\begin{bmatrix} 1 \\ 1 \\ -1 \end{bmatrix} = \dfrac{1}{6}\left(\begin{bmatrix} 1 \\ -2 \\ 1 \end{bmatrix} \cdot \begin{bmatrix} 1 \\ 1 \\ -1 \end{bmatrix} \right) \begin{bmatrix} 1 \\ -2 \\ 1 \end{bmatrix} = -\dfrac{1}{3}\begin{bmatrix} 1 \\ -2 \\ 1 \end{bmatrix}$ and

$T\begin{bmatrix} 5 \\ -4 \\ 1 \end{bmatrix} = \dfrac{1}{6}\left(\begin{bmatrix} 1 \\ -2 \\ 1 \end{bmatrix} \cdot \begin{bmatrix} 5 \\ -4 \\ 1 \end{bmatrix} \right) \begin{bmatrix} 1 \\ -2 \\ 1 \end{bmatrix} = \dfrac{7}{3}\begin{bmatrix} 1 \\ -2 \\ 1 \end{bmatrix}$, by Fact 2.2.5.

Also note that $\begin{bmatrix} 1 \\ -2 \\ 1 \end{bmatrix} = -\dfrac{2}{3}\begin{bmatrix} 1 \\ 1 \\ -1 \end{bmatrix} + \dfrac{1}{3}\begin{bmatrix} 5 \\ -4 \\ 1 \end{bmatrix}$, so that $\begin{bmatrix} 1 \\ -2 \\ 1 \end{bmatrix}_{\mathcal{B}} = \dfrac{1}{3}\begin{bmatrix} -2 \\ 1 \end{bmatrix}.$

Now $B = \left[\left[-\dfrac{1}{3}\begin{bmatrix} 1 \\ -2 \\ 1 \end{bmatrix} \right]_{\mathcal{B}} \ \ \left[\dfrac{7}{3}\begin{bmatrix} 1 \\ -2 \\ 1 \end{bmatrix} \right]_{\mathcal{B}} \right] = \dfrac{1}{9}\begin{bmatrix} 2 & -14 \\ -1 & 7 \end{bmatrix}.$

57. $T\begin{bmatrix} 1 \\ 1 \\ -1 \end{bmatrix} = \begin{bmatrix} -6 \\ 3 \\ 0 \end{bmatrix} = -\begin{bmatrix} 1 \\ 1 \\ -1 \end{bmatrix} - \begin{bmatrix} 5 \\ -4 \\ 1 \end{bmatrix}$ and $T\begin{bmatrix} 5 \\ -4 \\ 1 \end{bmatrix} = \begin{bmatrix} 3 \\ 3 \\ -3 \end{bmatrix} = 3\begin{bmatrix} 1 \\ 1 \\ -1 \end{bmatrix}.$

Thus $B = \left[\begin{bmatrix} -6 \\ 3 \\ 0 \end{bmatrix}_{\mathcal{B}} \ \ \begin{bmatrix} 3 \\ 3 \\ -3 \end{bmatrix}_{\mathcal{B}} \right] = \begin{bmatrix} -1 & 3 \\ -1 & 0 \end{bmatrix}.$

59. $T(f) = t \cdot f$ is linear and $\ker(T) = \{0\}$, but T is not an isomorphism since the constant function 1 is not in the image of T.

61. a.
$$[T(\cos t)]_\mathcal{B} = [0]_\mathcal{B} = \vec{0}$$
$$[T(\sin t)]_\mathcal{B} = [0]_\mathcal{B} = \vec{0}$$

$$[T(t\cos(t))]_\mathcal{B} = [-2\sin(t)]_\mathcal{B} = \begin{bmatrix} 0 \\ -2 \\ 0 \\ 0 \end{bmatrix}$$

$$[T(t\sin(t))]_\mathcal{B} = [2\cos(t)]_\mathcal{B} = \begin{bmatrix} 2 \\ 0 \\ 0 \\ 0 \end{bmatrix}$$

so $M = \begin{bmatrix} 0 & 0 & 0 & 2 \\ 0 & 0 & -2 & 0 \\ 0 & 0 & 0 & 0 \\ 0 & 0 & 0 & 0 \end{bmatrix}$.

b. The equation $T(f) = \cos(t)$ corresponds to $M\vec{x} = \begin{bmatrix} 1 \\ 0 \\ 0 \\ 0 \end{bmatrix}$, with solutions $\vec{x} = \begin{bmatrix} p \\ q \\ 0 \\ \frac{1}{2} \end{bmatrix}$, where p and

q are arbitrary. Thus $f(t) = p\cos(t) + q\sin(t) + \frac{1}{2}t\sin(t)$. Below we graph $f(t)$ for $p = q = 0$; note that $p\cos(t) + q\sin(t)$ is just a sinusoidal function

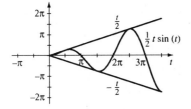

63. As the hint suggests, we find the kernel of $M = \begin{bmatrix} f_1(a_1) & f_2(a_1) & \cdots & f_n(a_1) \\ f_1(a_2) & f_2(a_2) & \cdots & f_n(a_2) \\ \vdots & \vdots & & \vdots \\ f_1(a_n) & f_2(a_n) & \cdots & f_n(a_n) \end{bmatrix}$.

If $M \begin{bmatrix} c_1 \\ c_2 \\ \vdots \\ c_n \end{bmatrix} = \begin{bmatrix} f_1(a_1) & f_2(a_1) & \cdots & f_n(a_1) \\ f_1(a_2) & f_2(a_2) & \cdots & f_n(a_2) \\ \vdots & \vdots & & \vdots \\ f_1(a_n) & f_2(a_n) & \cdots & f_n(a_n) \end{bmatrix} \begin{bmatrix} c_1 \\ c_2 \\ \vdots \\ c_n \end{bmatrix} = \begin{bmatrix} c_1 f_1(a_1) + \cdots + c_n f_n(a_1) \\ c_1 f_1(a_2) + \cdots + c_n f_n(a_2) \\ \vdots \\ c_1 f_1(a_n) + \cdots + c_n f_n(a_n) \end{bmatrix} = \begin{bmatrix} 0 \\ 0 \\ \vdots \\ 0 \end{bmatrix}$,

then the polynomial $c_1 f_1 + \cdots + c_n f_n$ in P_{n-1} has at least n zeros, namely, $a_1, a_2, \cdots, a_n$. It follows that $c_1 f_1 + c_2 f_2 + \cdots + c_n f_n = 0$ and therefore $c_1 = c_2 = \cdots = c_n = 0$ since the f_i are linearly independent. We have shown that $\ker(M) = \{\vec{0}\}$, so that M is invertible.

65. We need to show that there are constants $w_1, \ldots, w_n$ such that

$$w_1 f_1(a_1) + w_2 f_1(a_2) + \cdots + w_n f_1(a_n) = \int_{-1}^{1} f_1$$

$$w_1 f_2(a_1) + w_2 f_2(a_2) + \cdots + w_n f_2(a_n) = \int_{-1}^{1} f_2$$

$$\vdots \qquad\qquad \vdots$$

$$w_1 f_n(a_1) + w_2 f_n(a_2) + \cdots + w_n f_n(a_n) = \int_{-1}^{1} f_n.$$

In order to be able to use the matrix M introduced in Exercises 63, as the hint suggests, we write this system in a somewhat unusual way, as

$$\begin{bmatrix} w_1 & w_2 & \cdots & w_n \end{bmatrix} \underbrace{\begin{bmatrix} f_1(a_1) & f_2(a_1) & \cdots & f_n(a_1) \\ f_1(a_2) & f_2(a_2) & \cdots & f_n(a_2) \\ \cdots & \cdots & \cdots & \cdots \\ f_1(a_n) & f_2(a_n) & \cdots & f_n(a_n) \end{bmatrix}}_{M} = \begin{bmatrix} \int_{-1}^{1} f_1 & \int_{-1}^{1} f_2 & \cdots & \int_{-1}^{1} f_n \end{bmatrix}$$

Since M is invertible (Exercise 63), we have the unique solution

$$\begin{bmatrix} w_1 & w_2 & \cdots & w_n \end{bmatrix} = \begin{bmatrix} \int_{-1}^{1} f_1 & \int_{-1}^{1} f_2 & \cdots & \int_{-1}^{1} f_n \end{bmatrix} M^{-1}.$$

Now if f is any polynomial in P_{n-1} and $f = \sum_{j=1}^{n} c_j f_j$, then

$$\int_{-1}^{1} f = \sum_{j=1}^{n} c_j \int_{-1}^{1} f_j = \sum_{j=1}^{n} c_j \sum_{i=1}^{n} w_i f_j(a_i) = \sum_{i=1}^{n} w_i \sum_{j=1}^{n} c_j f_j(a_i) = \sum_{i=1}^{n} w_i f(a_i),$$

as claimed.

Chapter 5

5.1

1. $\|\vec{v}\| = \sqrt{7^2 + 11^2} = \sqrt{49 + 121} = \sqrt{170} \approx 13.04$

3. $\|\vec{v}\| = \sqrt{2^2 + 3^2 + 4^2 + 5^2} = \sqrt{4 + 9 + 16 + 25} = \sqrt{54} \approx 7.35$

5. $\alpha = \arccos \dfrac{\vec{u} \cdot \vec{v}}{\|\vec{u}\|\|\vec{v}\|} = \arccos \dfrac{2 + 6 + 12}{\sqrt{14}\sqrt{29}} \approx 0.122$ (radians)

7. Use the fact that $\vec{u} \cdot \vec{v} = \|\vec{u}\|\|\vec{v}\| \cos \alpha$, so that the angle is acute if $\vec{u} \cdot \vec{v} > 0$, and obtuse if $\vec{u} \cdot \vec{v} < 0$. Since $\vec{u} \cdot \vec{v} = 10 - 12 = -2$, the angle is obtuse.

9. Since $\vec{u} \cdot \vec{v} = 3 - 4 + 5 - 3 = 1$, the angle is acute (see Exercise 7).

11. a. $\alpha_n = \arccos \dfrac{\vec{u} \cdot \vec{v}}{\|\vec{u}\|\|\vec{v}\|} = \arccos \dfrac{1}{\sqrt{n}}$

    $\alpha_2 = \arccos \dfrac{1}{\sqrt{2}} = \dfrac{\pi}{4}(= 45°)$

    $\alpha_3 = \arccos \dfrac{1}{\sqrt{3}} \approx 0.955$ (radians)

    $a_4 = \arccos \dfrac{1}{2} = \dfrac{\pi}{3}(= 60°)$

    b. Since $y = \arccos(x)$ is a continuous function,
    $$\lim_{n \to \infty} \alpha_n = \arccos \left(\lim_{n \to \infty} \frac{1}{\sqrt{n}} \right) = \arccos(0) = \frac{\pi}{2}(= 90°)$$

13. The figure below shows that $\|\vec{F}_2 + \vec{F}_3\| = 2 \cos \left(\dfrac{\alpha}{2} \right) \|\vec{F}_2\| = 20 \cos \left(\dfrac{\alpha}{2} \right)$.

    It is required that $\|\vec{F}_2 + \vec{F}_3\| = 16$, so that $20 \cos \left(\dfrac{\alpha}{2} \right) = 16$, or $\alpha = 2 \arccos(0.8) \approx 74°$.

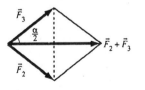

15. The subspace consists of all vectors $\vec{x}$ in $\mathbb{R}^4$ such that $\vec{x} \cdot \vec{v} = \begin{bmatrix} x_1 \\ x_2 \\ x_3 \\ x_4 \end{bmatrix} \cdot \begin{bmatrix} 1 \\ 2 \\ 3 \\ 4 \end{bmatrix} = x_1 + 2x_2 + 3x_3 + 4x_4 = 0$.

These are vectors of the form
$$\begin{bmatrix} -2r & -3s & -4t \\ r & & \\ & s & \\ & & t \end{bmatrix} = r\begin{bmatrix} -2 \\ 1 \\ 0 \\ 0 \end{bmatrix} + s\begin{bmatrix} -3 \\ 0 \\ 1 \\ 0 \end{bmatrix} + t\begin{bmatrix} -4 \\ 0 \\ 0 \\ 1 \end{bmatrix}.$$
The three vectors to the right give the desired basis.

17. The orthogonal complement $W^\perp$ of W consists of the vectors $\vec{x}$ in $\mathbb{R}^4$ such that
$$\begin{bmatrix} x_1 \\ x_2 \\ x_3 \\ x_4 \end{bmatrix} \cdot \begin{bmatrix} 1 \\ 2 \\ 3 \\ 4 \end{bmatrix} = 0 \text{ and } \begin{bmatrix} x_1 \\ x_2 \\ x_3 \\ x_4 \end{bmatrix} \cdot \begin{bmatrix} 5 \\ 6 \\ 7 \\ 8 \end{bmatrix} = 0.$$

Finding these vectors amounts to solving the system $\begin{vmatrix} x_1 + 2x_2 + 3x_3 + 4x_4 = 0 \\ 5x_1 + 6x_2 + 7x_3 + 8x_4 = 0 \end{vmatrix}.$

The solutions are of the form
$$\begin{bmatrix} x_1 \\ x_2 \\ x_3 \\ x_4 \end{bmatrix} = \begin{bmatrix} s + 2t \\ -2s - 3t \\ s \\ t \end{bmatrix} = s\begin{bmatrix} 1 \\ -2 \\ 1 \\ 0 \end{bmatrix} + t\begin{bmatrix} 2 \\ -3 \\ 0 \\ 1 \end{bmatrix}.$$
The two vectors to the right form a basis of $W^\perp$.

19.

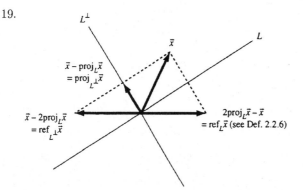

21. Call the three given vectors $\vec{v}_1, \vec{v}_2,$ and $\vec{v}_3$. Since $\vec{v}_2$ is required to be a unit vector, we must have $b = g = 0$. Now $\vec{v}_1 \cdot \vec{v}_2 = d$ must be zero, so that $d = 0$.

Likewise, $\vec{v}_2 \cdot \vec{v}_3 = e$ must be zero, so that $e = 0$.

Since $\vec{v}_3$ must be a unit vector, we have $\|\vec{v}_3\|^2 = c^2 + \frac{1}{4} = 1$, so that $c = \pm\frac{\sqrt{3}}{2}$.

Since we are asked to find just one solution, let us pick $c = \frac{\sqrt{3}}{2}$.

The condition $\vec{v}_1 \cdot \vec{v}_3 = 0$ now implies that $\frac{\sqrt{3}}{2}a + \frac{1}{2}f = 0$, or $f = -\sqrt{3}a$.

Finally, it is required that $\|\vec{v}_1\|^2 = a^2 + f^2 = a^2 + 3a^2 = 4a^2 = 1$, so that $a = \pm\frac{1}{2}$.

Let us pick $a = \frac{1}{2}$, so that $f = -\frac{\sqrt{3}}{2}$.

Summary:

$$\vec{v}_1 = \begin{bmatrix} \frac{1}{2} \\ 0 \\ -\frac{\sqrt{3}}{2} \end{bmatrix}, \vec{v}_2 = \begin{bmatrix} 0 \\ 1 \\ 0 \end{bmatrix}, \vec{v}_3 = \begin{bmatrix} \frac{\sqrt{3}}{2} \\ 0 \\ \frac{1}{2} \end{bmatrix}$$

There are other solutions; some components will have different signs.

23. We need to show that $V^{\perp}$ contains the zero vector and is closed under addition: $\vec{0} \cdot \vec{v} = 0$ for all $\vec{v}$ in V, so that $\vec{0}$ is in $V^{\perp}$.

    Now suppose that $\vec{u}$ and $\vec{w}$ are in $V^{\perp}$. To show that $\vec{u} + \vec{w}$ is in $V^{\perp}$, we need to verify that $(\vec{u} + \vec{w}) \cdot \vec{v} = 0$ for all $\vec{v}$ in V. Indeed, $(\vec{u} + \vec{w}) \cdot \vec{v} = \vec{u} \cdot \vec{v} + \vec{w} \cdot \vec{v} = 0 + 0 = 0$, since $\vec{u}$ and $\vec{w}$ are in $V^{\perp}$.

25. a. $\|k\vec{v}\|^2 = (k\vec{v}) \cdot (k\vec{v}) = k^2 (\vec{v} \cdot \vec{v}) = k^2 \|\vec{v}\|^2$

    Now take square roots of both sides; note that $\sqrt{k^2} = |k|$, the absolute value of k (think about the case when k is negative).

    $\|k\vec{v}\| = |k|\|\vec{v}\|$, as claimed.

    b. $\|\vec{u}\| = \left\| \dfrac{1}{\|\vec{v}\|} \vec{v} \right\| = \dfrac{1}{\|\vec{v}\|} \|\vec{v}\| = 1$, as claimed.
    $\qquad\qquad\quad \uparrow$
    $\qquad\qquad$ by part a

27. Since the two given vectors in the subspace are orthogonal, we have the orthonormal basis

    $$\vec{v}_1 = \frac{1}{3} \begin{bmatrix} 2 \\ 2 \\ 1 \\ 0 \end{bmatrix}, \vec{v}_2 = \frac{1}{3} \begin{bmatrix} -2 \\ 2 \\ 0 \\ 1 \end{bmatrix}.$$

    Now we can use Fact 5.1.6, with $\vec{x} = 9\vec{e}_1 : \text{proj}_V \vec{x} = (\vec{v}_1 \cdot \vec{x})\vec{v}_1 + (\vec{v}_2 \cdot \vec{x})\vec{v}_2 = 2 \begin{bmatrix} 2 \\ 2 \\ 1 \\ 0 \end{bmatrix} - 2 \begin{bmatrix} -2 \\ 2 \\ 0 \\ 1 \end{bmatrix} =$

    $\begin{bmatrix} 8 \\ 0 \\ 2 \\ -2 \end{bmatrix}.$

29. By the Pythagorean theorem (Fact 5.1.8),

    $$\|\vec{x}\|^2 = \|7\vec{v}_1 - 3\vec{v}_2 + 2\vec{v}_3 + \vec{v}_4 - \vec{v}_5\|^2$$
    $$= \|7\vec{v}_1\|^2 + \|3\vec{v}_2\|^2 + \|2\vec{v}_3\|^2 + \|\vec{v}_4\|^2 + \|\vec{v}_5\|^2$$
    $$= 49 + 9 + 4 + 1 + 1$$
    $$= 64, \text{ so that } \|\vec{x}\| = 8.$$

31. If $V = \text{span}(\vec{v}_1, \ldots, \vec{v}_m)$, then $\text{proj}_V \vec{x} = (\vec{v}_1 \cdot \vec{x})\vec{v}_1 + \cdots + (\vec{v}_m \cdot \vec{x})\vec{v}_m$, by Fact 5.1.6, and $\|\text{proj}_V \vec{x}\|^2 = (\vec{v}_1 \cdot \vec{x})^2 + \cdots + (\vec{v}_m \cdot \vec{x})^2 = p$, by the Pythagorean theorem (Fact 5.1.8). Therefore $p \le \|\vec{x}\|^2$, by Fact 5.1.9. The two quantities are equal if (and only if) $\vec{x}$ is in V.

33. Let $\vec{x} = \begin{bmatrix} x_1 \\ \cdots \\ x_n \end{bmatrix}$ be a vector in $\mathbb{R}^n$ whose components add up to 1, that is, $x_1 + \cdots + x_n = 1$. Let

$\vec{y} = \begin{bmatrix} 1 \\ \cdots \\ 1 \end{bmatrix}$ (all n components are 1). The Cauchy-Schwarz inequality (Fact 5.1.10) tells us that

$|\vec{x} \cdot \vec{y}| \le \|\vec{x}\| \|\vec{y}\|$, or, $|x_1 + \cdots + x_n| \le \|\vec{x}\| \sqrt{n}$, or $\|\vec{x}\| \ge \dfrac{1}{\sqrt{n}}$. By Fact 5.1.10, the equation $\|\vec{x}\| = \dfrac{1}{\sqrt{n}}$

holds if (and only if) the vectors $\vec{x}$ and $\vec{y}$ are parallel, that is, $x_1 = x_2 = \cdots = x_n = \dfrac{1}{n}$. Thus the

vector of minimal length is $\vec{x} = \begin{bmatrix} \frac{1}{n} \\ \cdots \\ \frac{1}{n} \end{bmatrix}$ $\left(\text{all components are } \dfrac{1}{n}\right)$.

The figure below illustrates the case $n = 2$.

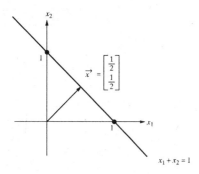

35. Applying the Cauchy-Schwarz inequality to $\vec{u} = \begin{bmatrix} x \\ y \\ z \end{bmatrix}$ and $\vec{v} = \begin{bmatrix} 1 \\ 2 \\ 3 \end{bmatrix}$ gives $|\vec{u} \cdot \vec{v}| \le \|\vec{u}\| \|\vec{v}\|$, or

$|x + 2y + 3z| \le \sqrt{14}$. The minimal value $x + 2y + 3z = -\sqrt{14}$ is attained when $\vec{u} = k\vec{v}$ for negative

k. Thus $\vec{u}$ must be a unit vector of the form $\vec{u} = \begin{bmatrix} k \\ 2k \\ 3k \end{bmatrix}$, for negative k. It is required that $14k^2 = 1$,

or, $k = -\dfrac{1}{\sqrt{14}}$. Thus $\vec{u} = \begin{bmatrix} -\frac{1}{\sqrt{14}} \\ -\frac{2}{\sqrt{14}} \\ -\frac{3}{\sqrt{14}} \end{bmatrix}$.

37. Using Definition 2.2.6 as a guide, we find that $\text{ref}_E \vec{x} = 2(\text{proj}_E \vec{x}) - \vec{x} = 2(\vec{v}_1 \cdot \vec{x})\vec{v}_1 + 2(\vec{v}_2 \cdot \vec{x})\vec{v}_2 - \vec{x}$.

39. No! By definition of a projection, the vector $\vec{x} - \text{proj}_L\vec{x}$ is perpendicular to $\text{proj}_L\vec{x}$, so that
$(\vec{x} - \text{proj}_L\vec{x}) \cdot (\text{proj}_L\vec{x}) = \vec{x} \cdot \text{proj}_L\vec{x} - \|\text{proj}_L\vec{x}\|^2 = 0$ and $\vec{x} \cdot \text{proj}_L\vec{x} = \|\text{proj}_L\vec{x}\|^2 \geq 0$.

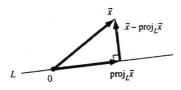

5.2

In Exercises 1–14, we will refer to the given vectors as $\vec{v}_1, \ldots, \vec{v}_m$, where $m = 1, 2,$ or 3.

1. $\vec{w}_1 = \dfrac{1}{\|\vec{v}_1\|}\vec{v}_1 = \dfrac{1}{3}\begin{bmatrix} 2 \\ 1 \\ -2 \end{bmatrix}$

3. $\vec{w}_1 = \dfrac{1}{\|\vec{v}_1\|}\vec{v}_1 = \dfrac{1}{5}\begin{bmatrix} 4 \\ 0 \\ 3 \end{bmatrix}$

   $\vec{w}_2 = \dfrac{\vec{v}_2 - (\vec{w}_1 \cdot \vec{v}_2)\vec{w}_1}{\text{length}} = \dfrac{1}{5}\begin{bmatrix} 3 \\ 0 \\ -4 \end{bmatrix}$

5. $\vec{w}_1 = \dfrac{1}{\|\vec{v}_1\|}\vec{v}_1 = \dfrac{1}{3}\begin{bmatrix} 2 \\ 2 \\ 1 \end{bmatrix}$

   $\vec{w}_2 = \dfrac{\vec{v}_2 - (\vec{w}_1 \cdot \vec{v}_2)\vec{w}_1}{\text{length}} = \dfrac{1}{\sqrt{18}}\begin{bmatrix} -1 \\ -1 \\ 4 \end{bmatrix} = \dfrac{1}{3\sqrt{2}}\begin{bmatrix} -1 \\ -1 \\ 4 \end{bmatrix}$

7. Note that $\vec{v}_1$ and $\vec{v}_2$ are orthogonal, so that $\vec{w}_1 = \dfrac{1}{\|\vec{v}_1\|}\vec{v}_1 = \dfrac{1}{3}\begin{bmatrix} 2 \\ 2 \\ 1 \end{bmatrix}$ and $\vec{w}_2 = \dfrac{1}{\|\vec{v}_2\|}\vec{v}_2 = \dfrac{1}{3}\begin{bmatrix} -2 \\ 1 \\ 2 \end{bmatrix}$.

   Then $\vec{w}_3 = \dfrac{\vec{v}_3 - (\vec{w}_1 \cdot \vec{v}_3)\vec{w}_1 - (\vec{w}_2 \cdot \vec{v}_3)\vec{w}_2}{\text{length}} = \dfrac{1}{\sqrt{36}}\begin{bmatrix} 2 \\ -4 \\ 4 \end{bmatrix} = \dfrac{1}{3}\begin{bmatrix} 1 \\ -2 \\ 2 \end{bmatrix}$.

9. $\vec{w}_1 = \dfrac{1}{\|\vec{v}_1\|}\vec{v}_1 = \dfrac{1}{2}\begin{bmatrix} 1 \\ 1 \\ 1 \\ 1 \end{bmatrix}$

$$\vec{w}_2 = \frac{\vec{v}_2 - (\vec{w}_1 \cdot \vec{v}_2)\vec{w}_1}{\text{length}} = \frac{1}{10}\begin{bmatrix} -1 \\ 7 \\ -7 \\ 1 \end{bmatrix}$$

11. $\vec{w}_1 = \dfrac{1}{\|\vec{v}_1\|}\vec{v}_1 = \dfrac{1}{5}\begin{bmatrix} 4 \\ 0 \\ 0 \\ 3 \end{bmatrix}$

$$\vec{w}_2 = \frac{\vec{v}_2 - (\vec{w}_1 \cdot \vec{v}_2)\vec{w}_1}{\text{length}} = \frac{1}{\sqrt{225}}\begin{bmatrix} -3 \\ 2 \\ 14 \\ 4 \end{bmatrix} = \frac{1}{15}\begin{bmatrix} -3 \\ 2 \\ 14 \\ 4 \end{bmatrix}$$

13. $\vec{w}_1 = \dfrac{1}{\|\vec{v}_1\|}\vec{v}_1 = \dfrac{1}{2}\begin{bmatrix} 1 \\ 1 \\ 1 \\ 1 \end{bmatrix}$

$$\vec{w}_2 = \frac{\vec{v}_2 - (\vec{w}_1 \cdot \vec{v}_2)\vec{w}_1}{\text{length}} = \begin{bmatrix} \frac{1}{2} \\ -\frac{1}{2} \\ -\frac{1}{2} \\ \frac{1}{2} \end{bmatrix}$$

$$\vec{w}_3 = \frac{\vec{v}_3 - (\vec{w}_1 \cdot \vec{v}_3)\vec{w}_1 - (\vec{w}_2 \cdot \vec{v}_3)\vec{w}_2}{\text{length}} = \begin{bmatrix} \frac{1}{2} \\ \frac{1}{2} \\ -\frac{1}{2} \\ -\frac{1}{2} \end{bmatrix}$$

15. $Q = \dfrac{1}{3}\begin{bmatrix} 2 \\ 1 \\ -2 \end{bmatrix}, R = [3]$

17. $Q = \dfrac{1}{5}\begin{bmatrix} 4 & 3 \\ 0 & 0 \\ 3 & -4 \end{bmatrix}, R = \begin{bmatrix} 5 & 5 \\ 0 & 35 \end{bmatrix}$

19. $Q = \dfrac{1}{3}\begin{bmatrix} 2 & -\frac{1}{\sqrt{2}} \\ 2 & -\frac{1}{\sqrt{2}} \\ 1 & \frac{4}{\sqrt{2}} \end{bmatrix}, R = 3\begin{bmatrix} 1 & 1 \\ 0 & \sqrt{2} \end{bmatrix}$

21. $Q = \dfrac{1}{3}\begin{bmatrix} 2 & -2 & 1 \\ 2 & 1 & -2 \\ 1 & 2 & 2 \end{bmatrix}, R = \begin{bmatrix} 3 & 0 & 12 \\ 0 & 3 & -12 \\ 0 & 0 & 6 \end{bmatrix}$

23. $Q = \begin{bmatrix} 0.5 & -0.1 \\ 0.5 & 0.7 \\ 0.5 & -0.7 \\ 0.5 & 0.1 \end{bmatrix}$, $R = \begin{bmatrix} 2 & 4 \\ 0 & 10 \end{bmatrix}$

25. $Q = \dfrac{1}{15} \begin{bmatrix} 12 & -3 \\ 0 & 2 \\ 0 & 14 \\ 9 & 4 \end{bmatrix}$, $R = \begin{bmatrix} 5 & 10 \\ 0 & 15 \end{bmatrix}$

27. $Q = \dfrac{1}{2} \begin{bmatrix} 1 & 1 & 1 \\ 1 & -1 & 1 \\ 1 & -1 & -1 \\ 1 & 1 & -1 \end{bmatrix}$, $R = \begin{bmatrix} 2 & 1 & 1 \\ 0 & 1 & -2 \\ 0 & 0 & 1 \end{bmatrix}$

29. $\vec{w}_1 = \dfrac{1}{\|\vec{v}_1\|} \vec{v}_1 = \dfrac{1}{5} \begin{bmatrix} -3 \\ 4 \end{bmatrix}$

$\vec{w}_2 = \dfrac{\vec{v}_2 - (\vec{w}_1 \cdot \vec{v}_2)\vec{w}_1}{\text{length}} = \dfrac{1}{5} \begin{bmatrix} 4 \\ 3 \end{bmatrix}$

31. $\vec{w}_1 = \dfrac{1}{\|\vec{v}_1\|} \vec{v}_1 = \begin{bmatrix} 1 \\ 0 \\ 0 \end{bmatrix} = \vec{e}_1$

$\vec{v}_2 - \text{proj}_{V_1}\vec{v}_2 = \begin{bmatrix} b \\ c \\ 0 \end{bmatrix} - \begin{bmatrix} b \\ 0 \\ 0 \end{bmatrix} = \begin{bmatrix} 0 \\ c \\ 0 \end{bmatrix}$, so that $\vec{w}_2 = \begin{bmatrix} 0 \\ 1 \\ 0 \end{bmatrix} = \vec{e}_2$

Note that $V_1 = \text{span}(\vec{e}_1) = x$ axis

$\vec{v}_3 - \text{proj}_{V_2}\vec{v}_3 = \begin{bmatrix} d \\ e \\ f \end{bmatrix} - \begin{bmatrix} d \\ e \\ 0 \end{bmatrix} = \begin{bmatrix} 0 \\ 0 \\ f \end{bmatrix}$, so that $\vec{w}_3 = \begin{bmatrix} 0 \\ 0 \\ 1 \end{bmatrix} = \vec{e}_3$.

Note that $V_2 = \text{span}(\vec{e}_1, \vec{e}_2) = x$-$y$ plane

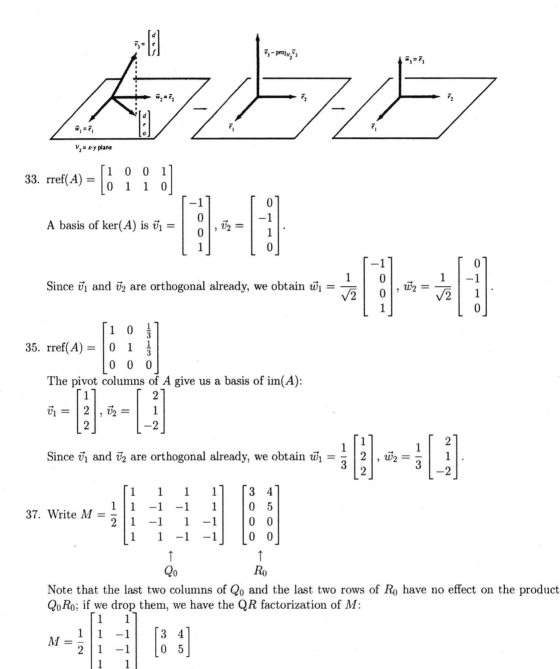

33. $\text{rref}(A) = \begin{bmatrix} 1 & 0 & 0 & 1 \\ 0 & 1 & 1 & 0 \end{bmatrix}$

A basis of $\ker(A)$ is $\vec{v}_1 = \begin{bmatrix} -1 \\ 0 \\ 0 \\ 1 \end{bmatrix}$, $\vec{v}_2 = \begin{bmatrix} 0 \\ -1 \\ 1 \\ 0 \end{bmatrix}$.

Since $\vec{v}_1$ and $\vec{v}_2$ are orthogonal already, we obtain $\vec{w}_1 = \dfrac{1}{\sqrt{2}} \begin{bmatrix} -1 \\ 0 \\ 0 \\ 1 \end{bmatrix}$, $\vec{w}_2 = \dfrac{1}{\sqrt{2}} \begin{bmatrix} 0 \\ -1 \\ 1 \\ 0 \end{bmatrix}$.

35. $\text{rref}(A) = \begin{bmatrix} 1 & 0 & \frac{1}{3} \\ 0 & 1 & \frac{1}{3} \\ 0 & 0 & 0 \end{bmatrix}$

The pivot columns of A give us a basis of $\text{im}(A)$:

$\vec{v}_1 = \begin{bmatrix} 1 \\ 2 \\ 2 \end{bmatrix}$, $\vec{v}_2 = \begin{bmatrix} 2 \\ 1 \\ -2 \end{bmatrix}$

Since $\vec{v}_1$ and $\vec{v}_2$ are orthogonal already, we obtain $\vec{w}_1 = \dfrac{1}{3} \begin{bmatrix} 1 \\ 2 \\ 2 \end{bmatrix}$, $\vec{w}_2 = \dfrac{1}{3} \begin{bmatrix} 2 \\ 1 \\ -2 \end{bmatrix}$.

37. Write $M = \dfrac{1}{2} \underset{\underset{Q_0}{\uparrow}}{\begin{bmatrix} 1 & 1 & 1 & 1 \\ 1 & -1 & -1 & 1 \\ 1 & -1 & 1 & -1 \\ 1 & 1 & -1 & -1 \end{bmatrix}} \underset{\underset{R_0}{\uparrow}}{\begin{bmatrix} 3 & 4 \\ 0 & 5 \\ 0 & 0 \\ 0 & 0 \end{bmatrix}}$

Note that the last two columns of Q_0 and the last two rows of R_0 have no effect on the product $Q_0 R_0$; if we drop them, we have the QR factorization of M:

$M = \dfrac{1}{2} \underset{\underset{Q}{\uparrow}}{\begin{bmatrix} 1 & 1 \\ 1 & -1 \\ 1 & -1 \\ 1 & 1 \end{bmatrix}} \underset{\underset{R}{\uparrow}}{\begin{bmatrix} 3 & 4 \\ 0 & 5 \end{bmatrix}}$

39. $\vec{w}_1 = \dfrac{1}{\sqrt{14}} \begin{bmatrix} 1 \\ 2 \\ 3 \end{bmatrix}$, $\vec{w}_2 = \dfrac{1}{\sqrt{3}} \begin{bmatrix} 1 \\ 1 \\ -1 \end{bmatrix}$, $\vec{w}_3 = \vec{w}_1 \times \vec{w}_2 = \dfrac{1}{\sqrt{42}} \begin{bmatrix} -5 \\ 4 \\ -1 \end{bmatrix}$

41. If all diagonal entries of A are positive, then we have $Q = I_n$ and $R = A$. A small modification is necessary if A has negative entries on the diagonal: if $a_{ii} < 0$ we let $r_{ij} = -a_{ij}$ for all j, and we let $q_{ii} = -1$; if $a_{ii} > 0$ we let $r_{ij} = a_{ij}$ and $q_{ii} = 1$. Furthermore, $q_{ij} = 0$ if $i \neq j$ (that is, Q is diagonal).

For example, $\begin{bmatrix} -1 & 2 & 3 \\ 0 & 4 & 5 \\ 0 & 0 & -6 \end{bmatrix} = \begin{bmatrix} -1 & 0 & 0 \\ 0 & 1 & 0 \\ 0 & 0 & -1 \end{bmatrix} \begin{bmatrix} 1 & -2 & -3 \\ 0 & 4 & 5 \\ 0 & 0 & 6 \end{bmatrix}$

$\qquad\qquad\qquad\;\; \uparrow \qquad\qquad\quad \uparrow \qquad\qquad\quad \uparrow$
$\qquad\qquad\qquad\;\; A \qquad\qquad\quad Q \qquad\qquad\quad R$

43. Partition the matrices Q and R in the QR factorization of A as follows:

$$\begin{bmatrix} A_1 & A_2 \end{bmatrix} = A = QR = \begin{bmatrix} Q_1 & Q_2 \end{bmatrix} \begin{bmatrix} R_1 & R_2 \\ 0 & R_3 \end{bmatrix} = \begin{bmatrix} Q_1 R_1 & Q_1 R_2 + Q_2 R_3 \end{bmatrix},$$

where Q_1 is $n \times m_1, Q_2$ is $n \times m_2, R_1$ is $m_1 \times m_1$, and R_3 is $m_2 \times m_2$.
Then, $A_1 = Q_1 R_1$ is the QR factorization of A_1: note that the columns of A_1 are orthonormal, and R_1 is upper triangular with positive diagonal entries.

45. Yes. Let $A = \begin{bmatrix} \vec{v}_1 & \cdots & \vec{v}_m \end{bmatrix}$. The idea is to perform the Gram-Schmidt process in reversed order, starting with $\vec{w}_m = \dfrac{1}{\|\vec{v}_m\|} \vec{v}_m$.

Then we can express $\vec{v}_j$ as a linear combination of $\vec{w}_j, \ldots, \vec{w}_m$, so that $\begin{bmatrix} \vec{v}_1 & \cdots & \vec{v}_j & \cdots & \vec{v}_m \end{bmatrix} = \begin{bmatrix} \vec{w}_1 & \cdots & \vec{w}_j & \cdots & \vec{w}_m \end{bmatrix} L$ for some *lower* triangular matrix L, with

$$\vec{v}_j = \begin{bmatrix} \vec{w}_1 & \cdots & \vec{w}_j & \cdots & \vec{w}_m \end{bmatrix} \begin{bmatrix} l_{1j} \\ \cdots \\ l_{jj} \\ \cdots \\ l_{mj} \end{bmatrix} = l_{jj}\vec{w}_j + \cdots + l_{mj}\vec{w}_m.$$

5.3

1. Using Facts 5.3.6 and 5.3.9a, we find that $(A\vec{v}) \cdot \vec{w} = (A\vec{v})^T \vec{w} = \vec{v}^T A^T \vec{w} = \vec{v} \cdot (A^T \vec{w})$, as claimed.

3. We will use the fact that L preserves length (by Definition 5.3.1) and the dot product (by Exercise 2):
$$\angle(L(\vec{v}), L(\vec{w})) = \arccos \frac{L(\vec{v}) \cdot L(\vec{w})}{\|L(\vec{v})\|\|L(\vec{w})\|} = \arccos \frac{\vec{v} \cdot \vec{w}}{\|\vec{v}\|\|\vec{w}\|} = \angle(\vec{v}, \vec{w}).$$

5. Yes, since the product of orthogonal matrices is orthogonal, by Fact 5.3.4a.

7. Yes! If A is orthogonal, then so is A^T, by Exercise 6. Since the columns of A are orthonormal, so are the rows of A^T.

9. Write $A = \begin{bmatrix} \vec{v}_1 & \vec{v}_2 \end{bmatrix}$. The unit vector $\vec{v}_1$ can be expressed as $\vec{v} = \begin{bmatrix} \cos(\phi) \\ \sin(\phi) \end{bmatrix}$, for some ϕ. Then $\vec{v}_2$ will be one of the two unit vectors orthogonal to $\vec{v}_1 : \vec{v}_2 = \begin{bmatrix} -\sin(\phi) \\ \cos(\phi) \end{bmatrix}$ or $\vec{v}_2 = \begin{bmatrix} \sin(\phi) \\ -\cos(\phi) \end{bmatrix}$.

Therefore, an orthogonal 2×2 matrix is either of the form $A = \begin{bmatrix} \cos(\phi) & -\sin(\phi) \\ \sin(\phi) & \cos(\phi) \end{bmatrix}$ or $A = \begin{bmatrix} \cos(\phi) & \sin(\phi) \\ \sin(\phi) & -\cos(\phi) \end{bmatrix}$, representing a rotation or a reflection.

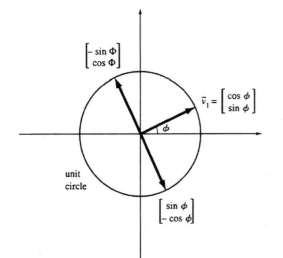

11. Let us first think about the inverse $L = T^{-1}$ of T.

Write $L(\vec{x}) = A\vec{x} = \begin{bmatrix} \vec{v}_1 & \vec{v}_2 & \vec{v}_3 \end{bmatrix} \vec{x}$. It is required that $L(\vec{e}_3) = \vec{v}_3 = \begin{bmatrix} \frac{2}{3} \\ \frac{2}{3} \\ \frac{1}{3} \end{bmatrix}$.

Furthermore, the vectors $\vec{v}_1, \vec{v}_2, \vec{v}_3$ must form an orthonormal basis of $\mathbb{R}^3$. By inspection, we find $\vec{v}_1 = \begin{bmatrix} -\frac{2}{3} \\ \frac{1}{3} \\ \frac{2}{3} \end{bmatrix}$.

Then $\vec{v}_2 = \vec{v}_1 \times \vec{v}_3 = \begin{bmatrix} -\frac{1}{3} \\ \frac{2}{3} \\ -\frac{2}{3} \end{bmatrix}$ does the job. In summary, we have $L(\vec{x}) = \frac{1}{3} \begin{bmatrix} -2 & -1 & 2 \\ 1 & 2 & 2 \\ 2 & -2 & 1 \end{bmatrix} \vec{x}$.

Since the matrix of L is orthogonal, the matrix of $T = L^{-1}$ is the transpose of the matrix of L:
$$T(\vec{x}) = \frac{1}{3} \begin{bmatrix} -2 & 1 & 2 \\ -1 & 2 & -2 \\ 2 & 2 & 1 \end{bmatrix} \vec{x}.$$
There are many other answers (since there are many choices for the vector $\vec{v}_1$ above).

13. No, since the vectors $\begin{bmatrix} 2 \\ 3 \\ 0 \end{bmatrix}$ and $\begin{bmatrix} -3 \\ 2 \\ 0 \end{bmatrix}$ are orthogonal, whereas $\begin{bmatrix} 3 \\ 0 \\ 2 \end{bmatrix}$ and $\begin{bmatrix} 2 \\ -3 \\ 0 \end{bmatrix}$ are not (see Fact 5.3.2).

15. No! If two symmetric matrices A and B do not commute, then $(AB)^T = B^T A^T = BA \neq AB$, so that AB is not symmetric.

    Example: $A = \begin{bmatrix} 1 & 0 \\ 0 & 0 \end{bmatrix}$ and $B = \begin{bmatrix} 0 & 1 \\ 1 & 0 \end{bmatrix}$

17. Yes! By Fact 5.3.9b, $(A^{-1})^T = (A^T)^{-1} = A^{-1}$.

19. By Fact 5.3.10, the matrix of the projection is $\vec{v}\vec{v}^T$; the ijth entry of this matrix is $v_i v_j$.

21. A unit vector on the line is $\vec{u} = \frac{1}{\sqrt{n}} \begin{bmatrix} 1 \\ \vdots \\ 1 \end{bmatrix}$.

    The matrix of the orthogonal projection is $\vec{u}\vec{u}^T$, the $n \times n$ matrix whose entries are all $\frac{1}{n}$ (compare with Exercise 19).

23. Examine how A acts on $\vec{u}$, and on a vector $\vec{v}$ orthogonal to $\vec{u}$:

    $A\vec{u} = (2\vec{u}\vec{u}^T - I_3)\vec{u} = 2\vec{u}\vec{u}^T\vec{u} - \vec{u} = \vec{u}$, since $\vec{u}^T\vec{u} = \vec{u} \cdot \vec{u} = \|\vec{u}\|^2 = 1$.

    $A\vec{v} = (2\vec{u}\vec{u}^T - I_3)\vec{v} = 2\vec{u}\vec{u}^T\vec{v} - \vec{v} = -\vec{v}$, since $\vec{u}^T\vec{v} = \vec{u} \cdot \vec{v} = 0$.

    Since A leaves the vectors in $L = \text{span}(\vec{u})$ unchanged and reverses the vectors in $V = L^\perp$, it represents the *reflection in L.*

    Note that $B = -A$, so that B reverses the vectors in L and leaves the vectors in V unchanged; that is, B represents the reflection in V.

25. Note that A^T is an $n \times m$ matrix. By Facts 3.3.5 and 5.3.9c, we have
    $\dim(\ker(A)) = n - \text{rank}(A)$ and $\dim(\ker(A^T)) = m - \text{rank}(A^T) = m - \text{rank}(A)$,
    so that $\dim(\ker(A)) = \dim(\ker(A^T))$ if (and only if) A is a square matrix.

27. By Fact 5.2.2, the columns $\vec{w}_1, \ldots, \vec{w}_m$ of Q are orthonormal. Therefore, $Q^T Q = I_m$, since the ijth entry of $Q^T Q$ is $\vec{w}_i \cdot \vec{w}_j$.

    By Fact 5.3.9a, we now have $A^T A = (QR)^T QR = R^T Q^T QR = R^T R$.

29. Yes! By Exercise 5.2.45, we can write $A^T = PL$, where P is orthogonal and L is lower triangular. By Fact 5.3.9a, $A = (PL)^T = L^T P^T$.

Note that $R = L^T$ is upper triangular, and $Q = P^T$ is orthogonal (by Exercise 6).

31. a. Using the terminology suggested in the hint, we observe that $I_m = Q_1^T Q_1 = (Q_2 S)^T Q_2 S = S^T Q_2^T Q_2 S = S^T S$, so that S is orthogonal, by Fact 5.3.7.

   b. Using the terminology suggested in the hint, we observe that $R_2 R_1^{-1}$ is both orthogonal (let $S = R_2 R_1^{-1}$ in part a) and upper triangular, with positive diagonal entries. By Exercise 30a, we have $R_2 R_1^{-1} = I_m$, so that $R_1 = R_2$. Then $Q_1 = Q_2 R_2 R_1^{-1} = Q_2$, as claimed.

33. Applying the strategy outlined on Page 155 to the general element $\begin{bmatrix} 0 & b & c \\ -b & 0 & e \\ -c & -e & 0 \end{bmatrix}$ of V, we find

the basis $\begin{bmatrix} 0 & 1 & 0 \\ -1 & 0 & 0 \\ 0 & 0 & 0 \end{bmatrix}, \begin{bmatrix} 0 & 0 & 1 \\ 0 & 0 & 0 \\ -1 & 0 & 0 \end{bmatrix}, \begin{bmatrix} 0 & 0 & 0 \\ 0 & 0 & 1 \\ 0 & -1 & 0 \end{bmatrix}$, so that $\dim(V) = 3$.

35. To write the general form of a symmetric $n \times n$ matrix A, we can place arbitrary constants on and above the diagonal, and then write the corresponding entries below the diagonal $(a_{ij} = a_{ji})$. See Exercise 32 for the case $n = 3$. Thus the dimension of the space equals the number of entries on and above the diagonal of an $n \times n$ matrix. Now there are n^2 entries in the matrix, $n^2 - n$ off the diagonal, and half of them, $(n^2 - n)/2$, above the diagonal. Since there are n entries on the diagonal, we have $\dim(V) = (n^2 - n)/2 + n = (n^2 + n)/2$.

37. Yes, L is linear, since $L(A + B) = (A + B)^T = A^T + B^T = L(A) + L(B)$ and $L(kA) = (kA)^T = kA^T = kL(A)$. Yes, L is an isomorphism; the inverse is the transformation $R(A) = A^T$ from $\mathbb{R}^{n \times m}$ to $\mathbb{R}^{m \times n}$.

39. The kernel consists of all matrixes A such that $L(A) = A - A^T = 0$, that is, $A^T = A$; those are the symmetric matrices.

The value $L(A) = A - A^T$ is always skew-symmetric, since $(A - A^T)^T = A^T - (A^T)^T = -(A - A^T)$, and every skew-symmetric matrix B can be written as $B = L(\frac{1}{2}B)$. Thus the image consists of all skew-symmetric matrices.

41. Using Fact 4.3.3, we find the matrix $\begin{bmatrix} 0 & 0 & 0 & 0 \\ 0 & 0 & 0 & 0 \\ 0 & 0 & 0 & 0 \\ 0 & 0 & 0 & 2 \end{bmatrix}$.

43. By Exercise 2.4.62b, the given LDU factorization of A is unique.

By Fact 5.3.9a, $A = A^T = (LDU)^T = U^T D^T L^T = U^T D L^T$ is another way to write the LDU factorization of A (since U^T is lower triangular and L^T is upper triangular). By the uniqueness of the LDU factorization, we have $U = L^T$ (and $L = U^T$), as claimed.

5.4

1. A basis of $\ker(A^T)$ is $\begin{bmatrix} -3 \\ 2 \end{bmatrix}$.

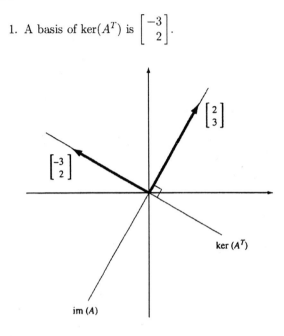

3. We will first show that the vectors $\vec{v}_1, \ldots, \vec{v}_p, \vec{w}_1, \ldots, \vec{w}_q$ span $\mathbb{R}^n$. Any vector $\vec{v}$ in $\mathbb{R}^n$ can be written as $\vec{v} = \text{proj}_V \vec{v} + (\vec{v} - \text{proj}_V \vec{v})$, where $\text{proj}_V \vec{v}$ is in V and $\vec{v} - \text{proj}_V \vec{v}$ is in $V^\perp$ (by definition of a projection, Fact 5.1.6).

   Now $\text{proj}_V \vec{v}$ is a linear combination of $\vec{v}_1, \ldots, \vec{v}_p$, and $\vec{v} - \text{proj}_V \vec{v}$ is a linear combination of $\vec{w}_1, \ldots, \vec{w}_q$, showing that the vectors $\vec{v}_1, \ldots, \vec{v}_p, \vec{w}_1, \ldots, \vec{w}_q$ span $\mathbb{R}^n$.

   Note that $p + q = n$, by Fact 5.4.2a; therefore, the vectors $\vec{v}_1, \ldots, \vec{v}_p, \vec{w}_1, \ldots, \vec{w}_q$ form a basis of $\mathbb{R}^n$, by Fact 3.3.4d.

5. $V = \ker(A)$, where $A = \begin{bmatrix} 1 & 1 & 1 & 1 \\ 1 & 2 & 5 & 4 \end{bmatrix}$.

   Then $V^\perp = (\ker A)^\perp = \text{im}(A^T)$, by Exercise 4.

   The two columns of A^T form a basis of $V^\perp$:

   $$\begin{bmatrix} 1 \\ 1 \\ 1 \\ 1 \end{bmatrix}, \begin{bmatrix} 1 \\ 2 \\ 5 \\ 4 \end{bmatrix}$$

7. $\text{im}(A)$ and $\ker(A)$ are orthogonal complements by Fact 5.4.1:
   $(\text{im} A)^\perp = \ker(A^T) = \ker(A)$

9.

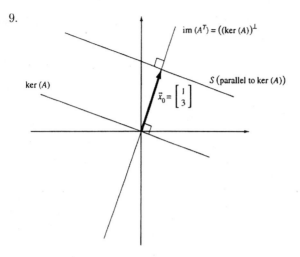

$\vec{x}_0$ is the shortest of all the vectors in S.

11. a. Note that $L^+(\vec{y}) = A^T(AA^T)^{-1}\vec{y}$; indeed, this vector is in $\text{im}(A^T) = (\ker A)^\perp$, and it is a solution of $L(\vec{x}) = A\vec{x} = \vec{y}$.

   b. $L(L^+(\vec{y})) = \vec{y}$, by definition of L^+.

   c. $L^+(L(\vec{x})) = A^T(AA^T)^{-1}A\vec{x} = \text{proj}_V\vec{x}$, where $V = \text{im}(A^T) = (\ker A)^\perp$, by Fact 5.4.8.

   d. $\text{im}(L^+) = \text{im}(A^T)$, by part c, and $\ker(L^+) = \{\vec{0}\}$ (if $\vec{y}$ is in $\ker(L^+)$, then $\vec{y} = L(L^+(\vec{y})) = L(\vec{0}) = \vec{0}$, by part b).

   e. Let $A = \begin{bmatrix} 1 & 0 & 0 \\ 0 & 1 & 0 \end{bmatrix}$; then the matrix of L^+ is $A^T(AA^T)^{-1} = A^T = \begin{bmatrix} 1 & 0 \\ 0 & 1 \\ 0 & 0 \end{bmatrix}$.

13. a. Suppose that $L^+(\vec{y}_1) = \vec{x}_1$ and $L^+(\vec{y}_2) = \vec{x}_2$; this means that $\vec{x}_1$ and $\vec{x}_2$ are both in $(\ker A)^\perp = \text{im}(A^T)$, $A^TA\vec{x}_1 = A^T\vec{y}_1$, and $A^TA\vec{x}_2 = A^T\vec{y}_2$. Then $\vec{x}_1 + \vec{x}_2$ is in $\text{im}(A^T)$ as well, and $A^TA(\vec{x}_1 + \vec{x}_2) = A^T(\vec{y}_1 + \vec{y}_2)$, so that $L^+(\vec{y}_1 + \vec{y}_2) = \vec{x}_1 + \vec{x}_2$.
   The verification of the property $L^+(k\vec{y}) = kL^+(\vec{y})$ is analogous.

   b. $L^+(L(\vec{x}))$ is the orthogonal projection of $\vec{x}$ onto $(\ker A)^\perp = \text{im}(A^T)$.

   c. $L(L^+(\vec{y}))$ is the orthogonal projection of $\vec{y}$ onto $\text{im}(A) = (\ker A^T)^\perp$.

   d. $\text{im}(L^+) = \text{im}(A^T)$ and $\ker(L^+) = \ker(A^T)$, by parts b and c.

   e. $L^+\begin{bmatrix} y_1 \\ y_2 \end{bmatrix} = \begin{bmatrix} \frac{y_1}{2} \\ 0 \\ 0 \end{bmatrix}$, so that the matrix of L^+ is $\begin{bmatrix} \frac{1}{2} & 0 \\ 0 & 0 \\ 0 & 0 \end{bmatrix}$.

15. Note that $(A^TA)^{-1}A^TA = I_n$; let $B = (A^TA)^{-1}A^T$.

17. Yes! By Fact 5.4.3, $\ker(A) = \ker(A^T A)$. Taking dimensions of both sides and using Fact 3.3.5, we find that $n - \text{rank}(A) = n - \text{rank}(A^T A)$; the claim follows.

19. $\vec{x}^* = (A^T A)^{-1} A^T \vec{b} = \begin{bmatrix} 1 \\ 1 \end{bmatrix}$, by Fact 5.4.7.

21. Using Fact 5.4.7, we find $\vec{x}^* = \begin{bmatrix} -1 \\ 2 \end{bmatrix}$ and $\vec{b} - A\vec{x}^* = \begin{bmatrix} -12 \\ 36 \\ -18 \end{bmatrix}$, so that $\|\vec{b} - A\vec{x}^*\| = 42$.

23. Using Fact 5.4.7, we find $\vec{x}^* = \vec{0}$; here $\vec{b}$ is perpendicular to $\text{im}(A)$.

25. In this case, the normal equation $A^T A\vec{x} = A^T \vec{b}$ is $\begin{bmatrix} 5 & 15 \\ 15 & 45 \end{bmatrix} \begin{bmatrix} x_1 \\ x_2 \end{bmatrix} = \begin{bmatrix} 5 \\ 15 \end{bmatrix}$, which simplifies to $x_1 + 3x_2 = 1$, or $x_1 = 1 - 3x_2$. The solutions are of the form $\vec{x}^* = \begin{bmatrix} 1 - 3t \\ t \end{bmatrix}$, where t is an arbitrary constant.

27. The least-squares solutions of the system $SA\vec{x} = S\vec{b}$ are the exact solutions of the normal equation $(SA)^T SA\vec{x} = (SA)^T S\vec{b}$.
Note that $S^T S = I_n$, since S is orthogonal; therefore, the normal equation simplifies as follows: $(SA)^T SA\vec{x} = A^T S^T SA\vec{x} = A^T A\vec{x}$ and $(SA)^T S\vec{b} = A^T S^T S\vec{b} = A^T \vec{b}$, so that the normal equation is $A^T A\vec{x} = A^T \vec{b}$, the same as the normal equation of the system $A\vec{x} = \vec{b}$. Therefore, the systems $A\vec{x} = \vec{b}$ and $SA\vec{x} = S\vec{b}$ have the same least-squares solution, $\vec{x}^* = \begin{bmatrix} 7 \\ 11 \end{bmatrix}$.

29. By Fact 5.4.7, $\vec{x}^* = (A^T A)^{-1} A^T \vec{b} = \begin{bmatrix} 1+\varepsilon & 1 \\ 1 & 1+\varepsilon \end{bmatrix}^{-1} \begin{bmatrix} 1+\varepsilon \\ 1+\varepsilon \end{bmatrix} = \frac{1}{2+\varepsilon} \begin{bmatrix} 1+\varepsilon \\ 1+\varepsilon \end{bmatrix} \approx \begin{bmatrix} \frac{1}{2} \\ \frac{1}{2} \end{bmatrix}$, where $\varepsilon = 10^{-20}$.
If we use a hand-held calculator, due to roundoff errors we find the normal equation $\begin{bmatrix} 1 & 1 \\ 1 & 1 \end{bmatrix} \begin{bmatrix} x_1 \\ x_2 \end{bmatrix} = \begin{bmatrix} 1 \\ 1 \end{bmatrix}$, with infinitely many solutions.

31. We want $\begin{bmatrix} c_0 \\ c_1 \end{bmatrix}$ such that

$$\begin{array}{l} 3 = c_0 + 0c_1 \\ 3 = c_0 + 1c_1 \\ 6 = c_0 + 1c_1 \end{array} \text{ or } \begin{bmatrix} 1 & 0 \\ 1 & 1 \\ 1 & 1 \end{bmatrix} \begin{bmatrix} c_1 \\ c_2 \end{bmatrix} = \begin{bmatrix} 3 \\ 3 \\ 6 \end{bmatrix}.$$

Since $\ker \begin{bmatrix} 1 & 0 \\ 1 & 1 \\ 1 & 1 \end{bmatrix} = \{\vec{0}\}, \begin{bmatrix} c_0 \\ c_1 \end{bmatrix}^* = \left(\begin{bmatrix} 1 & 1 & 1 \\ 0 & 1 & 1 \end{bmatrix} \begin{bmatrix} 1 & 0 \\ 1 & 1 \\ 1 & 1 \end{bmatrix} \right)^{-1} \begin{bmatrix} 1 & 1 & 1 \\ 0 & 1 & 1 \end{bmatrix} \begin{bmatrix} 3 \\ 3 \\ 6 \end{bmatrix} = \begin{bmatrix} 3 & 2 \\ 2 & 2 \end{bmatrix}^{-1} \begin{bmatrix} 12 \\ 9 \end{bmatrix}$
$= \begin{bmatrix} 3 \\ \frac{3}{2} \end{bmatrix}$ so $f^*(t) = 3 + \frac{3}{2}t$.

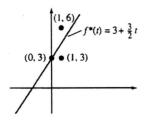

33. We want $\begin{bmatrix} c_0 \\ c_1 \\ c_2 \end{bmatrix}$ such that

$$\begin{array}{l} 0 = c_0 + \sin(0)c_1 + \cos(0)c_2 \\ 1 = c_0 + \sin(1)c_1 + \cos(1)c_2 \\ 2 = c_0 + \sin(2)c_1 + \cos(2)c_2 \\ 3 = c_0 + \sin(3)c_1 + \cos(3)c_2 \end{array} \text{ or } \begin{bmatrix} 1 & 0 & 1 \\ 1 & \sin(1) & \cos(1) \\ 1 & \sin(2) & \cos(2) \\ 1 & \sin(3) & \cos(3) \end{bmatrix} \begin{bmatrix} c_1 \\ c_2 \\ c_3 \end{bmatrix} = \begin{bmatrix} 0 \\ 1 \\ 2 \\ 3 \end{bmatrix}.$$

Since the coefficient matrix has kernel $\{\vec{0}\}$, we compute $\begin{bmatrix} c_1 \\ c_2 \\ c_3 \end{bmatrix}^*$ using Fact 5.4.7, obtaining

$$\begin{bmatrix} c_0 \\ c_1 \\ c_2 \end{bmatrix}^* \approx \begin{bmatrix} 1.5 \\ 0.1 \\ -1.41 \end{bmatrix} \text{ so } f^*(t) \approx 1.5 + 0.1\sin t - 1.41 \cos t.$$

35. a. The ijth entry of $A_n^T A_n$ is the dot product of the ith row of A_n^T and the jth column of A_n, i.e.

$$A_n^T A_n = \begin{bmatrix} n & \sum_{i=1}^{n} \sin a_i & \sum_{i=1}^{n} \cos a_i \\ \sum_{i=1}^{n} \sin a_i & \sum_{i=1}^{n} \sin^2 a_i & \sum_{i=1}^{n} \sin a_i \cos a_i \\ \sum_{i=1}^{n} \cos a_i & \sum_{i=1}^{n} \sin a_i \cos a_i & \sum_{i=1}^{n} \cos^2 a_i \end{bmatrix} \text{ and } A_n^T \vec{b} = \begin{bmatrix} \sum_{i=1}^{n} g(a_i) \\ \sum_{i=1}^{n} g(a_i) \sin a_i \\ \sum_{i=1}^{n} g(a_i) \cos a_i \end{bmatrix}.$$

b. $\displaystyle\lim_{n\to\infty} \frac{2\pi}{n} A_n^T A_n = \begin{bmatrix} 2\pi & \int_0^{2\pi} \sin t\, dt & \int_0^{2\pi} \cos t\, dt \\ \int_0^{2\pi} \sin t\, dt & \int_0^{2\pi} \sin^2 t\, dt & \int_0^{2\pi} \sin t \cos t\, dt \\ \int_0^{2\pi} \cos t\, dt & \int_0^{2\pi} \sin t \cos t\, dt & \int_0^{2\pi} \cos^2 t\, dt \end{bmatrix} = \begin{bmatrix} 2\pi & 0 & 0 \\ 0 & \pi & 0 \\ 0 & 0 & \pi \end{bmatrix}$

and $\displaystyle\lim_{n\to\infty} \frac{2\pi}{n} A_n^T \vec{b} = \begin{bmatrix} \int_0^{2\pi} g(t)\,dt \\ \int_0^{2\pi} g(t)\sin t\,dt \\ \int_0^{2\pi} g(t)\cos t\,dt \end{bmatrix}$

$\left(\text{Here } \dfrac{2\pi}{n} = \Delta t \text{ so } \displaystyle\lim_{n\to\infty} \frac{2\pi}{n} \sum_{i=1}^n \cos(t_i) = \lim_{n\to\infty} \sum_{i=1}^n \cos(t_i)\Delta t = \int_0^{2\pi} \cos t\,dt \text{ for instance. All other}\right.$

$\left.\text{limits are obtained similarly.}\vphantom{\sum}\right)$

c. $\begin{bmatrix} c \\ p \\ q \end{bmatrix} = \displaystyle\lim_{n\to\infty} \begin{bmatrix} c_n \\ p_n \\ q_n \end{bmatrix} = \begin{bmatrix} 2\pi & 0 & 0 \\ 0 & \pi & 0 \\ 0 & 0 & \pi \end{bmatrix}^{-1} \begin{bmatrix} \int_0^{2\pi} g(t)\,dt \\ \int_0^{2\pi} g(t)\sin t\,dt \\ \int_0^{2\pi} g(t)\cos t\,dt \end{bmatrix} = \begin{bmatrix} \frac{1}{2\pi}\int_0^{2\pi} g(t)\,dt \\ \frac{1}{\pi}\int_0^{2\pi} g(t)\sin t\,dt \\ \frac{1}{\pi}\int_0^{2\pi} g(t)\cos t\,dt \end{bmatrix}$ and $f(t) =$

$c + p\sin t + q\cos t$, where c, p, q are given above.

37. a. We want c_0, c_1 such that

$\begin{array}{l} c_0 + c_1(35) = \log 35 \\ c_0 + c_1(46) = \log 46 \\ c_0 + c_1(59) = \log 77 \\ c_0 + c_1(69) = \log 133 \end{array}$ or $\underbrace{\begin{bmatrix} 1 & 35 \\ 1 & 46 \\ 1 & 59 \\ 1 & 69 \end{bmatrix}}_{A} \begin{bmatrix} c_0 \\ c_1 \end{bmatrix} = \underbrace{\begin{bmatrix} \log 35 \\ \log 46 \\ \log 77 \\ \log 133 \end{bmatrix}}_{\vec{b}}$

so $\begin{bmatrix} c_0 \\ c_1 \end{bmatrix}^* = (A^T A)^{-1} A^T \vec{b} \approx \begin{bmatrix} 0.915 \\ 0.017 \end{bmatrix}$ so $\log(d) \approx 0.915 + 0.017t$.

b. $d \approx 10^{0.915} \cdot 10^{0.017t} \approx 8.22 \cdot 10^{0.017t}$

c. If $t = 88$ then $d \approx 258$. Since the Airbus has only 93 displays, new technologies must have rendered the old trends obsolete.

39. a. We want $\begin{bmatrix} c_0 \\ c_1 \end{bmatrix}$ such that

$\log(250) = c_0 + c_1 \log(600,000)$

$\log(60) = c_0 + c_1 \log(200,000)$

$\log(25) = c_0 + c_1 \log(60,000)$

$\log(12) = c_0 + c_1 \log(10,000)$

$\log(5) = c_0 + c_1 \log(2500)$

The least-squares solution to the above system is $\begin{bmatrix} c_0 \\ c_1 \end{bmatrix}^* \approx \begin{bmatrix} -1.616 \\ 0.664 \end{bmatrix}$ so $\log z \approx -1.616 + 0.664 \log g$.

b. Exponentiating both sides of the answer to a, we get $z \approx 10^{-1.616} \cdot g^{0.664} \approx 0.0242 \cdot g^{0.664}$.

c. This model is close since $\sqrt{g} = g^{0.5}$.

41. a. We want $\begin{bmatrix} c_0 \\ c_1 \end{bmatrix}$ such that $\log D = c_0 + c_1 t$ (t in years since 1970), i.e.

   $$\log 370 = c_0 + c_1(0)$$
   $$\log 533 = c_0 + c_1(5)$$
   $$\log 908 = c_0 + c_1(10)$$
   $$\log 1,823 = c_0 + c_1(15)$$
   $$\log 3,233 = c_0 + c_1(20)$$
   $$\log 4,871 = c_0 + c_1(25)$$

   The least-squares solution to the system is $\begin{bmatrix} c_0 \\ c_1 \end{bmatrix}^* \approx \begin{bmatrix} 2.53 \\ 0.047 \end{bmatrix}$, i.e. $\log D \approx 2.53 + 0.047t$ or $D \approx 10^{2.53} \cdot 10^{0.047t} = 339 \cdot 10^{0.047t}$.

b. In the year 2000, $t = 30$ and $D \approx 8,700$. The formula predicts a debt of about 8.7 trillion dollars.

c. In the late 1990's, the United States managed to balance their budget.

5.5

1. Since f is nonzero, there is a c on $[a,\ b]$ such that $f(c) = d \neq 0$. By continuity, there is an $\varepsilon > 0$ such that $|f(x)| > \dfrac{|d|}{2}$ for all x on the open interval $(c - \varepsilon, c + \varepsilon)$ where f is defined (see any good Calculus text).

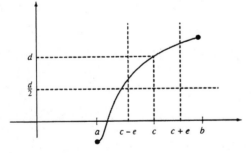

We assume that $c - \varepsilon \geq a$ and $c + \varepsilon \leq b$ and leave the other cases to the reader. Then $\langle f, f \rangle = \displaystyle\int_a^b (f(t))^2\, dt \geq \int_{c-\varepsilon}^{c+\varepsilon} \left(\frac{d}{2}\right)^2 dt = \frac{d^2 \varepsilon}{2} > 0$, as claimed.

3. Note that $\langle \vec{x}, \vec{y} \rangle = (S\vec{x})^T S\vec{y} = S\vec{x} \cdot S\vec{y}$.

   a. We will check the four parts of Definition 5.5.1
      α. $\langle \vec{x}, \vec{y} \rangle = S\vec{x} \cdot S\vec{y} = S\vec{y} \cdot S\vec{x} = \langle \vec{y}, \vec{x} \rangle$
      β. $\langle \vec{x} + \vec{y}, \vec{z} \rangle = S(\vec{x} + \vec{y}) \cdot S\vec{z} = (S\vec{x} + S\vec{y}) \cdot S\vec{z} = (S\vec{x} \cdot S\vec{z}) + (S\vec{y} \cdot S\vec{z}) = \langle \vec{x}, \vec{z} \rangle + \langle \vec{y}, \vec{z} \rangle$
      γ. $\langle c\vec{x}, \vec{y} \rangle = S(c\vec{x}) \cdot S\vec{y} = c(S\vec{x}) \cdot S\vec{y} = c\langle \vec{x}, \vec{y} \rangle$
      δ. If $\vec{x} \neq 0$, then $\langle \vec{x}, \vec{x} \rangle = S\vec{x} \cdot S\vec{x} = \|S\vec{x}\|^2$ is positive if $S\vec{x} \neq \vec{0}$, that is, if $\vec{x}$ is not in the
         kernel of S. It is required that $S\vec{x} \neq \vec{0}$ whenever $\vec{x} \neq \vec{0}$, that is, $\ker(S) = \{\vec{0}\}$.
      Answer: S must be invertible.

   b. It is required that $\langle \vec{x}, \vec{y} \rangle = (S\vec{x})^T S\vec{y} = \vec{x}^T S^T S\vec{y}$ equal $\vec{x} \cdot \vec{y} = \vec{x}^T \vec{y}$ for all $\vec{x}$ and $\vec{y}$. This is the
      case if and only if $S^T S = I_n$, that is, *S is orthogonal.*

5. a. $\langle\langle A, B \rangle\rangle = \mathrm{tr}(AB^T) = \mathrm{tr}((AB^T)^T) = \mathrm{tr}(BA^T) = \langle\langle B, A \rangle\rangle$ In the second step we have used the
      fact that $\mathrm{tr}(M) = \mathrm{tr}(M^T)$, for any square matrix M.

   b. $\langle\langle A + B, C \rangle\rangle = \mathrm{tr}((A + B)C^T) = \mathrm{tr}(AC^T + BC^T) = \mathrm{tr}(AC^T) + \mathrm{tr}(BC^T) = \langle\langle A, C \rangle\rangle + \langle\langle B, C \rangle\rangle$

   c. $\langle\langle cA, B \rangle\rangle = \mathrm{tr}(cAB^T) = c\,\mathrm{tr}(AB^T) = c\langle\langle A, B \rangle\rangle$

   d. $\langle\langle A, A \rangle\rangle = \mathrm{tr}(AA^T) = \sum_{i=1}^{n} \|\vec{v}_i\|^2 > 0$ if $A \neq 0$, where $\vec{v}_i$ is the ith row of A.

   We have shown that $\langle\langle \cdot, \cdot \rangle\rangle$ does indeed define an inner product.

7. Axioms *a, b,* and *c* hold for any choice of k (check this!). Also, it is required that $\langle\langle v, v \rangle\rangle = k\langle v, v \rangle$
   be positive for nonzero v. Since $\langle v, v \rangle$ is positive, this is the case if (and only if) k is *positive.*

9. If f is even and g is odd, then fg is odd, so that $\langle f, g \rangle = \int_{-1}^{1} fg = 0$.

11. $\langle f, g \rangle = \langle \cos(t), \cos(t + \delta) \rangle = \langle \cos(t), \cos(t) \cos(\delta) - \sin(t) \sin(\delta) \rangle = \cos(\delta)\langle \cos(t), \cos(t) \rangle - \sin(\delta)$
    $\langle \cos(t), \sin(t) \rangle = \cos(\delta)$, by Fact 5.5.4.
    Also, $\langle g, g \rangle = 1$ (left to reader).
    Thus, $\angle(f, g) = \arccos\left(\dfrac{\langle f, g \rangle}{\|f\|\|g\|} \right) = \arccos(\cos\delta) = \delta$.

13. The sequence $(a_0, b_1, c_1, b_2, c_2, \ldots)$ is "square-summable" by Fact 5.5.6, so that it is in ℓ_2. Also,
    $\|(a_0, b_1, c_1, b_2, c_2, \ldots)\|^2 = a_0^2 + b_1^2 + c_1^2 + b_2^2 + c_2^2 + \cdots = \|f\|^2$, by Fact 5.5.6, so that the two norms
    are equal.

15. First note that $b = \left\langle \begin{bmatrix} 1 \\ 0 \end{bmatrix}, \begin{bmatrix} 0 \\ 1 \end{bmatrix} \right\rangle = \left\langle \begin{bmatrix} 0 \\ 1 \end{bmatrix}, \begin{bmatrix} 1 \\ 0 \end{bmatrix} \right\rangle = c$, by part a of Definition 5.5.1, so that $b = c$.
    Check that if $b = c$ then $\langle \vec{v}, \vec{w} \rangle = \langle \vec{w}, \vec{v} \rangle$ for all $\vec{v}, \vec{w}$ in $\mathbb{R}^2$. Check that parts (b) and (c) of Definition
    5.5.1 are satisfied for all values of constants c, d. Next, we need to worry about part (d) of that

definition. It is required that $\left\langle \begin{bmatrix} x_1 \\ x_2 \end{bmatrix}, \begin{bmatrix} x_1 \\ x_2 \end{bmatrix} \right\rangle = x_1^2 + 2bx_1x_2 + dx_2^2$ be positive for all nonzero $\begin{bmatrix} x_1 \\ x_2 \end{bmatrix}$.
We can complete the square and write $x_1^2 + 2bx_1x_2 + dx_2^2 = (x_1 + bx_2)^2 + (d - b^2)x_2^2$; this quantity
is positive for all nonzero $\begin{bmatrix} x_1 \\ x_2 \end{bmatrix}$ if (and only if) $d - b^2 > 0$, or, $d > b^2$. In summary, the function is
an inner product if (and only if) $b = c$ and $d > b^2$.

17. We leave it to the reader to check that the first three axioms are satisfied for any such T. As for
    axiom d: It is required that $\langle v, v \rangle = T(v) \cdot T(v) = \|T(v)\|^2$ be positive for any nonzero v, that is,
    $T(v) \neq \vec{0}$. This means that the *kernel of T must be* $\{0\}$.

19. If we write $\vec{v} = \begin{bmatrix} x_1 \\ x_2 \end{bmatrix}, \vec{w} = \begin{bmatrix} y_1 \\ y_2 \end{bmatrix}$, and $A = \begin{bmatrix} p & q \\ r & s \end{bmatrix}$, then $\left\langle \begin{bmatrix} x_1 \\ x_2 \end{bmatrix}, \begin{bmatrix} y_1 \\ y_2 \end{bmatrix} \right\rangle = [x_1x_2] \begin{bmatrix} p & q \\ r & s \end{bmatrix} \begin{bmatrix} y_1 \\ y_2 \end{bmatrix} =$
    $px_1y_1 + qx_1y_2 + rx_2y_1 + sx_2y_2$. Note that in Exercise 15 we considered the special case $p = 1$. First
    it is required that $p = \left\langle \begin{bmatrix} 1 \\ 0 \end{bmatrix}, \begin{bmatrix} 1 \\ 0 \end{bmatrix} \right\rangle$ be positive.

    Now we can write $\left\langle \begin{bmatrix} x_1 \\ x_2 \end{bmatrix}, \begin{bmatrix} y_1 \\ y_2 \end{bmatrix} \right\rangle = p \left[x_1y_1 + \frac{q}{p}x_1y_2 + \frac{r}{p}x_2y_1 + \frac{s}{p}x_2y_2 \right]$ and use our work in Exer-

    cise 15 $\left(\text{with } b = \frac{q}{p}, c = \frac{r}{p}, d = \frac{s}{p} \right)$ to see that the conditions $q = r$ and $q^2 < ps$ must hold. In

    summary, the function is an inner product if (and only if) the entries of matrix $A = \begin{bmatrix} p & q \\ r & s \end{bmatrix}$
    satisfy the conditions $p > 0$, $q = r$ and $\det(A) = ps - q^2 > 0$.

21. Note that $\langle \vec{v}, \vec{w} \rangle = (\vec{v} + \vec{w}) \cdot (\vec{v} + \vec{w}) - \vec{v} \cdot \vec{v} - \vec{w} \cdot \vec{w} = 2(\vec{v} \cdot \vec{w})$, double the dot product. Thus it's
    an inner product, by Exercise 7.

23. We start with the standard basis $1, t$ of P_1 and use the Gram-Schmidt process to construct and
    orthonormal basis $g_1(t), g_2(t)$.
    $\|1\| = \sqrt{\frac{1}{2}(1 \cdot 1) + 1 \cdot 1} = 1$, so that we can let $g_1(t) = 1$. Then $g_2(t) = \dfrac{t - \langle 1, t \rangle 1}{\|t - (1,t)1\|} = \dfrac{t - \frac{1}{2}}{\|t - \frac{1}{2}\|} =$
    $2t - 1$.
    Summary: $g_1(t) = 1$ and $g_2(t) = 2t - 1$ is an orthonormal basis.

25. Using the inner product defined in Example 2, we find that
    $$\|\vec{x}\| = \sqrt{\langle \vec{x}, \vec{x} \rangle} = \sqrt{1 + \frac{1}{4} + \frac{1}{9} + \cdots + \frac{1}{n^2} + \cdots} = \sqrt{\frac{\pi^2}{6}} = \frac{\pi}{\sqrt{6}} \text{ (see the text right after Fact 5.5.6)}.$$

27. $a_0 = \dfrac{1}{\sqrt{2\pi}} \displaystyle\int_{-\pi}^{\pi} f(t)\, dt = \dfrac{1}{\sqrt{2}}.$

    $b_k = \dfrac{1}{\pi} \displaystyle\int_{-\pi}^{\pi} f(t) \sin(kt)\, dt = \dfrac{1}{\pi} \displaystyle\int_0^{\pi} \sin(kt)\, dt = -\dfrac{1}{k\pi}[\cos(kt)]_0^{\pi} = \begin{cases} 0 & \text{if } k \text{ is even} \\ \dfrac{2}{k\pi} & \text{if } k \text{ is odd} \end{cases}$

    $c_k = \dfrac{1}{\pi} \displaystyle\int_{-\pi}^{\pi} f(t) \cos(kt)\, dt = \dfrac{1}{\pi} \displaystyle\int_0^{\pi} \cos(kt)\, dt = \dfrac{1}{k\pi}[\sin(kt)]_0^{\pi} = 0$

$$f_1(t) = f_2(t) = \frac{1}{2} + \frac{2}{\pi}\sin(t), \; f_3(t) = f_4(t) = \frac{1}{2} + \frac{2}{\pi}\sin(t) + \frac{2}{3\pi}\sin(3t)$$

$$\vdots$$

29. $\|f\|^2 = \langle f, f \rangle = \dfrac{1}{\pi}\displaystyle\int_{-\pi}^{\pi}(f(t))^2\,dt = \dfrac{1}{\pi}\displaystyle\int_0^{\pi} 1\,dt = 1$

Now Fact 5.5.6 tells us that $\dfrac{1}{2} + \dfrac{4}{\pi^2} + \dfrac{4}{9\pi^2} + \dfrac{4}{25\pi^2} + \cdots = 1$, or $\dfrac{1}{2} + \dfrac{4}{\pi^2}\left(\displaystyle\sum_{k\,\text{odd}} \dfrac{1}{k^2}\right) = 1$ or

$$\sum_{k\,\text{odd}} \frac{1}{k^2} = 1 + \frac{1}{9} + \frac{1}{25} + \frac{1}{49} + \cdots = \frac{\frac{1}{2}}{\frac{4}{\pi^2}} = \frac{\pi^2}{8}.$$

31. An orthonormal basis of P_2 of the desired form is $f_0(t) = \dfrac{1}{\sqrt{2}}, f_1(t) = \sqrt{\dfrac{3}{2}}\,t, f_2(t) = \dfrac{1}{2}\sqrt{\dfrac{5}{2}}(3t^2 - 1)$

(compare with Exercise 10), and the zeros of $f_2(t)$ are $a_{1,2} = \pm\dfrac{1}{\sqrt{3}}$.

Next we find the weights w_1, w_2 such that $\displaystyle\int_{-1}^{1} f(t)\,dt = \sum_{i=1}^{2} w_i f(a_i)$ for all f in P_1. We need to make sure that the equation holds for 1 and t.

$\begin{vmatrix} 2 = w_1 + w_2 \\ 0 = \frac{1}{\sqrt{3}}w_1 - \frac{1}{\sqrt{3}}w_2 \end{vmatrix}$, with solution $w_1 = w_2 = 1$.

It follows that the equation $\displaystyle\int_{-1}^{1} f(t)\,dt = f(a_1) + f(a_2) = f\left(\dfrac{1}{\sqrt{3}}\right) + f\left(-\dfrac{1}{\sqrt{3}}\right)$ holds for all polynomials f in P_1. We can check that it holds for t^2 and t^3 as well, that is, it holds in fact for all cubic polynomials.

$$\int_{-1}^{1} t^2\,dt = \frac{2}{3} \text{ equals } \left(\frac{1}{\sqrt{3}}\right)^2 + \left(-\frac{1}{\sqrt{3}}\right)^2 = \frac{2}{3}, \text{ and } \int_{-1}^{1} t^3\,dt = 0 \text{ equals } \left(\frac{1}{\sqrt{3}}\right)^3 + \left(-\frac{1}{\sqrt{3}}\right)^3 = 0.$$

True or False

1. T, by Fact 5.3.4.a

3. T, since $(A + B)^T = A^T + B^T = A + B$

5. F. Consider $\begin{bmatrix} 1 & 1 \\ 1 & 1 \end{bmatrix}$.

7. F. The correct formula is $\text{proj}_L(\vec{x}) = (\vec{x} \cdot \vec{v})\vec{v}$, by Fact 2.2.5.

9. F. Consider $T(\vec{x}) = \begin{bmatrix} 1 & 1 \\ 0 & 0 \end{bmatrix}\vec{x}$.

11. T, since $(ABBA)^T = A^T B^T B^T A^T = ABBA$, by Fact 5.3.9.a

13. F. $\dim(V) + \dim(V^\perp) = 5$, by Fact 5.4.2.a. Thus one of the dimensions is even and the other odd.

15. F. The Pythagorean Theorem holds for orthogonal vectors $\vec{x}, \vec{y}$ only (Fact 5.1.8)

17. T. If A is orthogonal, then $A^T A = I_n$, by Fact 5.3.7, so that $(A^T)^T = A = (A^T)^{-1}$. Again by Fact 5.3.7, this implies that matrix A^T is orthogonal.

19. T, since $\vec{x} \cdot (\text{proj}_V \vec{x}) = (\text{proj}_V \vec{x} + (\vec{x} - \text{proj}_V \vec{x})) \cdot \text{proj}_V \vec{x} = \|\text{proj}_V \vec{x}\|^2 \geq 0$. Note that $\vec{x} - \text{proj}_V \vec{x}$ is orthogonal to $\text{proj}_V \vec{x}$, by the definition of a projection.

21. T, since the columns are unit vectors.

23. F. The columns fail to be unit vectors (use Fact 5.3.3.b)

25. F. As a counterexample, consider $\begin{bmatrix} 1 & 0 \\ 0 & -1 \end{bmatrix}$ and $\begin{bmatrix} 0 & -1 \\ 1 & 0 \end{bmatrix}$.

27. T, by Fact 5.4.3.a.

29. T. If $A = \begin{bmatrix} a & b \\ b & c \end{bmatrix}$ is a symmetric matrix, then $A - xI_2 = \begin{bmatrix} a-x & b \\ b & c-x \end{bmatrix}$. This matrix fails to be invertible if (and only if) $\det(A - xI_2) = (a-x)(c-x) - b^2 = 0$. We use the quadratic formula to find the (real) solutions $x = \dfrac{a+c \pm \sqrt{(a+c)^2 - 4ac + 4b^2}}{2} = \dfrac{a+c \pm \sqrt{(a-c)^2 + 4b^2}}{2}$. Note that the discriminant $(a-c)^2 + 4b^2$ is positive or zero.

31. F. Consider $A = \begin{bmatrix} -1 & 1 \\ 0 & 1 \end{bmatrix}$.

33. T. In Fact 5.4.1, let $A = B^T$ to see that $(\text{im}(B^T))^\perp = \ker(B)$. Now take the orthogonal complements of both sides and use Fact 5.4.2.b.

35. F. Verify that matrices $A = \begin{bmatrix} 1 & 0 \\ 0 & -1 \end{bmatrix}$ and $B = \begin{bmatrix} 1 & 1 \\ 0 & -1 \end{bmatrix}$ are similar.

37. T. We know that $A^T = A$ and $S^{-1} = S^T$. Now $(S^{-1}AS)^T = S^T A^T (S^{-1})^T = S^{-1}AS$, by Fact 5.3.9.a.

39. T. Try $A = \begin{bmatrix} 1 & 0 \\ 0 & 1 \end{bmatrix}$ and $B = \begin{bmatrix} \cos\alpha & -\sin\alpha \\ \sin\alpha & \cos\alpha \end{bmatrix}$, so that $A + B = \begin{bmatrix} 1+\cos\alpha & -\sin\alpha \\ \sin\alpha & 1+\cos\alpha \end{bmatrix}$. It is required that $\begin{bmatrix} 1+\cos\alpha \\ \sin a \end{bmatrix}$ and $\begin{bmatrix} -\sin\alpha \\ 1+\cos\alpha \end{bmatrix}$ be unit vectors, meaning that $1 + 2\cos\alpha +$

$\cos^2 \alpha + \sin^2 \alpha = 2 + 2\cos\alpha = 1$, or $\cos\alpha = -\dfrac{1}{2}$, and $\sin\alpha = \pm\dfrac{\sqrt{3}}{2}$. Thus $A = \begin{bmatrix} 1 & 0 \\ 0 & 1 \end{bmatrix}$ and $B = \begin{bmatrix} -\frac{1}{2} & -\frac{\sqrt{3}}{2} \\ \frac{\sqrt{3}}{2} & -\frac{1}{2} \end{bmatrix}$ is a solution.

41. T. We attempt to write $A = S + Q$, where S is symmetric and Q is skew-symmetric. Then $A^T = S^T + Q^T = S - Q$. Adding the equations $A = S + Q$ and $A^T = S - Q$ together gives $2S = A + A^T$ and $S = \frac{1}{2}(A + A^T)$. Similarly we find $Q = \frac{1}{2}(A - A^T)$. Check that the decomposition $A = S + Q = (\frac{1}{2}(A + A^T)) + (\frac{1}{2}(A - A^T))$ does the job.

43. T. Let $A = \begin{bmatrix} x & y \\ z & t \end{bmatrix}$. We know that $AA^T = A^2$, or $\begin{bmatrix} x^2 + y^2 & xz + yt \\ xz + yt & z^2 + t^2 \end{bmatrix} = \begin{bmatrix} x^2 + yz & xy + yt \\ zx + tz & yz + t^2 \end{bmatrix}$. We need to show that $y = z$. If $y \neq 0$, this follows from the equation $x^2 + y^2 = x^2 + yz$; if $z \neq 0$, it follows from $z^2 + t^2 = yz + t^2$; if both y and z are zero, we are all set.

Chapter 6

6.1

1. $\det \begin{bmatrix} 1 & 2 \\ 3 & 4 \end{bmatrix} = -2$

3. $\det \begin{bmatrix} 1 & 2 & 3 \\ 0 & 2 & 3 \\ 0 & 0 & 3 \end{bmatrix} = 6$, by Fact 6.1.3.

5. $\det \begin{bmatrix} 0 & 0 & 2 \\ 0 & 3 & 0 \\ 4 & 0 & 0 \end{bmatrix} = -24$

7. $\det \begin{bmatrix} 1 & 2 & 3 \\ 4 & 5 & 6 \\ 7 & 8 & 9 \end{bmatrix} = 0$

9. $\det \begin{bmatrix} 7 & 8 & 9 \\ 0 & 0 & 0 \\ 5 & 6 & 7 \end{bmatrix} = 0$

11. $\det \begin{bmatrix} 1 & 1 & 1 \\ 1 & 1 & 1 \\ 1 & 1 & 1 \end{bmatrix} = 0$

13. $\det \begin{bmatrix} 2 & 3 & 4 & 5 \\ 0 & 6 & 7 & 8 \\ 0 & 0 & 3 & 2 \\ 0 & 0 & 0 & 1 \end{bmatrix} = 36$, by Fact 6.1.3.

15. $\det \begin{bmatrix} 0 & 2 & 3 & 4 \\ 1 & 2 & 3 & 4 \\ 0 & 0 & 0 & 4 \\ 0 & 0 & 3 & 4 \end{bmatrix} = 24$

17. $\det \begin{bmatrix} 0 & 0 & 1 & 0 & 0 \\ 0 & 0 & 0 & 1 & 0 \\ 1 & 0 & 0 & 0 & 0 \\ 0 & 0 & 0 & 0 & 1 \\ 0 & 1 & 0 & 0 & 0 \end{bmatrix} = -1$

19. $\det \begin{bmatrix} a & b & c \\ 0 & p & q \\ 0 & r & s \end{bmatrix} = aps - aqr$

21. Invertible since its determinant is 2 (i.e. $\neq 0$).

23. Invertible if $a \neq 0, b \neq 0$, and $c \neq 0$ since its determinant is abc.

25. Invertible since its determinant is 6 (i.e. $\neq 0$).

27. We will compute $\det(\lambda I_2 - A) = \det \begin{bmatrix} \lambda - 4 & -2 \\ -2 & \lambda - 7 \end{bmatrix} = \lambda^2 - 11\lambda + 24 = (\lambda - 3)(\lambda - 8)$, so the matrix is not invertible when $(\lambda - 3)(\lambda - 8) = 0$, i.e., when $\lambda = 3$ or $\lambda = 8$.

29. We will compute $\det(\lambda I_2 - A) = \det \begin{bmatrix} \lambda - 3 & -1 \\ 4 & \lambda + 1 \end{bmatrix} = (\lambda + 1)^2$, so the matrix is not invertible when $(\lambda - 1)^2 = 0$, i.e., when $\lambda = 1$.

31. We will compute $\det(\lambda I_3 - A) = \det \begin{bmatrix} \lambda & 0 & -1 \\ 0 & \lambda & -1 \\ -1 & -1 & \lambda - 1 \end{bmatrix} = \lambda(\lambda - 2)(\lambda + 1)$, so the matrix is not invertible when $\lambda(\lambda - 2)(\lambda + 1) = 0$, i.e., when $\lambda = 0, \lambda = 2$, or $\lambda = -1$.

33. Its determinant is zero, since each pattern will contain an entry from the row or column of zeros. Hence, each product associated with a pattern will be zero, and the determinant will be zero as well.

35. $\det(A) = 1$ since there is only one pattern which does not contain a 0, and since the number of inversions in that pattern is $1 + 2 + 3 + \cdots + 99 = \dfrac{99 \cdot 100}{2} = 99 \cdot 50$, which is even.

37. Let $A = \begin{bmatrix} a_1 & a_2 \\ a_3 & a_4 \end{bmatrix}$ and $C = \begin{bmatrix} c_1 & c_2 \\ c_3 & c_4 \end{bmatrix}$.

    Then $\det(M) = a_1 a_4 c_1 c_4 - a_2 a_3 c_1 c_4 - a_1 a_4 c_2 c_3 + a_2 a_3 c_2 c_3 = \det(A)\det(C)$.

39. Pick any pattern other than the diagonal pattern. Let a_{ii} be the left-most diagonal entry of the matrix such that a_{ii} is *not* in the chosen pattern. Then the chosen pattern must have an entry in row i to the right of a_{ii} and in column i below a_{ii}. This is the case since the rows above a_{ii} and the columns to the left of a_{ii} were already represented in the pattern by diagonal entries.

41. $\det(A) = -x(x - 1)^2$ so A is invertible when $x \neq 0$ and $x \neq 1$.

    In Exercises 42 to 45, let $A = \begin{bmatrix} a_1 & a_2 \\ a_3 & a_4 \end{bmatrix}$.

43. $\det C = \det \begin{bmatrix} a_3 & a_4 \\ a_1 & a_2 \end{bmatrix} = a_2 a_3 - a_1 a_4 = -\det(A)$ so $\det(C) = -\det(A) = -k$.

45. $\det(A^T) = \det \begin{bmatrix} a_1 & a_3 \\ a_2 & a_4 \end{bmatrix} = a_1 a_4 - a_2 a_3 = \det(A)$ so $\det(A^T) = \det(A) = k$.

47. Consider a pattern in A, with entries $a_1, \ldots, a_n$; the corresponding pattern in $-A$ will have the entries $-a_1, \ldots, -a_n$. The products associated with these patterns will be $a_1 a_2 \cdots a_n$ and $(-1)^n a_1 a_2 \cdots a_n$, respectively. Since these observations apply to all patterns, we can say that $\det(-A) = (-1)^n \det(A)$.

49. Let $A = \begin{bmatrix} a_1 & a_2 \\ a_3 & a_4 \end{bmatrix}$. If $a_1 a_4 - a_2 a_3 \neq 0$, then $A^{-1} = \dfrac{1}{\det(A)} \begin{bmatrix} a_4 & -a_2 \\ -a_3 & a_1 \end{bmatrix}$. By Exercise 48,

    $\det(A^{-1}) = \left(\dfrac{1}{\det(A)} \right)^2 (a_1 a_4 - a_2 a_3) = \left(\dfrac{1}{\det(A)} \right)^2 \cdot \det(A)$ so $\det(A^{-1}) = \dfrac{1}{\det(A)}$.

51. Only one pattern makes a nonzero contribution. The number of inversions in this pattern is n^2: for each 1 in the lower I_n, there are n inversions corresponding to the n entries of the upper I_n, so

    $$\det(A) = \begin{cases} 1 & \text{if } n \text{ (and } n^2 \text{) is even} \\ -1 & \text{if } n \text{ (and } n^2 \text{) is odd.} \end{cases}$$

6.2

1. $\det \begin{bmatrix} 1 & 2 & 3 \\ 4 & 5 & 6 \\ 7 & 8 & 10 \end{bmatrix} = -3$

3. $\det \begin{bmatrix} 1 & -1 & 2 & -2 \\ -1 & 2 & 1 & 6 \\ 2 & 1 & 14 & 10 \\ -2 & 6 & 10 & 33 \end{bmatrix} = 9$

5. $\det \begin{bmatrix} 1 & 1 & 1 & 1 & 1 \\ 1 & 2 & 2 & 2 & 2 \\ 1 & 1 & 3 & 3 & 3 \\ 1 & 1 & 1 & 4 & 4 \\ 1 & 1 & 1 & 1 & 5 \end{bmatrix} = 24$

7. $\det(A) = 1$

9. By Fact 6.2.4a, the desired determinant is $(-9)(8) = -72$.

11. By Fact 6.2.4b, applied twice, since there are two row swaps, the desired determinant is $(-1)(-1)(8) = 8$.

13. By Fact 6.2.4c, the desired determinant is 8.

15. If a square matrix A has two equal columns, then its columns are linearly dependent, hence A is not invertible, and $\det(A) = 0$.

17. a. If $n = 1$, then $A = \begin{bmatrix} 1 & 1 \\ a_0 & a_1 \end{bmatrix}$ so $\det(A) = a_1 - a_0$ (and the product formula holds).

    b. Expanding the given determinant about the right-most column, we see that the coefficient k of t^n is the $n - 1$ Vandermonde determinant which we assume is $\displaystyle\prod_{n-1 \geq i > j} (a_i - a_j)$.

    $f(a_0) = f(a_1) = \cdots = f(a_{n-1}) = 0$ since in each case the given matrix has two identical columns, hence its determinant equals zero (see Exercise 15).

    Therefore $f(t) = \left(\displaystyle\prod_{n-1 \geq i > j} (a_i - a_j) \right) (t - a_0)(t - a_1) \cdots (t - a_{n-1})$ and $\det(A) = f(a_n) =$
    $\displaystyle\prod_{n \geq i > j} (a_i - a_j)$, as required.

19. Think of the ith column of the given matrix as $a_i \begin{bmatrix} 1 \\ a_i \\ a_i^2 \\ \vdots \\ a_i^{n-1} \end{bmatrix}$ so by Fact 6.2.3b, the determinant can

    be written as $(a_1 a_2 \cdots a_n) \det \begin{bmatrix} 1 & 1 & \cdots & 1 \\ a_1 & a_2 & \cdots & a_n \\ a_1^2 & a_2^2 & \cdots & a_n^2 \\ \vdots & \vdots & & \vdots \\ a_1^{n-1} & a_2^{n-1} & \cdots & a_n^{n-1} \end{bmatrix}$.

    The new determinant is a Vandermonde determinant (see Exercise 17), and we get $\displaystyle\prod_{i=1}^{n} a_i \prod_{i > j} (a_i - a_j)$.

21. $\begin{bmatrix} x_1 \\ x_2 \end{bmatrix}$ must satisfy $\det \begin{bmatrix} 1 & 1 & 1 \\ x_1 & a_1 & b_1 \\ x_2 & a_2 & b_2 \end{bmatrix} = 0$, i.e. must satisfy the linear equation

    $(a_1 b_2 - a_2 b_1) - x_1(b_2 - a_2) + x_2(b_1 - a_1) = 0.$

    We can see that $\begin{bmatrix} x_1 \\ x_2 \end{bmatrix} = \begin{bmatrix} a_1 \\ a_2 \end{bmatrix}$ and $\begin{bmatrix} x_1 \\ x_2 \end{bmatrix} = \begin{bmatrix} b_1 \\ b_2 \end{bmatrix}$ satisfy this equation, since the matrix has two identical columns in these cases.

23. Applying Fact 6.2.7 to the equation $AA^{-1} = I_n$ we see that $\det(A)\det(A^{-1}) = 1$.
    The only way the product of the two integers $\det(A)$ and $\det(A^{-1})$ can be 1 is that they are both 1 or both -1. Therefore, $\det(A) = 1$ or $\det(A) = -1$.

25. $\det(A^T A) = \det(A^T)\det(A) = [\det(A)]^2 > 0$
    $\qquad\qquad\;\; \uparrow \qquad\qquad\;\; \uparrow$
    $\qquad\;\;$ Fact 6.2.7 $\qquad$ Fact 6.2.1

27. $\det(A) = \det(A^T) = \det(-A) = (-1)^n(\det A) = -\det(A)$, so that $\det(A) = 0$. We have used Facts 6.2.1 and 6.2.3.b.

29. $\det(A^T A) = \det\left(\begin{bmatrix} \vec{v}^T \\ \vec{w}^T \end{bmatrix} \begin{bmatrix} \vec{v} & \vec{w} \end{bmatrix}\right) = \det\begin{bmatrix} \vec{v}\cdot\vec{v} & \vec{v}\cdot\vec{w} \\ \vec{v}\cdot\vec{w} & \vec{w}\cdot\vec{w} \end{bmatrix} = \det\begin{bmatrix} \|\vec{v}\|^2 & \vec{v}\cdot\vec{w} \\ \vec{v}\cdot\vec{w} & \|\vec{w}\|^2 \end{bmatrix} =$
    $\|\vec{v}\|^2\|\vec{w}\|^2 - (\vec{v}\cdot\vec{w})^2 \geq 0$ by the Cauchy-Schwarz inequality (Fact 5.1.10).

31. $f(x)$ is a linear function so $f'(x)$ is the coefficient of x (the slope). But, by Fact 6.2.10, the coefficient
    of x is given by $-\det\begin{bmatrix} 1 & 2 & 3 & 4 \\ 0 & 2 & 3 & 4 \\ 0 & 0 & 3 & 4 \\ 0 & 0 & 0 & 4 \end{bmatrix} = -24$ so $f'(x) = -24$.

33. Yes! For example $T\begin{bmatrix} x & b \\ y & d \end{bmatrix} = dx + by$ is given by the matrix $\begin{bmatrix} d & b \end{bmatrix}$, so that T is linear in the first column.

35. $\det(Q_1) = \det(Q_2) = \det(Q_3) = 1$
    $\det(Q_n) = 2\det(Q_{n-1}) - \det(Q_{n-2})$ (expand along the first column), so that $\det(Q_n) = 1$ for all n.

37. Expand along the first column, realizing that all but the first contribution is zero, since the other minors will have two equal rows. Therefore, $\det(P_n) = \det(P_{n-1})$.
    Since $\det(P_1) = 1$ we can conclude that $\det(P_n) = 1$, for all n.

39. a. See Exercise 23.

    b. If $A = \begin{bmatrix} a & b \\ c & d \end{bmatrix}$, then $A^{-1} = \dfrac{1}{\det(A)}\begin{bmatrix} d & -b \\ -c & a \end{bmatrix}$ has integer entries.

41. Mimicking the proof of Fact 6.2.4c we can show:
    If B is obtained from A by adding a multiple of a row of A to another row, then $D(B) = D(A)$.
    As in the proof of Algorithm 6.2.6 it follows that $D(A) = (-1)^s k_1 k_2 \ldots k_r D(\text{rref } A)$.
    If A is not invertible, then $D(\text{rref } A) = 0$, by the linearity of D in the last row, so that $D(A) = \det(A) = 0$. If A is invertible, then $\text{rref}(A) = I_n$ and $D(\text{rref } A) = 1$, by property c of the function D. Therefore,
    $D(A) = (-1)^s k_1 k_2 \cdots k_r = \det(A)$.
    We have shown that $D(A) = \det(A)$ for all $n \times n$ matrices A, as claimed.

43. Note that matrix A_1 is invertible, since $\det(A_1) \neq 0$. Now

    $T\begin{bmatrix} \vec{y} \\ \vec{x} \end{bmatrix} = [A_1\ A_2]\begin{bmatrix} \vec{y} \\ \vec{x} \end{bmatrix} = A_1\vec{y} + A_2\vec{x} = \vec{0}$ when $A_1\vec{y} = -A_2\vec{x}$, or,

    $\vec{y} = -A_1^{-1}A_2\vec{x}$. This shows that for every $\vec{x}$ there is a unique $\vec{y}$ (that is, $\vec{y}$ is a function of $\vec{x}$); furthermore, this function is linear, with matrix $M = -A_1^{-1}A_2$.

45. The standard matrix of T is $A = \begin{bmatrix} 2 & 3 & 0 \\ 0 & 2 & 6 \\ 0 & 0 & 2 \end{bmatrix}$, so that $\det(T) = \det(A) = 8$.

47. The standard matrix of T is $A = \begin{bmatrix} 1 & 0 & 0 \\ 0 & -1 & 0 \\ 0 & 0 & 1 \end{bmatrix}$, so that $\det(T) = \det(A) = -1$.

49. The standard matrix of T is $A = \begin{bmatrix} 1 & 0 & 0 & 0 \\ 0 & -1 & 0 & 0 \\ 0 & 0 & 1 & 0 \\ 0 & 0 & 0 & -1 \end{bmatrix}$, so that $\det(T) = \det(A) = 1$.

51. Consider the matrix M of T with respect to a basis consisting of $n(n+1)/2$ symmetric matrices and $n(n-1)/2$ skew-symmetric matrices (see Exercises 34 and 35 of Section 5.4). Matrix M will be diagonal, with $n(n+1)/2$ entries 1 and $n(n-1)/2$ entries -1 on the diagonal. Thus $\det(T) = \det(M) = (-1)^{n(n-1)/2}$.

53. The standard matrix of T is $A = \begin{bmatrix} 2 & 0 & 0 \\ 0 & 2 & 3 \\ 0 & 0 & 4 \end{bmatrix}$, so that $\det(T) = \det(A) = 16$.

55. The matrix of T with respect to the basis $\cos(x), \sin(x)$ is $A = \begin{bmatrix} -b & a \\ -a & -b \end{bmatrix}$, so that $\det(T) = \det(A) = a^2 + b^2$.

6.3

1. By Fact 6.3.3 Area $= \left| \det \begin{bmatrix} 3 & 8 \\ 7 & 2 \end{bmatrix} \right| = |-50| = 50$.

3. Area of triangle $= \dfrac{1}{2} \left| \det \begin{bmatrix} 6 & 1 \\ -2 & 4 \end{bmatrix} \right| = 13$ (See figure.)

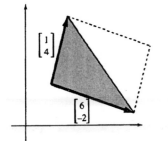

5. The volume of the tetrahedron T_0 defined by $\vec{e}_1, \vec{e}_2, \vec{e}_3$ is $\frac{1}{3}$(base)(height) = $\frac{1}{6}$ (formula for the volume of a pyramid).

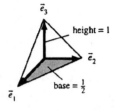

The tetrahedron T defined by $\vec{v}_1, \vec{v}_2, \vec{v}_3$ can be obtained by applying the linear transformation with matrix $[\vec{v}_1 \ \vec{v}_2 \ \vec{v}_3]$ to T_0.
Now we have $\text{vol}(T) = |\det[\vec{v}_1 \ \vec{v}_2 \ \vec{v}_3]|\text{vol}(T_0) = \frac{1}{6}|\det[\vec{v}_1 \ \vec{v}_2 \ \vec{v}_3]| = \frac{1}{6}V(\vec{v}_1, \vec{v}_2, \vec{v}_3)$.

$\uparrow$ $\uparrow$

Fact 6.3.8 and page 277   Fact 6.3.5

7. Area $= \frac{1}{2}\left|\det\begin{bmatrix} 10 & -2 \\ 11 & 13 \end{bmatrix}\right| + \frac{1}{2}\left|\det\begin{bmatrix} 8 & 10 \\ 2 & 11 \end{bmatrix}\right| = 110$ (See Figure.)

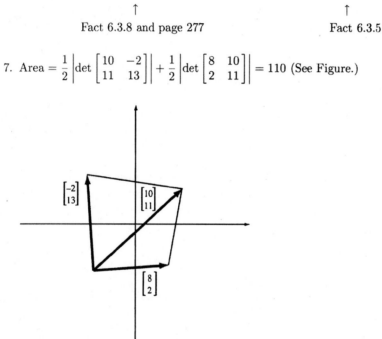

9. By Fact 6.3.3, $|\det[\vec{v}_1 \ \vec{v}_2]| = $ area of the parallelogram defined by $\vec{v}_1$ and $\vec{v}_2$. But $\|\vec{v}_1\|$ is the base of that parallelogram and $\|\vec{v}_2\|\sin\alpha$ is its height, hence $|\det[\vec{v}_1 \ \vec{v}_2]| = \|\vec{v}_1\|\|\vec{v}_2\|\sin\alpha$.

11. The matrix of transformation T with respect to the basis $\vec{v}_1, \vec{v}_2$ is $B = \begin{bmatrix} 3 & 0 \\ 0 & 4 \end{bmatrix}$, so that $\det(A) = \det(B) = 12$, by Definition 6.2.11.

13. By Fact 6.3.7, the desired 2-volume is $\sqrt{\det\left(\begin{bmatrix} 1 & 1 & 1 & 1 \\ 1 & 2 & 3 & 4 \end{bmatrix}\begin{bmatrix} 1 & 1 \\ 1 & 2 \\ 1 & 3 \\ 1 & 4 \end{bmatrix}\right)} = \sqrt{\det\begin{bmatrix} 4 & 10 \\ 10 & 30 \end{bmatrix}} = \sqrt{20}.$

15. If $\vec{v}_1, \vec{v}_2, \ldots, \vec{v}_k$ are linearly dependent and if $A = [\vec{v}_1 \cdots \vec{v}_k]$, then $\det(A^T A) = 0$ since $A^T A$ and A have equal and nonzero kernels (by Fact 5.3.3), hence $A^T A$ is not invertible.

    On the other hand, since the $\vec{v}_i$'s are linearly dependent, $\vec{v}_i = a_1 \vec{v}_1 + \cdots + a_{i-1} \vec{v}_{i-1}$ for some i.

    Hence $\|\vec{v}_i - \text{proj}_{V_{i-1}} \vec{v}_i\| = 0$, so $V(\vec{v}_1, \ldots, \vec{v}_k) = 0$. The above shows that both sides of the equation in Fact 6.3.7 are 0 if $\vec{v}_1, \ldots, \vec{v}_k$ are linearly dependent.

17. a. Let $\vec{w} = \vec{v}_1 \times \vec{v}_2 \times \vec{v}_3$. Note that $\vec{w}$ is orthogonal to $\vec{v}_1, \vec{v}_2$ and $\vec{v}_3$, by Exercise 6.2.30c. Then
    $$V(\vec{v}_1, \vec{v}_2, \vec{v}_3, \vec{w}) = V(\vec{v}_1, \vec{v}_2, \vec{v}_3)\|\vec{w} - \text{proj}_{V_3} \vec{w}\| = V(\vec{v}_1, \vec{v}_2, \vec{v}_3)\|\vec{w}\|.$$
    $$\uparrow \qquad\qquad\qquad\qquad\qquad\qquad \uparrow$$
    $$\text{Definition 6.3.6} \qquad\qquad\qquad \text{proj}_{V_3} \vec{w} = \vec{0}$$

    b. By Exercise 6.2.30e,
    $$V(\vec{v}_1, \vec{v}_2, \vec{v}_3, \vec{v}_1 \times \vec{v}_2 \times \vec{v}_3) = |\det[\,\vec{v}_1\ \vec{v}_2\ \vec{v}_3\ \vec{v}_1 \times \vec{v}_2 \times \vec{v}_3\,]|$$
    $$= |\det[\vec{v}_1 \times \vec{v}_2 \times \vec{v}_3\ \vec{v}_1\ \vec{v}_2 \vec{v}_3]| = \|\vec{v}_1 \times \vec{v}_2 \times \vec{v}_3\|^2.$$

    c. By parts a and b $V(\vec{v}_1, \vec{v}_2, \vec{v}_3) = \|\vec{v}_1 \times \vec{v}_2 \times \vec{v}_3\|$. If the vectors $\vec{v}_1, \vec{v}_2, \vec{v}_3$ are linearly dependent, then both sides of the equation are 0, by Exercise 15 and Exercise 6.2.30a.

19. $\det[\,\vec{v}_1\ \ \vec{v}_2\ \ \vec{v}_3\,] = \vec{v}_1 \cdot (\vec{v}_2 \times \vec{v}_3) = \|\vec{v}_1\|\|\vec{v}_2 \times \vec{v}_3\| \cos\alpha$ where α is the angle between $\vec{v}_1$ and $\vec{v}_2 \times \vec{v}_3$ so $\det[\,\vec{v}_1\ \ \vec{v}_2\ \ \vec{v}_3\,] > 0$ if and only if $\cos\alpha > 0$, i.e., if and only if α is acute $\left(0 \le \alpha < \dfrac{\pi}{2}\right)$.

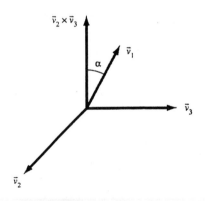

21. a. Reverses
    Consider $\vec{v}_2$ and $\vec{v}_3$ in the plane (not parallel), and let $\vec{v}_1 = \vec{v}_2 \times \vec{v}_3$; then $\vec{v}_1, \vec{v}_2, \vec{v}_3$ is a positively oriented basis, but $T(\vec{v}_1) = -\vec{v}_1, T(\vec{v}_2) = \vec{v}_2, T(\vec{v}_3) = \vec{v}_3$ is negatively oriented.

b. Preserves

Consider $\vec{v}_2$ and $\vec{v}_3$ orthogonal to the line (not parallel), and let $\vec{v}_1 = \vec{v}_2 \times \vec{v}_3$; then $\vec{v}_1, \vec{v}_2, \vec{v}_3$ is a positively oriented basis, and $T(\vec{v}_1) = \vec{v}_1, T(\vec{v}_2) = -\vec{v}_2, T(\vec{v}_3) = -\vec{v}_3$ is positively oriented as well.

c. Reverses

The standard basis $\vec{e}_1, \vec{e}_2, \vec{e}_3$ is positively oriented, but $T(\vec{e}_1) = -\vec{e}_1, T(\vec{e}_2) = -\vec{e}_2, T(\vec{e}_3) = -\vec{e}_3$ is negatively oriented.

23. Here $A = \begin{bmatrix} 5 & -3 \\ -6 & 7 \end{bmatrix}$, $\det(A) = 17$, $\vec{b} = \begin{bmatrix} 1 \\ 0 \end{bmatrix}$, so by Fact 6.3.9

$$x_1 = \frac{\det \begin{bmatrix} 1 & -3 \\ 0 & 7 \end{bmatrix}}{17} = \frac{7}{17}, \; x_2 = \frac{\det \begin{bmatrix} 5 & 1 \\ -6 & 0 \end{bmatrix}}{17} = \frac{6}{17}.$$

25. By Fact 6.3.10, the ijth entry of adj(A) is given by $(-1)^{i+j} \det(A_{ji})$ so since $A = \begin{bmatrix} 1 & 0 & 1 \\ 0 & 1 & 0 \\ 2 & 0 & 1 \end{bmatrix}$ for

$i = 1, j = 1$, we get $(-1)^2 \det \begin{bmatrix} 1 & 0 \\ 0 & 1 \end{bmatrix} = 1$, and for $i = 1, j = 2$ we get $(-1)^3 \det \begin{bmatrix} 0 & 1 \\ 0 & 1 \end{bmatrix} = 0$, etc.

Completing this process gives adj$(A) = \begin{bmatrix} 1 & 0 & -1 \\ 0 & -1 & 0 \\ -2 & 0 & 1 \end{bmatrix}$, hence by Fact 6.3.10,

$$A^{-1} = \frac{1}{\det(A)} \text{adj}(A) = \frac{1}{-1} \begin{bmatrix} 1 & 0 & -1 \\ 0 & -1 & 0 \\ -2 & 0 & 1 \end{bmatrix} = \begin{bmatrix} -1 & 0 & 1 \\ 0 & 1 & 0 \\ 2 & 0 & -1 \end{bmatrix}.$$

27. By Fact 6.3.9, using $A = \begin{bmatrix} a & -b \\ b & a \end{bmatrix}$, $\det(A) = a^2 + b^2$, $\vec{b} = \begin{bmatrix} 1 \\ 0 \end{bmatrix}$, we get

$$x = \frac{\det \begin{bmatrix} 1 & -b \\ 0 & a \end{bmatrix}}{a^2 + b^2} = \frac{a}{a^2 + b^2}, y = \frac{\det \begin{bmatrix} a & 1 \\ b & 0 \end{bmatrix}}{a^2 + b^2} = \frac{-b}{a^2 + b^2}, \text{ so } x \text{ is positive, } y \text{ is negative (since } a, b > $$
0), and as b increases, x decreases.

29. By Fact 6.3.9

$$dx_1 = \frac{\det \begin{bmatrix} 0 & R_1 & -(1 - \alpha) \\ 0 & 1 - \alpha & -(1 - \alpha)^2 \\ -R_2 de_2 & -R_2 & \frac{(1 - \alpha)^2}{\alpha} \end{bmatrix}}{D} = \frac{R_1 R_2 (1 - \alpha)^2 de_2 - R_2 (1 - \alpha)^2 de_2}{D}$$

$$dy_1 = \frac{\det \begin{bmatrix} -R_1 & 0 & -(1-\alpha) \\ \alpha & 0 & -(1-\alpha)^2 \\ R_2 & -R_2de_2 & -\dfrac{(1-\alpha)^2}{\alpha} \end{bmatrix}}{D} = \frac{R_2de_2(R_1(1-\alpha)^2 + \alpha(1-\alpha))}{D} > 0$$

$$dp = \frac{\det \begin{bmatrix} -R_1 & R_1 & 0 \\ \alpha & 1-\alpha & 0 \\ R_2 & -R_2 & -R_2de_2 \end{bmatrix}}{D} = \frac{R_1R_2de_2}{D} > 0 \quad \bullet$$

31. In what follows, we will freely use the fact that an invertible linear transformation L from $\mathbb{R}^2$ to $\mathbb{R}^2$ maps an ellipse into an ellipse (see Exercise 52 of Section 2.2).

    Now consider a linear transformation L that transforms our 3-4-5 right triangle R into an equilateral triangle T. If we place the vertices of the right triangle R at the points $\begin{bmatrix} 0 \\ 0 \end{bmatrix}, \begin{bmatrix} 4 \\ 0 \end{bmatrix}, \begin{bmatrix} 0 \\ 3 \end{bmatrix}$, and the vertices of the equilateral triangle T at $\begin{bmatrix} 0 \\ 0 \end{bmatrix}, \begin{bmatrix} 2 \\ 0 \end{bmatrix}, \begin{bmatrix} 1 \\ \sqrt{3} \end{bmatrix}$, then the transformation L has the matrix $A = \begin{bmatrix} \frac{1}{2} & \frac{1}{3} \\ 0 & \frac{1}{\sqrt{3}} \end{bmatrix}$, with $\det(A) = \frac{1}{2\sqrt{3}}$.

    According to the hint, L will map the largest ellipse E inscribed into R into the circle C inscribed into T. The accompanying figure illustrates that the radius of C is $\tan(\pi/6) = 1/\sqrt{3}$, so that the area of C is $\pi/3$. Using the interpretation of the determinant as an expansion fact, we find that (area of C) = (det A)(area of E), or (area of E) = $\dfrac{\text{area of } C}{\det(A)} = \dfrac{2\pi}{\sqrt{3}} \approx 3.6$

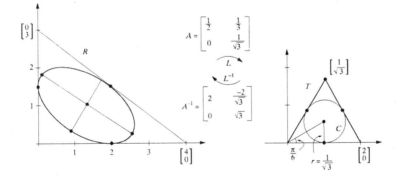

True or False

1. T, by Fact 6.1.3 (a diagonal matrix is triangular as well)

3. T; See work on Page 243

5. F; Let $A = B = I_5$, for example

7. F; If fact, $\det(A) = 0$, since A is noninvertible

9. T, by Fact 6.2.4

11. T, by Example 6 of Section 6.2

13. T, by Fact 6.2.7.

15. F; If $k = -1$ or $k = -2$, then the matrix has two equal columns, so that it fails to be invertible.

17. T; The pattern with the four entries 100 guarantees a nonzero determinant.

19. T; Matrix A is invertible

21. T, by Fact 6.3.4.

23. F; Let $A = \begin{bmatrix} 3 & 2 \\ 5 & 3 \end{bmatrix}$, for example

25. T; Let $A = \begin{bmatrix} 1 & 1 & 1 & 1 \\ 1 & 1 & -1 & -1 \\ 1 & -1 & 1 & -1 \\ 1 & -1 & -1 & 1 \end{bmatrix}$. The columns of A are orthogonal; now use Fact 6.3.4.

27. F; In fact, $\vec{v} \cdot (\vec{u} \times \vec{w}) = -(\det A)$.

29. F; Note that $\det \begin{bmatrix} 1 & 1 & 0 \\ 0 & 1 & 1 \\ 1 & 0 & 1 \end{bmatrix} = 2$.

31. F; Let $A = 2I_2$, for example

33. F; Let $A = I_2$ and $B = -I_2$, for example.

35. T; Let's do Laplace expansion along the first row, for example (see Fact 6.2.10).
Then $\det(A) = \sum_{j=1}^{n} (-1)^{1+j} a_{1j} \det(A_{1j}) \neq 0$. Thus $\det(A_{1j}) \neq 0$ for at least one j, so that A_{1j} is invertible.

37. T, since $\mathrm{adj}(A) = (\det A)(A^{-1})$, by Fact 6.3.10.

39. F; Note that $\det(S^{-1}AS) = \det(A)$ but $\det(2A) = 2^3(\det A) = 8(\det A)$.

41. T; The diagonal pattern makes an odd contribution to the determinant, while all the other contributions are even. Thus the determinant is odd; in particular, it is nonzero.

43. T; Let $A = \begin{bmatrix} a & b \\ c & d \end{bmatrix}$. If $a \neq 0$, let $B = \begin{bmatrix} 0 & 0 \\ 0 & 1 \end{bmatrix}$; if $b \neq 0$, let $B = \begin{bmatrix} 0 & 0 \\ 1 & 0 \end{bmatrix}$; if $c \neq 0$, let $B = \begin{bmatrix} 0 & 1 \\ 0 & 0 \end{bmatrix}$, and if $d \neq 0$, let $B = \begin{bmatrix} 1 & 0 \\ 0 & 0 \end{bmatrix}$.

Chapter 7

7.1

1. If $\vec{v}$ is an eigenvector of A, then $A\vec{v} = \lambda\vec{v}$.

   Hence $A^3\vec{v} = A^2(A\vec{v}) = A^2(\lambda\vec{v}) = A(A\lambda\vec{v}) = A(\lambda A\vec{v}) = A(\lambda^2\vec{v}) = \lambda^2 A\vec{v} = \lambda^3\vec{v}$, so $\vec{v}$ is an eigenvector of A^3 with eigenvalue λ^3.

3. We know $A\vec{v} = \lambda\vec{v}$, so $(A + 2I_n)\vec{v} = A\vec{v} + 2I_n\vec{v} = \lambda\vec{v} + 2\vec{v} = (\lambda + 2)\vec{v}$, hence $\vec{v}$ is an eigenvector of $(A + 2I_n)$ with eigenvalue $\lambda + 2$.

5. Assume $A\vec{v} = \lambda\vec{v}$ and $B\vec{v} = \beta\vec{v}$ for some eigenvalues λ, β. Then $(A + B)\vec{v} = A\vec{v} + B\vec{v} = \lambda\vec{v} + \beta\vec{v} = (\lambda + \beta)\vec{v}$ so $\vec{v}$ is an eigenvector of $A + B$ with eigenvalue $\lambda + \beta$.

7. We know $A\vec{v} = \lambda\vec{v}$ so $(\lambda I_n - A)\vec{v} = \lambda I_n\vec{v} - A\vec{v} = \lambda\vec{v} - \lambda\vec{v} = \vec{0}$ so a nonzero vector $\vec{v}$ is in the kernel of $(\lambda I_n - A)$ so $\ker(\lambda I_n - A) \neq \{\vec{0}\}$ and $\lambda I_n - A$ is not invertible.

9. We want $\begin{bmatrix} a & b \\ c & d \end{bmatrix} \begin{bmatrix} 1 \\ 0 \end{bmatrix} = \lambda \begin{bmatrix} 1 \\ 0 \end{bmatrix}$ for any λ. Hence $\begin{bmatrix} a \\ c \end{bmatrix} = \begin{bmatrix} \lambda \\ 0 \end{bmatrix}$, i.e. the desired matrices must have the form $\begin{bmatrix} \lambda & b \\ 0 & d \end{bmatrix}$, they must be upper triangular.

11. We want $\begin{bmatrix} a & b \\ c & d \end{bmatrix} \begin{bmatrix} 1 \\ 2 \end{bmatrix} = \lambda \begin{bmatrix} 1 \\ 2 \end{bmatrix}$ for some λ, so

    $a + 2b = \lambda$
    $c + 2d = 2\lambda$ i.e.

    $c + 2d = 2(a + 2b)$ or $c = 2a + 4b - 2d$.

    Hence the desired form is $\begin{bmatrix} a & b \\ 2a + 4b - 2d & d \end{bmatrix}$.

13. Solving $\begin{bmatrix} -6 & 6 \\ -15 & 13 \end{bmatrix} \begin{bmatrix} v_1 \\ v_2 \end{bmatrix} = 4 \begin{bmatrix} v_1 \\ v_2 \end{bmatrix}$, we get $\begin{bmatrix} v_1 \\ v_2 \end{bmatrix} = \begin{bmatrix} \frac{3}{5}t \\ t \end{bmatrix}$ (with $t \neq 0$).

15. Any vector on L is unaffected by the reflection, so that a nonzero vector on L is an eigenvector with eigenvalue 1. Any vector on $L^\perp$ is flipped about L, so that a nonzero vector on $L^\perp$ is an eigenvector with eigenvalue -1. Picking a nonzero vector from L and one from $L^\perp$, we obtain a basis consisting of eigenvectors.

17. No (real) eigenvalues

19. Any nonzero vector in L is an eigenvector with eigenvalue 1, and any nonzero vector in the plane $L^\perp$ is an eigenvector with eigenvalue 0. Form an eigenbasis by picking any nonzero vector in L and any two noncollinear vectors in $L^\perp$.

21. Any nonzero vector in $\mathbb{R}^3$ is an eigenvector with eigenvalue 5. Any basis for $\mathbb{R}^3$ consists of eigenvectors.

23. a. Since $S = [\vec{v}_1 \cdots \vec{v}_n]$, $S^{-1}\vec{v}_i = S^{-1}(S\vec{e}_i) = \vec{e}_i$.

    b. ith column of $S^{-1}AS$
       $= S^{-1}AS\vec{e}_i$
       $= S^{-1}A\vec{v}_i$ (by definition of S)
       $= S^{-1}\lambda_i\vec{v}_i$ (since $\vec{v}_i$ is an eigenvector)
       $= \lambda_i S^{-1}\vec{v}_i$
       $= \lambda_i \vec{e}_i$ (by part a)

       hence $S^{-1}AS = \begin{bmatrix} \lambda_1 & 0 & 0 & \cdots & 0 \\ 0 & \lambda_2 & 0 & \cdots & 0 \\ \vdots & & & & \\ 0 & 0 & 0 & \cdots & \lambda_n \end{bmatrix}$.

25.

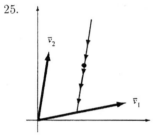

27.

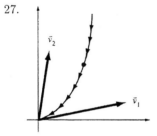

29.

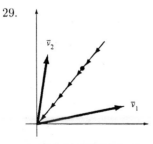

In Exercises 30−32, since the matrix is diagonal, $\vec{e}_1$ and $\vec{e}_2$ are eigenvectors.

31.

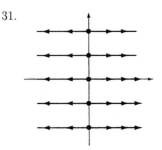

33. The eigenvalues of the system are $\lambda_1 = 1.1$, and $\lambda_2 = 0.9$ and corresponding eigenvectors are $\vec{v}_1 = \begin{bmatrix} 100 \\ 300 \end{bmatrix}$ and $\vec{v}_2 = \begin{bmatrix} 200 \\ 100 \end{bmatrix}$ respectively. So if $\vec{x}_0 = \begin{bmatrix} 100 \\ 800 \end{bmatrix}$, we can see that $\vec{x}_0 = 3\vec{v}_1 - \vec{v}_2$. Therefore, by Fact 7.1.3 $\vec{x}(t) = 3(1.1)^t \begin{bmatrix} 100 \\ 300 \end{bmatrix} - (0.9)^t \begin{bmatrix} 200 \\ 100 \end{bmatrix}$, i.e. $c(t) = 300(1.1)^t - 200(0.9)^t$ and $r(t) = 900(1.1)^t - 100(0.9)^t$.

35. We are given that $\vec{x}(t) = 2^t \begin{bmatrix} 1 \\ 1 \end{bmatrix} + 6^t \begin{bmatrix} -1 \\ 1 \end{bmatrix}$, hence we know that the eigenvalues are 2 and 6 with corresponding eigenvectors $\begin{bmatrix} 1 \\ 1 \end{bmatrix}$ and $\begin{bmatrix} -1 \\ 1 \end{bmatrix}$ respectively (see Fact 7.1.3), so we want a matrix A such that $A \begin{bmatrix} 1 & -1 \\ 1 & 1 \end{bmatrix} = \begin{bmatrix} 2 & -6 \\ 2 & 6 \end{bmatrix}$. Multiplying on the right by $\begin{bmatrix} 1 & -1 \\ 1 & 1 \end{bmatrix}^{-1}$, we get $A = \begin{bmatrix} 4 & -2 \\ -2 & 4 \end{bmatrix}$.

37. a. $A = 5 \begin{bmatrix} 0.6 & 0.8 \\ 0.8 & -0.6 \end{bmatrix}$ is a scalar multiple of an orthogonal matrix. By Fact 7.1.2, the possible eigenvalues of the orthogonal matrix are ± 1, so that the possible eigenvalues of A are ± 5. In part b we see that both are indeed eigenvalues.

   b. Solve $A\vec{v} = \pm 5\vec{v}$ to get $\vec{v}_1 = \begin{bmatrix} 2 \\ 1 \end{bmatrix}, \vec{v}_2 = \begin{bmatrix} -1 \\ 2 \end{bmatrix}$.

39. Let λ be an eigenvalue of $S^{-1}AS$. Then for some nonzero vector $\vec{v}$, $S^{-1}AS\vec{v} = \lambda\vec{v}$, i.e., $AS\vec{v} = S\lambda\vec{v} = \lambda S\vec{v}$ so λ is an eigenvalue of A with eigenvector $S\vec{v}$.
    Conversely, if α is an eigenvalue of A with eigenvector $\vec{w}$, then $A\vec{w} = \alpha\vec{w}$.
    Therefore, $S^{-1}AS(S^{-1}\vec{w}) = S^{-1}A\vec{w} = S^{-1}\alpha\vec{w} = \alpha S^{-1}\vec{w}$, so $S^{-1}\vec{w}$ is an eigenvector of $S^{-1}AS$ with eigenvalue α.

7.2

1. $\lambda_1 = 1$, $\lambda_2 = 3$ by Fact 7.2.2.

3. $\det(\lambda I_2 - A) = \det \begin{bmatrix} \lambda - 5 & 4 \\ -2 & \lambda + 1 \end{bmatrix} = (\lambda - 1)(\lambda - 3) = 0$ so $\lambda_1 = 1, \lambda_2 = 3$.

5. $\det(\lambda I_2 - A) = \det \begin{bmatrix} \lambda - 11 & 15 \\ -6 & \lambda + 7 \end{bmatrix} = \lambda^2 - 4\lambda + 13$ so $\det(\lambda I_2 - A) = 0$ for no real λ.

7. $\lambda = 1$ with algebraic multiplicity 3, by Fact 7.2.2.

9. $f_A(\lambda) = (\lambda - 2)^2(\lambda - 1)$ so
   $\lambda_1 = 2$ (Algebraic multiplicity 2)
   $\lambda_2 = 1$.

11. $f_A(\lambda) = \lambda^3 + \lambda^2 + \lambda + 1 = (\lambda + 1)(\lambda^2 + 1) = 0$
    $\lambda = -1$ (Algebraic multiplicity 1).

13. $f_A(\lambda) = \lambda^3 - 1 = (\lambda - 1)(\lambda^2 + \lambda + 1)$ so $\lambda = 1$ (Algebraic multiplicity 1).

15. $f_A(\lambda) = \lambda^2 - 2\lambda + (1 - k) = 0$ if $\lambda_{1,2} = \dfrac{2 \pm \sqrt{4 - 4(1 - k)}}{2} = 1 \pm \sqrt{k}$
    The matrix has 2 distinct real eigenvalues when $k > 0$, no real eigenvalues when $k < 0$.

17. $f_A(\lambda) = \lambda^2 - a^2 - b^2 = 0$ so $\lambda_{1,2} = \pm\sqrt{a^2 + b^2}$.
    The matrix represents a reflection about a line followed by a dilation by $\sqrt{a^2 + b^2}$, hence the eigenvalues.

19. True, since $f_A(\lambda) = \lambda^2 - \mathrm{tr}(A)\lambda + \det(A)$ and the discriminant $[\mathrm{tr}(A)]^2 - 4\det(A)$ is positive if $\det(A)$ is negative.

21. By Fact 7.2.5, $f_A(\lambda) = \lambda^n - \mathrm{tr}(A)\lambda^{n-1} + \cdots + (-1)^n \det(A)$.
    On the other hand, since the λ_i are all distinct and there are n of them,
    $f_A(\lambda) = (\lambda - \lambda_1)(\lambda - \lambda_2)\cdots(\lambda - \lambda_n) = \lambda^n - (\lambda_1 + \lambda_2 + \cdots + \lambda_n)\lambda^{n-1} + \cdots + (-1)^n \lambda_1\lambda_2\cdots\lambda_n$.

    Equating the second and last coefficients, we get $\mathrm{tr}(A) = \displaystyle\sum_{i=1}^{n} \lambda_i, \det(A) = \prod_{i=1}^{n} \lambda_i$.

23. $f_B(\lambda) = \det(\lambda I_n - B) = \det(\lambda I_n - S^{-1}AS)$
    $= \det(\lambda S^{-1}I_n S - S^{-1}AS)$
    $= \det(S^{-1}(\lambda I_n - A)S) = \det(S^{-1})\det(\lambda I_n - A)\det(S)$
    $= (\det(S))^{-1}\det(\lambda I_n - A)\det(S) = \det(\lambda I_n - A) = f_A(\lambda)$
    Hence, since $f_A(\lambda) = f_B(\lambda)$, A and B have the same eigenvalues.

25. $A \begin{bmatrix} c \\ b \end{bmatrix} = \begin{bmatrix} ac + bc \\ bc + bd \end{bmatrix} = \begin{bmatrix} (a + b)c \\ (c + d)b \end{bmatrix} = \begin{bmatrix} c \\ b \end{bmatrix}$ since $a + b = c + d = 1$; therefore, $\begin{bmatrix} c \\ b \end{bmatrix}$ is an eigenvector
    with eigenvalue $\lambda_1 = 1$.

    Also, $A \begin{bmatrix} 1 \\ -1 \end{bmatrix} = \begin{bmatrix} a - c \\ b - d \end{bmatrix} = (a - c) \begin{bmatrix} 1 \\ -1 \end{bmatrix}$ since $a - c = -(b - d)$; therefore, $\begin{bmatrix} 1 \\ -1 \end{bmatrix}$ is an eigen-
    vector with eigenvalue $\lambda_2 = a - c$. Notice that $|a - c| < 1$ so a possible phase portrait is

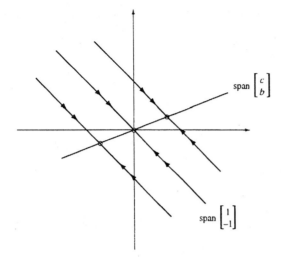

27. a. We know $\vec{v}_1 = \begin{bmatrix} 1 \\ 2 \end{bmatrix}, \lambda_1 = 1$ and $\vec{v}_2 = \begin{bmatrix} 1 \\ -1 \end{bmatrix}, \lambda_2 = \frac{1}{4}$. If $\vec{x}_0 = \begin{bmatrix} 1 \\ 0 \end{bmatrix}$ then $\vec{x}_0 = \frac{1}{3}\vec{v}_1 + \frac{2}{3}\vec{v}_2$, so by Fact 7.1.3,

$$x_1(t) = \frac{1}{3} + \frac{2}{3}\left(\frac{1}{4}\right)^t$$

$$x_2(t) = \frac{2}{3} - \frac{2}{3}\left(\frac{1}{4}\right)^t.$$

If $\vec{x}_0 = \begin{bmatrix} 0 \\ 1 \end{bmatrix}$ then $\vec{x}_0 = \frac{1}{3}\vec{v}_1 - \frac{1}{3}\vec{v}_2$, so by Fact 7.1.3,

$$x_1(t) = \frac{1}{3} - \frac{1}{3}\left(\frac{1}{4}\right)^t$$

$$x_2(t) = \frac{2}{3} + \frac{1}{3}\left(\frac{1}{4}\right)^t$$

b. A^t approaches $\frac{1}{3}\begin{bmatrix} 1 & 1 \\ 2 & 2 \end{bmatrix}$, as $t \to \infty$. See part c for a justification.

c. Let us think about the first column of A^t, which is $A^t \vec{e}_1$. We can use Fact 7.1.3 to compute $A^t \vec{e}_1$. Start by writing $\vec{e}_1 = c_1 \begin{bmatrix} c \\ b \end{bmatrix} + c_2 \begin{bmatrix} 1 \\ -1 \end{bmatrix}$; a straightforward computation shows that $c_1 = \dfrac{1}{c+b}$ and $c_2 = \dfrac{b}{c+b}$.

Now $A^t \vec{e}_1 = \dfrac{1}{c+b} \begin{bmatrix} c \\ b \end{bmatrix} + \dfrac{b}{c+b} (\lambda_2)^t \begin{bmatrix} 1 \\ -1 \end{bmatrix}$, where $\lambda_2 = a - c$.

Since $|\lambda_2| < 1$, the second summand goes to zero, so that $\lim\limits_{t \to \infty} (A^t \vec{e}_1) = \dfrac{1}{c+b} \begin{bmatrix} c \\ b \end{bmatrix}$.

Likewise, $\lim\limits_{t \to \infty} (A^t \vec{e}_2) = \dfrac{1}{c+b} \begin{bmatrix} c \\ b \end{bmatrix}$, so that $\lim\limits_{t \to \infty} A^t = \dfrac{1}{c+b} \begin{bmatrix} c & c \\ b & b \end{bmatrix}$.

29. The ith entry of $A\vec{e}$ is $[a_{i1} a_{i2} \cdots a_{in}]\vec{e} = \sum\limits_{j=1}^{n} a_{ij} = 1$, so $A\vec{e} = \vec{e}$ and $\lambda = 1$ is an eigenvalue of A, corresponding to the eigenvector $\vec{e}$.

31. Since A and A^T have the same eigenvalues (by Exercise 22), Exercise 29 states that $\lambda = 1$ is an eigenvalue of A, and Exercise 30 says that $|\lambda| \le 1$ for all eigenvalues λ. Vector $\vec{e}$ need not be an eigenvector of A; consider $A = \begin{bmatrix} 0.9 & 0.9 \\ 0.1 & 0.1 \end{bmatrix}$.

33. a. $f_A(\lambda) = \det(\lambda I_3 - A) = \lambda^3 - c\lambda^2 - b\lambda - a$

   b. By part a, $c = 17$, $b = -5$ and $a = \pi$, so $M = \begin{bmatrix} 0 & 1 & 0 \\ 0 & 0 & 1 \\ \pi & -5 & 17 \end{bmatrix}$.

34. Consider the possible graphs of $f_A(\lambda)$ assuming that it has 2 distinct real roots.

35. $A = \begin{bmatrix} 0 & -1 & 0 & 0 \\ 1 & 0 & 0 & 0 \\ 0 & 0 & 0 & -1 \\ 0 & 0 & 1 & 0 \end{bmatrix}$, $f_A(\lambda) = (\lambda^2 + 1)^2$

37. We can write $f_A(\lambda) = (\lambda - \lambda_0)^2 g(\lambda)$, for some polynomial g. The product rule for derivatives tells us that $f_A'(\lambda) = 2(\lambda - \lambda_0)g(\lambda) + (\lambda - \lambda_0)^2 g'(\lambda)$, so that $f_A'(\lambda_0) = 0$, as claimed.

7.3

1. $\lambda_1 = 7$, $\lambda_2 = 9$, $E_7 = \text{span} \begin{bmatrix} 1 \\ 0 \end{bmatrix}$, $E_9 = \text{span} \begin{bmatrix} 4 \\ 1 \end{bmatrix}$,

   Eigenbasis: $\begin{bmatrix} 1 \\ 0 \end{bmatrix}, \begin{bmatrix} 4 \\ 1 \end{bmatrix}$

3. $\lambda_1 = 4$, $\lambda_2 = 9$, $E_4 = \text{span} \begin{bmatrix} 3 \\ -2 \end{bmatrix}$, $E_9 = \text{span} \begin{bmatrix} 1 \\ 1 \end{bmatrix}$

   Eigenbasis: $\begin{bmatrix} 3 \\ -2 \end{bmatrix}, \begin{bmatrix} 1 \\ 1 \end{bmatrix}$

5. No real eigenvalues as $f_A(\lambda) = \lambda^2 - 2\lambda + 2$.

7. $\lambda_1 = 1$, $\lambda_2 = 2$, $\lambda_3 = 3$, eigenbasis: $\vec{e}_1$, $\vec{e}_2$, $\vec{e}_3$

9. $\lambda_1 = \lambda_2 = 1$, $\lambda_3 = 0$, eigenbasis: $\begin{bmatrix} 1 \\ 0 \\ 0 \end{bmatrix}, \begin{bmatrix} 0 \\ 1 \\ 0 \end{bmatrix}, \begin{bmatrix} -1 \\ 0 \\ 1 \end{bmatrix}$

11. $\lambda_1 = \lambda_2 = 0$, $\lambda_3 = 3$, eigenbasis: $\begin{bmatrix} 1 \\ -1 \\ 0 \end{bmatrix}, \begin{bmatrix} 1 \\ 0 \\ -1 \end{bmatrix}, \begin{bmatrix} 1 \\ 1 \\ 1 \end{bmatrix}$

13. $\lambda_1 = 0$, $\lambda_2 = 1$, $\lambda_3 = -1$, eigenbasis: $\begin{bmatrix} 0 \\ 1 \\ 0 \end{bmatrix}, \begin{bmatrix} 1 \\ -3 \\ 1 \end{bmatrix}, \begin{bmatrix} 1 \\ -1 \\ 2 \end{bmatrix}$

15. $\lambda_1 = 0$, $\lambda_2 = \lambda_3 = 1$, $E_0 = \text{span} \begin{bmatrix} 0 \\ 1 \\ 0 \end{bmatrix}$, $E_1 = \text{span} \begin{bmatrix} 1 \\ -1 \\ 2 \end{bmatrix}$

    No eigenbasis

17. $\lambda_1 = \lambda_2 = 0$, $\lambda_3 = \lambda_4 = 1$

    with eigenbasis $\begin{bmatrix} 1 \\ 0 \\ 0 \\ 0 \end{bmatrix}, \begin{bmatrix} 0 \\ -1 \\ 1 \\ 0 \end{bmatrix}, \begin{bmatrix} 0 \\ 1 \\ 0 \\ 0 \end{bmatrix}, \begin{bmatrix} 0 \\ 0 \\ 0 \\ 1 \end{bmatrix}$

19. We find the eigenspace $E_1 = \ker(I_3 - A) = \ker \begin{bmatrix} 0 & -a & -b \\ 0 & 0 & -c \\ 0 & 0 & 0 \end{bmatrix} = \ker \begin{bmatrix} 0 & a & b \\ 0 & 0 & c \\ 0 & 0 & 0 \end{bmatrix}$.

    If $a = b = c = 0$ then E_1 is 3-dimensional with eigenbasis $\vec{e}_1$, $\vec{e}_2$, $\vec{e}_3$.
    If $a \neq 0$ and $c \neq 0$ then E_1 is 1-dimensional and otherwise E_1 is 2-dimensional. The geometric multiplicity of the eigenvalue 1 is $\dim(E_1)$.

21. We want A such that $A \begin{bmatrix} 1 \\ 2 \end{bmatrix} = \begin{bmatrix} 1 \\ 2 \end{bmatrix}$ and $A \begin{bmatrix} 2 \\ 3 \end{bmatrix} = 2 \begin{bmatrix} 2 \\ 3 \end{bmatrix} = \begin{bmatrix} 4 \\ 6 \end{bmatrix}$, i.e. $A \begin{bmatrix} 1 & 2 \\ 2 & 3 \end{bmatrix} = \begin{bmatrix} 1 & 4 \\ 2 & 6 \end{bmatrix}$ so

    $A = \begin{bmatrix} 1 & 4 \\ 2 & 6 \end{bmatrix} \begin{bmatrix} 1 & 2 \\ 2 & 3 \end{bmatrix}^{-1} = \begin{bmatrix} 5 & -2 \\ 6 & -2 \end{bmatrix}$.
    The answer is unique.

23. $\lambda_1 = \lambda_2 = 1$ and $E_1 = \text{span}(\vec{e}_1)$, hence there is no eigenbasis. The matrix represents a shear parallel to the x-axis.

25. If λ is an eigenvalue of A, then $E_\lambda = \ker(\lambda I_3 - A) = \ker \begin{bmatrix} \lambda & -1 & 0 \\ 0 & \lambda & -1 \\ -a & -b & \lambda - c \end{bmatrix}$.

   The row-reduced echelon form of the above matrix will contain two leading 1's hence E_λ is always 1-dimensional, i.e. the geometric multiplicity of λ is 1.

27. By Fact 7.2.4, $f_A(\lambda) = \lambda^2 - 5\lambda + 6 = (\lambda - 3)(\lambda - 2)$ so $\lambda_1 = 2$, $\lambda_2 = 3$.

29. Note that r is the number of nonzero diagonal entries of A, since the nonzero columns of A form a basis of $\text{im}(A)$. Therefore, there are $n - r$ zeros on the diagonal, so that the algebraic multiplicity of the eigenvalue 0 is $n - r$. It is true for any $n \times n$ matrix A that the geometric multiplicity of the eigenvalue 0 is $\dim(\ker(A))$
   $= n - \text{rank}(A) = n - r$.

31. They must be the same. For if they are not, by Fact 7.3.3, the geometric multiplicities would not add up to n.

33. If $S^{-1}AS = B$, then
   $S^{-1}(\lambda I_n - A)S = S^{-1}(\lambda S - AS) = \lambda S^{-1}S - S^{-1}AS = \lambda I_n - B$.

35. No, since the two matrices have different eigenvalues (see Fact 7.3.8.c).

37. a. $A\vec{v} \cdot \vec{w} = (A\vec{v})^T \vec{w} = (\vec{v}^T A^T)\vec{w} = (\vec{v}^T A)\vec{w} = v^T(A\vec{w}) = \vec{v} \cdot A\vec{w}$
   $$\uparrow$$
   $$A \text{ symmetric}$$

   b. Assume $A\vec{v} = \lambda \vec{v}$ and $A\vec{w} = \alpha \vec{w}$ for $\lambda \neq \alpha$, then $(A\vec{v}) \cdot \vec{w} = (\lambda \vec{v}) \cdot \vec{w} = \lambda(\vec{v} \cdot \vec{w})$, and
   $\vec{v} \cdot A\vec{w} = \vec{v} \cdot \alpha \vec{w} = \alpha(\vec{v} \cdot \vec{w})$.
   By part a, $\lambda(\vec{v} \cdot \vec{w}) = \alpha(\vec{v} \cdot \vec{w})$ i.e. $(\lambda - \alpha)(\vec{v} \cdot \vec{w}) = 0$.
   Since $\lambda \neq \alpha$, it must be that $\vec{v} \cdot \vec{w} = 0$, i.e. $\vec{v}$ and $\vec{w}$ are perpendicular.

39. a. There are two eigenvalues, $\lambda_1 = 1$ (with $E_1 = V$) and $\lambda_2 = 0$ (with $E_0 = V^\perp$).
   Now geometric multiplicity$(1) = \dim(E_1) = \dim(V) = m$, and
   geometric multiplicity$(0) = \dim(E_0) = \dim(V^\perp) = n - \dim(V) = n - m$.
   Since geometric multiplicity$(\lambda) \leq$ algebraic multiplicity(λ), by Fact 7.3.3, and the algebraic multiplicities cannot add up to more than n, the geometric and algebraic multiplicities of the eigenvalues are the same here.

   b. Analogous to part a: $E_1 = V$ and $E_{-1} = V^\perp$.
   geometric multiplicity$(1) =$ algebraic multiplicity$(1) = \dim(V) = m$, and
   geometric multiplicity$(-1) =$ algebraic multiplicity$(-1) = \dim(V^\perp) = n - m$.

41. The eigenvalues of A are 1.2, -0.8, -0.4 with eigenvectors $\begin{bmatrix} 9 \\ 6 \\ 2 \end{bmatrix}$, $\begin{bmatrix} 2 \\ -2 \\ 1 \end{bmatrix}$, $\begin{bmatrix} 1 \\ -2 \\ 2 \end{bmatrix}$.

Since $\vec{x}_0 = 50 \begin{bmatrix} 9 \\ 6 \\ 2 \end{bmatrix} + 50 \begin{bmatrix} 2 \\ -2 \\ 1 \end{bmatrix} + 50 \begin{bmatrix} 1 \\ -2 \\ 2 \end{bmatrix}$ we have $\vec{x}(t) = 50(1.2)^t \begin{bmatrix} 9 \\ 6 \\ 2 \end{bmatrix} + 50(-0.8)^t \begin{bmatrix} 2 \\ -2 \\ 1 \end{bmatrix} +$

$50(-0.4)^t \begin{bmatrix} 1 \\ -2 \\ 2 \end{bmatrix}$ so as t goes to infinity $j(t) : n(t) : a(t)$ approaches the proportion $9 : 6 : 2$.

43. a. $A = \dfrac{1}{2} \begin{bmatrix} 0 & 1 & 1 \\ 1 & 0 & 1 \\ 1 & 1 & 0 \end{bmatrix}$

    b. After 10 rounds, we have $A^{10} \begin{bmatrix} 7 \\ 11 \\ 5 \end{bmatrix} \approx \begin{bmatrix} 7.6660156 \\ 7.6699219 \\ 7.6640625 \end{bmatrix}$.

    After 50 rounds, we have $A^{50} \begin{bmatrix} 7 \\ 11 \\ 5 \end{bmatrix} \approx \begin{bmatrix} 7.66666666667 \\ 7.66666666667 \\ 7.66666666667 \end{bmatrix}$.

    c. The eigenvalues of A are 1 and $-\dfrac{1}{2}$ with $E_1 = \operatorname{span} \begin{bmatrix} 1 \\ 1 \\ 1 \end{bmatrix}$ and $E_{-\frac{1}{2}} = \operatorname{span} \left(\begin{bmatrix} 0 \\ 1 \\ -1 \end{bmatrix}, \begin{bmatrix} -1 \\ -1 \\ 2 \end{bmatrix} \right)$

    so $\vec{x}(t) = \left(1 + \dfrac{c_0}{3} \right) \begin{bmatrix} 1 \\ 1 \\ 1 \end{bmatrix} + \left(-\dfrac{1}{2} \right)^t \begin{bmatrix} 0 \\ 1 \\ -1 \end{bmatrix} + \left(-\dfrac{1}{2} \right)^t \dfrac{c_0}{3} \begin{bmatrix} -1 \\ -1 \\ 2 \end{bmatrix}$.

    After 1001 rounds, Alberich will be ahead of Brunnhilde $\left(\text{by } \left(\tfrac{1}{2} \right)^{1001} \right)$, so that Carl needs to beat Alberich to win the game. A straightforward computation shows that $c(1001) - a(1001) = \left(\tfrac{1}{2} \right)^{1001} (1 - c_0)$; Carl wins if this quantity is positive, which is the case if c_0 is less than 1. Alternatively, observe that the ranking of the players is reversed in each round: Whoever is first will be last after the next round. Since the total number of rounds is odd (1001), Carl wants to be last initially to win the game; he wants to choose a smaller number than both Alberich and Brunnhilde.

45. a. $A = \begin{bmatrix} 0.1 & 0.2 \\ 0.4 & 0.3 \end{bmatrix}, \vec{b} = \begin{bmatrix} 1 \\ 2 \end{bmatrix}$

    b. $B = \begin{bmatrix} A & \vec{b} \\ 0 & 1 \end{bmatrix}$

    c. The eigenvalues of A are 0.5 and -0.1 with associated eigenvectors $\begin{bmatrix} 1 \\ 2 \end{bmatrix}$ and $\begin{bmatrix} 1 \\ -1 \end{bmatrix}$.

The eigenvalues of B are 0.5, -0.1, and 1. If $A\vec{v} = \lambda\vec{v}$ then $B\begin{bmatrix} \vec{v} \\ 0 \end{bmatrix} = \lambda\begin{bmatrix} \vec{v} \\ 0 \end{bmatrix}$ so $\begin{bmatrix} \vec{v} \\ 0 \end{bmatrix}$ is an eigenvector of B.

Furthermore, $\begin{bmatrix} 2 \\ 4 \\ 1 \end{bmatrix}$ is an eigenvector of B corresponding to the eigenvalue 1. Note that this vector is $\begin{bmatrix} -(A - I_2)^{-1}\vec{b} \\ 1 \end{bmatrix}$.

d. Write $\vec{y}(0) = \begin{bmatrix} x_1(0) \\ x_2(0) \\ 1 \end{bmatrix} = c_1\begin{bmatrix} 1 \\ 2 \\ 0 \end{bmatrix} + c_2\begin{bmatrix} 1 \\ -1 \\ 0 \end{bmatrix} + c_3\begin{bmatrix} 2 \\ 4 \\ 1 \end{bmatrix}$.

Note that $c_3 = 1$.

Now $\vec{y}(t) = c_1(0.5)^t\begin{bmatrix} 1 \\ 2 \\ 0 \end{bmatrix} + c_2(-0.1)^t\begin{bmatrix} 1 \\ -1 \\ 0 \end{bmatrix} + \begin{bmatrix} 2 \\ 4 \\ 1 \end{bmatrix} \xrightarrow{t\to\infty} \begin{bmatrix} 2 \\ 4 \\ 1 \end{bmatrix}$ so that $\vec{x}(t) \xrightarrow{t\to\infty} \begin{bmatrix} 2 \\ 4 \end{bmatrix}$.

47. a. If $\vec{x}(t) = \begin{bmatrix} r(t) \\ p(t) \\ w(t) \end{bmatrix}$, then $\vec{x}(t+1) = A\vec{x}(t)$ with $A = \begin{bmatrix} \frac{1}{2} & \frac{1}{4} & 0 \\ \frac{1}{2} & \frac{1}{2} & \frac{1}{2} \\ 0 & \frac{1}{4} & \frac{1}{2} \end{bmatrix}$.

The eigenvalues of A are $0, \dfrac{1}{2}, 1$ with eigenvectors $\begin{bmatrix} 1 \\ -2 \\ 1 \end{bmatrix}, \begin{bmatrix} 1 \\ 0 \\ -1 \end{bmatrix}, \begin{bmatrix} 1 \\ 2 \\ 1 \end{bmatrix}$.

Since $\vec{x}(0) = \begin{bmatrix} 1 \\ 0 \\ 0 \end{bmatrix} = \dfrac{1}{4}\begin{bmatrix} 1 \\ -2 \\ 1 \end{bmatrix} + \dfrac{1}{2}\begin{bmatrix} 1 \\ 0 \\ -1 \end{bmatrix} + \dfrac{1}{4}\begin{bmatrix} 1 \\ 2 \\ 1 \end{bmatrix}$, $\vec{x}(t) = \dfrac{1}{2}\left(\dfrac{1}{2}\right)^t\begin{bmatrix} 1 \\ 0 \\ -1 \end{bmatrix} + \dfrac{1}{4}\begin{bmatrix} 1 \\ 2 \\ 1 \end{bmatrix}$ for $t > 0$.

b. As $t \to \infty$ the ratio is $1 : 2 : 1$ (since the first term of $\vec{x}(t)$ drops out).

49. This "random" matrix $A = [\vec{0}\ \vec{v}_2\ \cdots\ \vec{v}_n]$ is unlikely to have any zeros above the diagonal. In this case, the columns $\vec{v}_2, \ldots, \vec{v}_n$ will be linearly independent (none of them is a linear combination of the previous ones), so that $\text{rank}(A) = n - 1$ and geometric multiplicity$(0) = \dim(\ker(A)) = n - \text{rank}(A) = 1$. Alternatively, you can argue in terms of $\text{rref}(A)$.

7.4

1. Matrix A is diagonal already, so it's certainly diagonalizable. Let $S = I_2$

3. Diagonalizable. The eigenvalues are $0,3$, with associated eigenvectors $\begin{bmatrix} -1 \\ 1 \end{bmatrix}, \begin{bmatrix} 1 \\ 2 \end{bmatrix}$. If we let $S = \begin{bmatrix} -1 & 1 \\ 1 & 2 \end{bmatrix}$, then $S^{-1}AS = D = \begin{bmatrix} 0 & 0 \\ 0 & 3 \end{bmatrix}$.

5. Fails to be diagonalizable. There is only one eigenvalue, 1, with a one-dimensional eigenspace.

7. Diagonalizable. The eigenvalues are $2, -3$, with associated eigenvectors $\begin{bmatrix} 4 \\ 1 \end{bmatrix}, \begin{bmatrix} -1 \\ 1 \end{bmatrix}$. If we let $S = \begin{bmatrix} 4 & -1 \\ 1 & 1 \end{bmatrix}$, then $S^{-1}AS = D = \begin{bmatrix} 2 & 0 \\ 0 & -3 \end{bmatrix}$.

9. Fails to be diagonalizable. There is only one eigenvalue, 1, with a one-dimensional eigenspace.

11. Fails to be diagonalizable. The eigenvalues are $1,2,1$, and the eigenspace $E_1 = \ker(I_3 - A) = \text{span}(\vec{e}_1)$ is only one-dimensional.

13. Diagonalizable. The eigenvalues are $1,2,3$, with associated eigenvectors $\begin{bmatrix} 1 \\ 0 \\ 0 \end{bmatrix}, \begin{bmatrix} 1 \\ 1 \\ 0 \end{bmatrix}, \begin{bmatrix} 1 \\ 2 \\ 1 \end{bmatrix}$. If we let $S = \begin{bmatrix} 1 & 1 & 1 \\ 0 & 1 & 2 \\ 0 & 0 & 1 \end{bmatrix}$, then $S^{-1}AS = D = \begin{bmatrix} 1 & 0 & 0 \\ 0 & 2 & 0 \\ 0 & 0 & 3 \end{bmatrix}$.

15. Diagonalizable. The eigenvalues are $1, -1, 1$, with associated eigenvectors $\begin{bmatrix} 2 \\ 1 \\ 0 \end{bmatrix}, \begin{bmatrix} 1 \\ 1 \\ 0 \end{bmatrix}, \begin{bmatrix} 0 \\ 0 \\ 1 \end{bmatrix}$. If we let $S = \begin{bmatrix} 2 & 1 & 0 \\ 1 & 1 & 0 \\ 0 & 0 & 1 \end{bmatrix}$, then $S^{-1}AS = D = \begin{bmatrix} 1 & 0 & 0 \\ 0 & -1 & 0 \\ 0 & 0 & 1 \end{bmatrix}$.

17. Diagonalizable. The eigenvalues are $0,3,0$, with associated eigenvectors $\begin{bmatrix} 1 \\ -1 \\ 0 \end{bmatrix}, \begin{bmatrix} 1 \\ 1 \\ 1 \end{bmatrix}, \begin{bmatrix} 1 \\ 0 \\ -1 \end{bmatrix}$. If we let $S = \begin{bmatrix} 1 & 1 & 1 \\ -1 & 1 & 0 \\ 0 & 1 & -1 \end{bmatrix}$, then $S^{-1}AS = D = \begin{bmatrix} 0 & 0 & 0 \\ 0 & 3 & 0 \\ 0 & 0 & 0 \end{bmatrix}$.

19. Fails to be diagonalizable. The eigenvalues are $1,0,1$, and the eigenspace $E_1 = \ker(I_3 - A) = \text{span}(\vec{e}_1)$ is only one-dimensional.

21. Diagonalizable for all values of a, since there are always two distinct eigenvalues, 1 and 2. See Fact 7.4.3.

23. Diagonalizable for positive a. The characteristic polynomial is $(\lambda - 1)^2 - a$, so that the eigenvalues are $\lambda = 1 \pm \sqrt{a}$. If a is positive, then we have two distinct real eigenvalues, so that the matrix is diagonalizable. If a is negative, then there are no real eigenvalues. If a is 0, then 1 is the only eigenvalue, with a one-dimensional eigenspace.

25. Diagonalizable for all values of a, b, and c, since we have three distinct eigenvalues, 1, 2, and 3.

27. Diagonalizable only if $a = b = c = 0$. Since 1 is the only eigenvalue, it is required that $E_1 = \mathbb{R}^3$, that is, the matrix must be the identity matrix.

29. Not diagonalizable for any a. The characteristic polynomial is $\lambda^3 - a$, so that there is only one real eigenvalue, $\sqrt[3]{a}$, for all a. Since the corresponding eigenspace isn't all of $\mathbb{R}^3$, the matrix fails to be diagonalizable.

31. In Example 1 of this section we see that the eigenvalues of $A = \begin{bmatrix} 1 & 2 \\ 4 & 3 \end{bmatrix}$ are -1 and 5, with associated eigenvectors $\begin{bmatrix} 1 \\ -1 \end{bmatrix}$ and $\begin{bmatrix} 1 \\ 2 \end{bmatrix}$. If we let $S = \begin{bmatrix} 1 & 1 \\ -1 & 2 \end{bmatrix}$, then $S^{-1}AS = D = \begin{bmatrix} -1 & 0 \\ 0 & 5 \end{bmatrix}$.

Thus $A = SDS^{-1}$ and $A^t = SD^tS^{-1} = \dfrac{1}{3} \begin{bmatrix} 1 & 1 \\ -1 & 2 \end{bmatrix} \begin{bmatrix} (-1)^t & 0 \\ 0 & 5^5 \end{bmatrix} \begin{bmatrix} 2 & -1 \\ 1 & 1 \end{bmatrix}$

$$= \dfrac{1}{3} \begin{bmatrix} 2(-1)^t + 5^t & (-1)^{t+1} + 5^t \\ 2(5^t) - 2(-1)^t & 2(5^t) + (-1)^t \end{bmatrix}$$

33. The eigenvalues of $A = \begin{bmatrix} 1 & 2 \\ 3 & 6 \end{bmatrix}$ are 0 and 7, with associated eigenvectors $\begin{bmatrix} -2 \\ 1 \end{bmatrix}$ and $\begin{bmatrix} 1 \\ 3 \end{bmatrix}$.

If we let $S = \begin{bmatrix} -2 & 1 \\ 1 & 3 \end{bmatrix}$, then $S^{-1}AS = D = \begin{bmatrix} 0 & 0 \\ 0 & 7 \end{bmatrix}$. Thus $A = SDS^{-1}$ and $A^t = SD^tS^{-1} = \dfrac{1}{7} \begin{bmatrix} -2 & 1 \\ 1 & 3 \end{bmatrix} \begin{bmatrix} 0 & 0 \\ 0 & 7^t \end{bmatrix} \begin{bmatrix} -3 & 1 \\ 1 & 2 \end{bmatrix} = \dfrac{1}{7} \begin{bmatrix} 7^t & 2(7^t) \\ 3(7^t) & 6(7^t) \end{bmatrix} = 7^{t-1}A$. We can find the same result more directly by observing that $A^2 = 7A$.

35. Matrix $\begin{bmatrix} -1 & 6 \\ -2 & 6 \end{bmatrix}$ has the eigenvalues 3 and 2. If $\vec{v}$ and $\vec{w}$ are associated eigenvectors, and if we let $S = [\vec{v}\,\vec{w}]$, then $S^{-1} \begin{bmatrix} -1 & 6 \\ -2 & 6 \end{bmatrix} S = \begin{bmatrix} 3 & 0 \\ 0 & 2 \end{bmatrix}$, so that matrix $\begin{bmatrix} -1 & 6 \\ -2 & 6 \end{bmatrix}$ is indeed similar to $\begin{bmatrix} 3 & 0 \\ 0 & 2 \end{bmatrix}$.

37. Yes. Matrices A and B have the same characteristic polynomial, $\lambda^2 - 7\lambda + 7$, so that they have the same two distinct real eigenvalues $\lambda_{1,2} = \dfrac{7 \pm \sqrt{21}}{2}$. Thus both A and B are similar to the diagonal matrix $\begin{bmatrix} \lambda_1 & 0 \\ 0 & \lambda_2 \end{bmatrix}$, by Algorithm 7.4.4. Therefore A is similar to B, by parts b and c of Fact 3.4.6.

39. The eigenfunctions with eigenvalue λ are the nonzero functions $f(x)$ such that $T(f(x)) = f'(x) - f(x) = \lambda f(x)$, or $f'(x) = (\lambda + 1)f(x)$. From calculus we recall that those are the exponential functions of the form $f(x) = Ce^{(\lambda+1)x}$, where C is a nonzero constant. Thus all real numbers are eigenvalues of T, and the eigenspace E_λ is one-dimensional, spanned by $e^{(\lambda+1)x}$.

41. The nonzero symmetric matrices are eigenmatrices with eigenvalue 2, since $L(A) = A + A^T = 2A$ in this case. The nonzero skew-symmetric matrices have eigenvalue 0, since $L(A) = A + A^T = A -$

$A = 0$. Yes, L is diagonalizable, since we have the eigenbasis $\begin{bmatrix} 1 & 0 \\ 0 & 0 \end{bmatrix}, \begin{bmatrix} 0 & 1 \\ 1 & 0 \end{bmatrix}, \begin{bmatrix} 0 & 0 \\ 0 & 1 \end{bmatrix}, \begin{bmatrix} 0 & 1 \\ -1 & 0 \end{bmatrix}$ (three symmetric matrices, and one skew-symmetric one).

43. The nonzero real numbers are "eigenvectors" with eigenvalue 1, and the nonzero imaginary numbers (of the form iy) are "eigenvectors" with eigenvalue -1. Yes, T is diagonalizable, since we have the eigenbasis $1, i$.

45. The nonzero sequence $(x_0, x_1, x_2, \ldots)$ is an eigensequence with eigenvalue λ if $T(x_0, x_1, x_2, \ldots)$ $= (0, x_0, x_1, x_2, \ldots) = \lambda(x_0, x_1, x_2, \ldots) = (\lambda x_0, \lambda x_1, \lambda x_2, \ldots)$. This means that $0 = \lambda x_0, x_0 = \lambda x_1$, $x_1 = \lambda x_2, \ldots, x_n = \lambda x_{n+1}, \ldots$. If λ is nonzero, then these equations imply that $x_0 = \dfrac{1}{\lambda} 0 = 0, x_1 = \dfrac{1}{\lambda} x_0 = 0, x_2 = \dfrac{1}{\lambda} x_1 = 0, \ldots$, so that there are no eigensequences in this case. If $\lambda = 0$, then we have $x_0 = \lambda x_1 = 0, x_1 = \lambda x_2 = 0, x_2 = \lambda x_3 = 0, \ldots$, so that there aren't any eigensequences either. In summary: There are no eigenvalues and eigensequences for T.

47. The nonzero even functions, of the form $f(x) = a + cx^2$, are eigenfunctions with eigenvalue 1, and the nonzero odd functions, of the form $f(x) = bx$, have eigenvalue -1. Yes, T is diagonalizable, since the standard basis, $1, x, x^2$, is an eigenbasis for T.

49. The matrix of T with respect to the standard basis $1, x, x^2$ is $B = \begin{bmatrix} 1 & -1 & 1 \\ 0 & 3 & -6 \\ 0 & 0 & 9 \end{bmatrix}$. The eigenvalues of B are 1, 3, 9, with corresponding eigenvectors $\begin{bmatrix} 1 \\ 0 \\ 0 \end{bmatrix}, \begin{bmatrix} -1 \\ 2 \\ 0 \end{bmatrix}, \begin{bmatrix} 1 \\ -4 \\ 4 \end{bmatrix}$. The eigenvalues of T are 1,3,9, with corresponding eigenfunctions $1, 2x - 1, 4x^2 - 4x + 1 = (2x - 1)^2$. Yes, T is diagonalizable, since the functions $1, 2x - 1, (2x - 1)^2$ from an eigenbasis.

51. The nonzero constant functions $f(x) = b$ are the eigenfunctions with eigenvalue 0. If $f(x)$ is a polynomial of degree ≥ 1, then the degree of $f(x)$ exceeds the degree of $f'(x)$ by 1 (by the power rule of calculus), so that $f'(x)$ cannot be a scalar multiple of $f(x)$. Thus 0 is the only eigenvalue of T, and the eigenspace E_0 consists of the constant functions.

53. Suppose basis $\mathcal{D}$ consists of $f_1, \ldots, f_n$. We are told that the $\mathcal{D}$-matrix B of T is diagonal; let $\lambda_1, \lambda_2, \ldots, \lambda_n$ be the diagonal entries of B. By Fact 4.3.3., we know that $[T(f_i)]_{\mathcal{D}} = $ (ith column of B) $= \lambda_i \vec{e}_i$, for $i = 1, 2, \ldots, n$, so that $T(f_i) = \lambda_i f_i$, by definition of coordinates. Thus $f_1, \ldots, f_n$ is an eigenbasis for T, as claimed.

55. Let $A = \begin{bmatrix} 0 & 1 \\ 0 & 0 \end{bmatrix}$ and $B = \begin{bmatrix} 1 & 0 \\ 0 & 0 \end{bmatrix}$, for example.

57. Modifying the hint in Exercise 56 slightly, we can write $\begin{bmatrix} AB & 0 \\ B & 0 \end{bmatrix} \begin{bmatrix} I_m & A \\ 0 & I_n \end{bmatrix} = \begin{bmatrix} I_m & A \\ 0 & I_n \end{bmatrix}$ $\begin{bmatrix} 0 & 0 \\ B & BA \end{bmatrix}$. Thus matrix $M = \begin{bmatrix} AB & 0 \\ B & 0 \end{bmatrix}$ is similar to $N = \begin{bmatrix} 0 & 0 \\ B & BA \end{bmatrix}$. By Fact 7.3.8, matrices M and N have the same characteristic polynomial. Now $f_M(\lambda) = \det \begin{bmatrix} \lambda I_m - AB & 0 \\ -B & \lambda I_n \end{bmatrix} =$ $\lambda^n \det(\lambda I_m - AB) = \lambda^n f_{AB}(\lambda)$. To understand the second equality, expand repeatedly down the last column. Likewise, $f_N(\lambda) = \det \begin{bmatrix} \lambda I_m & 0 \\ -B & \lambda I_n - BA \end{bmatrix} = \lambda^m f_{BA}(\lambda)$. It follows that $\lambda^n f_{AB}(\lambda) = \lambda^m f_{BA}(\lambda)$. Thus matrices AB and BA have the same *nonzero* eigenvalues, with the same algebraic multiplicities.

59. If $\vec{v}$ is an eigenvector with eigenvalue λ, then
    $f_A(A)\vec{v} = (A^n + a_{n-1}A^{n-1} + \cdots + a_1 A + a_0 I_n)\vec{v}$
    $= \lambda^n \vec{v} + a_{n-1}\lambda^{n-1}\vec{v} + \cdots + a_1\lambda\vec{v} + a_0\vec{v}$
    $= (\lambda^n + a_{n-1}\lambda^{n-1} + \cdots + a_1\lambda + a_0)\vec{v}$
    $= f_A(\lambda)\vec{v} = 0\vec{v} = \vec{0}$.
    Since A is diagonalizable, any vector $\vec{x}$ in $\mathbb{R}^n$ can be written as a linear combination of eigenvectors, so that $f_A(A)\vec{x} = \vec{0}$. Since this equation holds for all $\vec{x}$ in $\mathbb{R}^n$, we have $f_A(A) = 0$, as claimed.

61. a. B is diagonalizable since it has three distinct eigenvalues, so that $S^{-1}BS$ is diagonal for some invertible S. But $S^{-1}AS = S^{-1}I_3 S = I_3$ is diagonal as well. Thus A and B are indeed simultaneously diagonalizable.

    b. There is an invertible S such that $S^{-1}AS = D_1$ and $S^{-1}BS = D_2$ are both diagonal. Then $A = SD_1 S^{-1}$ and $B = SD_2 S^{-1}$, so that $AB = (SD_1 S^{-1})(SD_2 S^{-1}) = SD_1 D_2 S^{-1}$ and $BA = (SD_2 S^{-1})(SD_1 S^{-1}) = SD_2 D_1 S^{-1}$. These two results agree, since $D_1 D_2 = D_2 D_1$ for the diagonal matrices D_1 and D_2.

    c. Let A be I_n and B a nondiagonalizable $n \times n$ matrix, for example, $A = \begin{bmatrix} 1 & 0 \\ 0 & 1 \end{bmatrix}$ and $B = \begin{bmatrix} 1 & 1 \\ 0 & 1 \end{bmatrix}$.

    d. Suppose $BD = DB$ for a diagonal D with distinct diagonal entries. The ijth entry of the matrix $BD = DB$ is $b_{ij}d_{jj} = d_{ii}b_{ij}$. For $i \neq j$ this implies that $b_{ij} = 0$. Thus B must be diagonal.

    e. Since A has n distinct eigenvalues, A is diagonalizable, that is, there is an invertible S such that $S^{-1}AS = D$ is a diagonal matrix with n distinct diagonal entries. We claim that $S^{-1}BS$ is diagonal as well; by part d it suffices to show that $S^{-1}BS$ commutes with $D = S^{-1}AS$. This is easy to verify:
    $(S^{-1}BS)D = (S^{-1}BS)(S^{-1}AS) = S^{-1}BAS = S^{-1}ABS = (S^{-1}AS)(S^{-1}BS) = D(S^{-1}BS)$.

63. Recall from Exercise 62 that all the eigenspaces are two-dimensional.

   a. We need to solve the differential equation $f''(x) = f(x)$. As in Example 18 of Section 4.1, we will look for *exponential* solutions. The function $f(x) = e^{kx}$ is a solution if $k^2 = 1$, or $k = \pm 1$. Thus the eigenspace E_1 is the span of functions e^x and e^{-x}.

   b. We need to solve the differential equation $f''(x) = 0$. Integration gives $f'(x) = C$, a constant. If we integrate again, we find $f(x) = Cx + c$, where c is another arbitrary constant. Thus $E_0 = \text{span}(1, x)$.

   c. The solutions of the differential equation $f''(x) = -f(x)$ are the functions $f(x) = a\cos(x) + b\sin(x)$, so that $E_{-1} = \text{span}(\cos x, \sin x)$. See the introductory example of Section 4.1.

   d. Modifying part c, we see that the solutions of the differential equation $f''(x) = -4f(x)$ are the functions $f(x) = a\cos(2x) + b\sin(2x)$, so that $E_{-4} = \text{span}(\cos(2x), \sin(2x))$.

7.5

1. $z = 3 - 3i$ so $|z| = \sqrt{3^2 + (-3)^2} = \sqrt{18}$ and $\arg(z) = -\dfrac{\pi}{4}$, so $z = \sqrt{18}\left(\cos\left(-\dfrac{\pi}{4}\right) + i\sin\left(-\dfrac{\pi}{4}\right)\right)$.

3. If $z = r(\cos\phi + i\sin\phi)$, then $z^n = r^n(\cos(n\phi) + i\sin(n\phi))$.

   $z^n = 1$ if $r = 1, \cos(n\phi) = 1, \sin(n\phi) = 0$ so $n\phi = 2k\pi$ for an integer k, and $\phi = \dfrac{2k\pi}{n}$,

   i.e. $z = \cos\left(\dfrac{2k\pi}{n}\right) + i\sin\left(\dfrac{2k\pi}{n}\right)$, $k = 0, 1, 2, \ldots, n - 1$.

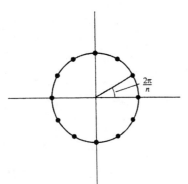

5. Let $z = r(\cos\phi + i\sin\phi)$ then $w = \sqrt[n]{r}\left(\cos\left(\dfrac{\phi + 2\pi k}{n}\right) + i\sin\left(\dfrac{\phi + 2\pi k}{n}\right)\right)$, $k = 0, 1, 2, \ldots, n - 1$.

7. $|T(z)| = |z|\sqrt{2}$ and $\arg(T(z)) = \arg(1 - i) + \arg(z) = -\dfrac{\pi}{4} + \arg(z)$ so T is a clockwise rotation by $\dfrac{\pi}{4}$ followed by a dilation by $\sqrt{2}$.

9. $|z| = \sqrt{0.8^2 + 0.7^2} = \sqrt{1.15}$, $\arg(z) = \arctan\left(-\dfrac{0.7}{0.8}\right) \approx -0.72$

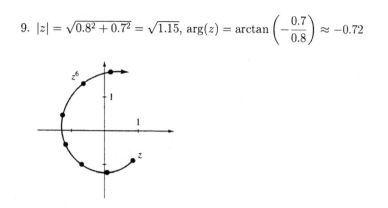

Trajectory spirals outward, in the clockwise direction.

11. Notice that $f(1) = 0$ so $\lambda = 1$ is a root of f. Hence $f(\lambda) = (\lambda - 1)g(\lambda)$, where $g(\lambda) = \dfrac{f(\lambda)}{\lambda - 1} = \lambda^2 - 2\lambda + 5$. Setting $g(\lambda) = 0$ we get $\lambda = 1 \pm 2i$ so that $f(\lambda) = (\lambda - 1)(\lambda - 1 - 2i)(\lambda - 1 + 2i)$.

13. Yes, $\mathbb{Q}$ is a field. Check the axioms on p 347.

15. Yes, check the axioms on p 347. (additive identity 0 and multiplicative identity 1)

17. No, since multiplication is not commutative; Axiom 5 does not hold.

19. a. Since A has eigenvalues 1 and 0 associated with V and $V^\perp$ respectively and since V is the eigenspace of $\lambda = 1$, by Fact 7.5.5, $\operatorname{tr}(A) = m$, $\det(A) = 0$.

    b. Since B has eigenvalues 1 and -1 associated with V and $V^\perp$ respectively and since V is the eigenspace associated with $\lambda = 1$, $\operatorname{tr}(A) = m - (n - m) = 2m - n$, $\det B = (-1)^{n-m}$.

21. $f_A(\lambda) = (\lambda - 11)(\lambda + 7) + 90 = \lambda^2 - 4\lambda + 13$ so $\lambda_{1,2} = 2 \pm 3i$.

23. $f_A(\lambda) = \lambda^3 + 1 = (\lambda - 1)(\lambda^2 + \lambda + 1)$ so $\lambda_1 = 1$, $\lambda_{2,3} = \dfrac{-1 \pm \sqrt{3}i}{2}$.

25. $f_A(\lambda) = \lambda^4 - 1 = (\lambda^2 - 1)(\lambda^2 + 1) = (\lambda - 1)(\lambda + 1)(\lambda - i)(\lambda + i)$ so $\lambda_{1,2} = \pm 1$ and $\lambda_{3,4} = \pm i$

27. By Fact 7.5.5 $\operatorname{tr}(A) = \lambda_1 + \lambda_2 + \lambda_3$, $\det(A) = \lambda_1 \lambda_2 \lambda_3$ but $\lambda_1 = \lambda_2 \neq \lambda_3$ by assumption, so $\operatorname{tr}(A) = 1 = 2\lambda_2 + \lambda_3$ and $\det(A) = 3 = \lambda_2^2 \lambda_3$.
    Solving for λ_2, λ_3 we get $-1, 3$ hence $\lambda_1 = \lambda_2 = -1$ and $\lambda_3 = 3$. (Note that the eigenvalues must be real; why?)

29. $\operatorname{tr}(A) = 0$ so $\lambda_1 + \lambda_2 + \lambda_3 = 0$.
    Also, we can compute $\det(A) = bcd > 0$ since $b, c, d > 0$. Therefore, $\lambda_1 \lambda_2 \lambda_3 > 0$.

Hence two of the eigenvalues must be negative, and the largest one (in absolute value) must be positive.

31. No matter how we choose A, $\frac{1}{15}A$ is a regular transition matrix, so that $\lim\limits_{t\to\infty}\left(\frac{1}{15}A\right)^t$ is a matrix with identical columns by Exercise 30. Therefore, the columns of A^t "become more and more alike" as t approaches infinity, in the sense that $\lim\limits_{t\to\infty}\dfrac{ij\text{th entry of }A^t}{ik\text{th entry of }A^t}=1$ for all i, j, k.

33. a. C is obtained from B by dividing each column of B by its first component. Thus, the first row of C will consist of 1's.

    b. We observe that the columns of C are almost identical, so that the columns of B are "almost parallel" (that is, almost scalar multiples of each other).

    c. Let $\lambda_1, \lambda_2, \ldots, \lambda_5$ be the eigenvalues. Assume λ_1 real and positive and $\lambda_1 > |\lambda_j|$ for $2 \le j \le 5$.

       Let $\vec{v}_1, \ldots, \vec{v}_5$ be corresponding eigenvectors. For a fixed i, write $\vec{e}_i = \sum\limits_{j=1}^{5} c_j \vec{v}_j$; then

       $(i\text{th column of }A^t) = A^t\vec{e}_i = c_1\lambda_1^t\vec{v}_1 + \cdots + c_5\lambda_5^t\vec{v}_5$.
       But in the last expression, for large t, the first term is dominant, so the ith column of A^t is almost parallel to $\vec{v}_1$, the eigenvector corresponding to the dominant eigenvalue.

    d. By part c, the columns of B and C are almost eigenvectors of A associated with the largest eigenvalue, λ_1. Since the first row of C consists of 1's, the entries in the first row of AC will be close to λ_1.

35. If $f_A(\lambda)$ is the characteristic polynomial of A, then, by Fact 7.5.2
    $$f_A(\lambda) = (\lambda - \lambda_1)(\lambda - \lambda_2)\cdots(\lambda - \lambda_n) = \lambda^n - (\lambda_1 + \lambda_2 + \lambda_3 + \cdots + \lambda_n)\lambda^{n-1} + \cdots + (-1)^n\lambda_1\cdots\lambda_n.$$
    But, by Fact 7.2.5, the coefficient of λ^{n-1} is -tr(A), hence tr$(A) = \lambda_1 + \cdots + \lambda_n$.

37. a. Use that $\overline{w} + \overline{z} = \overline{w + z}$ and $\overline{w}\overline{z} = \overline{wz}$.
    $$\begin{bmatrix} w_1 & -\overline{z}_1 \\ z_1 & \overline{w}_1 \end{bmatrix} + \begin{bmatrix} w_2 & -\overline{z}_2 \\ z_2 & \overline{w}_2 \end{bmatrix} = \begin{bmatrix} w_1 + w_2 & -(\overline{z_1 + z_2}) \\ z_1 + z_2 & \overline{w_1 + w_2} \end{bmatrix} \text{ is in } \mathbb{H}.$$
    $$\begin{bmatrix} w_1 & -\overline{z}_1 \\ z_1 & \overline{w}_1 \end{bmatrix}\begin{bmatrix} w_2 & -\overline{z}_2 \\ z_2 & \overline{w}_2 \end{bmatrix} = \begin{bmatrix} w_1 w_2 - \overline{z}_1 z_2 & -(\overline{z_1 w_2 + \overline{w}_1 z_2}) \\ z_1 w_2 + \overline{w}_1 z_2 & \overline{w_1 w_2 - \overline{z}_1 z_2} \end{bmatrix} \text{ is in } \mathbb{H}.$$

    b. If A in $\mathbb{H}$ is nonzero, then $\det(A) = w\overline{w} + z\overline{z} = |w|^2 + |z|^2 > 0$, so that A is invertible.

    c. Yes; if $A = \begin{bmatrix} w & -\overline{z} \\ z & \overline{w} \end{bmatrix}$, then $A^{-1} = \dfrac{1}{|w|^2 + |z|^2}\begin{bmatrix} \overline{w} & \overline{z} \\ -z & w \end{bmatrix}$ is in $\mathbb{H}$.

    d. For example, if $A = \begin{bmatrix} i & 0 \\ 0 & -i \end{bmatrix}$ and $B = \begin{bmatrix} 0 & -1 \\ 1 & 0 \end{bmatrix}$, then $AB = \begin{bmatrix} 0 & -i \\ -i & 0 \end{bmatrix}$ and $BA = \begin{bmatrix} 0 & i \\ i & 0 \end{bmatrix}$.

39. The diagram below illustrates how C_n acts on the basis $\vec{e}_1, \vec{e}_2, \ldots, \vec{e}_n$ of $\mathbb{R}^n$:

a. Based on the diagram above we see that C_n^k takes $\vec{e}_i$ to $\vec{e}_{i+k}$ "modulo n," that is, if $i + k$ exceeds n then C_n^k takes $\vec{e}_i$ to $\vec{e}_{i+k-n}$ (for $k = 1, \ldots, n-1$).
   To put it differently: C_n^k is the matrix whose ith column is $\vec{e}_{i+k}$ if $i + k \le n$ and $\vec{e}_{i+k-n}$ if $i + k > n$ (for $k = 1, \ldots, n-1$).

b. The characteristic polynomial is $\lambda^n - 1$, so that the eigenvalues are the n distinct solutions of the equation $\lambda^n = 1$ (the so-called nth roots of unity), equally spaced points along the unit circle, $\lambda_k = \cos\left(\dfrac{2\pi k}{n}\right) + i \sin\left(\dfrac{2\pi k}{n}\right)$, for $k = 0, 1, \ldots, n-1$ (compare with Exercise 5). For each eigenvalue λ_k,

$$\vec{v}_k = \begin{bmatrix} \lambda_k^{n-1} \\ \vdots \\ \lambda_k^2 \\ \lambda_k \\ 1 \end{bmatrix} \text{ is an associated eigenvector.}$$

c. The eigenbasis $\vec{v}_0, \vec{v}_1, \ldots, \vec{v}_{n-1}$ for C_n we found in part b is in fact an eigenbasis for all circulant $n \times n$ matrices.

41. Substitute $\rho = \dfrac{1}{x}$ into $14\rho^2 + 12\rho^3 - 1 = 0$;

$$\frac{14}{x^2} + \frac{12}{x^3} - 1 = 0$$

$$14x + 12 - x^3 = 0$$

$$\underline{x^3 - 14x = 12}$$

Now use the formula derived in Exercise 40 to find x, with $p = -14$ and $q = 12$. There is only one positive solution, $x \approx 4.114$, so that $\rho = \dfrac{1}{x} \approx 0.243$.

43. Note that $f(x)$ is not the zero polynomial, since $f(i) = \det(S_1 + S_2) = \det(S) \ne 0$, as S is invertible. A nonzero polynomial has only finitely many zeros, so that there is a real number x_0 such that $f(x_0) = \det(S_1 + x_0 S_2) \ne 0$, that is, $S_1 + x_0 S_2$ is invertible. Now $SB = AS$ or $(S_1 + iS_2)B = A(S_1 + iS_2)$. Considering the real and the imaginary part, we can conclude that $S_1 B = AS_1$ and

$S_2 B = A S_2$ and therefore $(S_1 + x_0 S_2)B = A(S_1 + x_0 S_2)$. Since $S_1 + x_0 S_2$ is invertible, we have $B = (S_1 + x_0 S_2)^{-1} A(S_1 + x_0 S_2)$, as claimed.

45. If $a \neq 0$, then there are two distinct eigenvalues, $1 \pm \sqrt{a}$, so that the matrix is diagonalizable. If $a = 0$, then $\begin{bmatrix} 1 & 1 \\ a & 1 \end{bmatrix} = \begin{bmatrix} 1 & 1 \\ 0 & 1 \end{bmatrix}$ fails to be diagonalizable.

47. If $a \neq 0$, then there are three distinct eigenvalues, $0, \pm \sqrt{a}$, so that the matrix is diagonalizable. If $a = 0$, then $\begin{bmatrix} 0 & 0 & 0 \\ 1 & 0 & a \\ 0 & 1 & 0 \end{bmatrix} = \begin{bmatrix} 0 & 0 & 0 \\ 1 & 0 & 0 \\ 0 & 1 & 0 \end{bmatrix}$ fails to be diagonalizable.

49. The eigenvalues are $0, 1, a - 1$. If a is neither 1 nor 2, then there are three distinct eigenvalues, so that the matrix is diagonalizable. Conversely, if $a = 1$ or $a = 2$, then the matrix fails to be diagonalizable, since all the eigenspaces will be one-dimensional (verify this!).

7.6

1. $\lambda_1 = 0.9, \lambda_2 = 0.8$, so by Fact 7.6.2, $\vec{0}$ is a stable equilibrium.

3. $\lambda_{1,2} = 0.8 \pm (0.7)i$ so $|\lambda_1| = |\lambda_2| = \sqrt{0.64 + 0.49} > 1$ so $\vec{0}$ is not a stable equilibrium.

5. $\lambda_1 = 0.8, \lambda_2 = 1.1$ so $\vec{0}$ is not a stable equilibrium.

7. $\lambda_{1,2} = 0.9 \pm (0.5)i$ so $|\lambda_1| = |\lambda_2| = \sqrt{0.81 + 0.25} > 1$ and $\vec{0}$ is not a stable equilibrium.

9. $\lambda_{1,2} = 0.8 \pm (0.6)i, \lambda_3 = 0.7$, so $|\lambda_1| = |\lambda_2| = 1$ and $\vec{0}$ is not a stable equilibrium.

11. $\lambda_1 = k, \lambda_2 = 0.9$ so $\vec{0}$ is a stable equilibrium if $|k| < 1$.

13. Since $\lambda_1 = 0.7, \lambda_2 = -0.9, \vec{0}$ is a stable equilibrium regardless of the value of k.

15. $\lambda_{1,2} = 1 \pm \dfrac{1}{10}\sqrt{k}$

    If $k \geq 0$ then $\lambda_1 = 1 + \dfrac{1}{10}\sqrt{k} \geq 1$. If $k < 0$ then $|\lambda_1| = |\lambda_2| > 1$. Thus, the zero state isn't a stable equilibrium for any real k.

17. $\lambda_{1,2} = 0.6 \pm (0.8)i = 1(\cos\phi \pm i \cdot \sin\phi)$, where

    $$\phi = \arctan\left(\frac{0.8}{0.6}\right) = \arctan\left(\frac{0.8}{0.6}\right) = \arctan\left(\frac{4}{3}\right) \approx 0.927.$$

    $$E_{\lambda_1} = \ker \begin{bmatrix} 0.8i & 0.8 \\ -0.8 & 0.8i \end{bmatrix} = \operatorname{span}\begin{bmatrix} -1 \\ i \end{bmatrix} \text{ so } \vec{w} = \begin{bmatrix} 0 \\ 1 \end{bmatrix}, \vec{v} = \begin{bmatrix} -1 \\ 0 \end{bmatrix}.$$

    $\vec{x}_0 = \begin{bmatrix} 0 \\ 1 \end{bmatrix} = 1\vec{w} + 0\vec{v}$, so $a = 1$ and $b = 0$. Now we use Fact 7.6.3:

$$\vec{x}(t) = \begin{bmatrix} 0 & -1 \\ 1 & 0 \end{bmatrix} \begin{bmatrix} \cos(\phi t) & -\sin(\phi t) \\ \sin(\phi t) & \cos \phi t \end{bmatrix} \begin{bmatrix} 1 \\ 0 \end{bmatrix} = \begin{bmatrix} 0 & -1 \\ 1 & 0 \end{bmatrix} \begin{bmatrix} \cos \phi t \\ \sin \phi t \end{bmatrix} = \begin{bmatrix} -\sin \phi t \\ \cos \phi t \end{bmatrix}, \text{ where}$$

$$\phi = \arctan\left(\frac{4}{3}\right) \approx 0.927.$$

The trajectory is a circle:

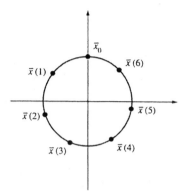

19. $\lambda_{1,2} = 2 \pm 3i$, $r = \sqrt{13}$, and $\phi = \arctan\left(\frac{3}{2}\right) \approx 0.98$, so

$$\lambda_1 \approx \sqrt{13}(\cos(0.98) + i\sin(0.98)), [\vec{w}\ \vec{v}] = \begin{bmatrix} 0 & -1 \\ 1 & 0 \end{bmatrix}, \begin{bmatrix} a \\ b \end{bmatrix} = \begin{bmatrix} 1 \\ 0 \end{bmatrix} \text{ and } \vec{x}(t) \approx \sqrt{13}^{\,t} \begin{bmatrix} -\sin(0.98t) \\ \cos(0.98t) \end{bmatrix}.$$

Spirals outwards (rotation-dilation).

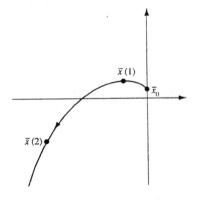

21. $\lambda_{1,2} = 4 \pm i$, $r = \sqrt{17}$, $\phi = \arctan\left(\frac{1}{4}\right) \approx 0.245$ so

$$\lambda_1 \approx \sqrt{17}(\cos(0.245) + i\sin(0.245)), [\vec{w}\ \vec{v}] = \begin{bmatrix} 0 & 5 \\ 1 & 3 \end{bmatrix}, \begin{bmatrix} a \\ b \end{bmatrix} = \begin{bmatrix} 1 \\ 0 \end{bmatrix}$$

$$\text{and } \vec{x}(t) \approx \sqrt{17}^{\,t} \begin{bmatrix} 5\sin(0.245t) \\ \cos(0.245t) + 3\sin(0.245t) \end{bmatrix}$$

Spirals outwards.

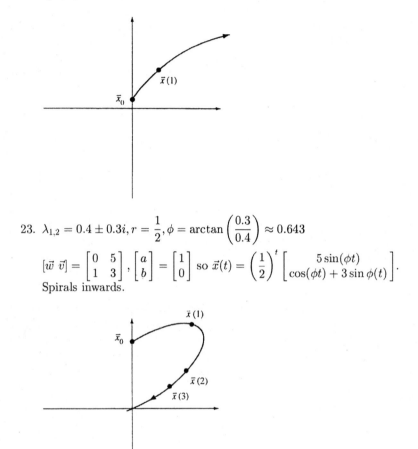

23. $\lambda_{1,2} = 0.4 \pm 0.3i, r = \dfrac{1}{2}, \phi = \arctan\left(\dfrac{0.3}{0.4}\right) \approx 0.643$

$[\vec{w} \ \vec{v}] = \begin{bmatrix} 0 & 5 \\ 1 & 3 \end{bmatrix}, \begin{bmatrix} a \\ b \end{bmatrix} = \begin{bmatrix} 1 \\ 0 \end{bmatrix}$ so $\vec{x}(t) = \left(\dfrac{1}{2}\right)^t \begin{bmatrix} 5\sin(\phi t) \\ \cos(\phi t) + 3\sin\phi(t) \end{bmatrix}$.

Spirals inwards.

25. Not stable since if λ is an eigenvalue of A, then $\dfrac{1}{\lambda}$ is an eigenvalue of A^{-1} and $\left|\dfrac{1}{\lambda}\right| = \dfrac{1}{|\lambda|} > 1$.

27. Stable since if λ is an eigenvalue of $-A$, then $-\lambda$ is an eigenvalue of $-A$ and $|-\lambda| = |\lambda|$.

29. Cannot tell; for example, if $A = \begin{bmatrix} \frac{1}{2} & 0 \\ 0 & \frac{1}{2} \end{bmatrix}$, then $A + I_2$ is $\begin{bmatrix} \frac{3}{2} & 0 \\ 0 & \frac{3}{2} \end{bmatrix}$ and the zero state is not stable,

but if $A = \begin{bmatrix} -\frac{1}{2} & 0 \\ 0 & -\frac{1}{2} \end{bmatrix}$ then $A + I_2 = \begin{bmatrix} \frac{1}{2} & 0 \\ 0 & \frac{1}{2} \end{bmatrix}$ and the zero state is stable.

31. We need to determine for which values of $\det(A)$ and $\operatorname{tr}(A)$ the modulus of both eigenvalues is less than 1. We will first think about the border line case and examine when one of the moduli is exactly 1: If one of the eigenvalues is 1 and the other is λ, then $\operatorname{tr}(A) = \lambda + 1$ and $\det(A) = \lambda$, so that $\det(A) = \operatorname{tr}(A) - 1$. If one of the eigenvalues is -1 and the other is λ, then $\operatorname{tr}(A) = \lambda - 1$ and $\det(A) = -\lambda$, so that $\det(A) = -\operatorname{tr}(A) - 1$. If the eigenvalues are complex conjugates with modulus 1, then $\det(A) = 1$ and $|\operatorname{tr}(A)| < 2$ (think about it!). It is convenient to represent these conditions in the tr-det plane, where each 2×2 matrix A is represented by the point $(\operatorname{tr}A, \det A)$:

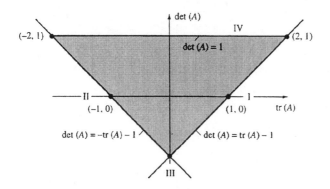

If $\operatorname{tr}(A) = \det(A) = 0$, then both eigenvalues of A are zero. We can conclude that throughout the shaded triangle above the modulus of both eigenvalues will be less than 1, since the modulus of the eigenvalues changes continuously with $\operatorname{tr}(A)$ and $\det(A)$ (consider the quadratic formula!). Conversely, we can choose sample points to show that in all the other four regions above the modulus of at least one of the eigenvalues exceeds one; consider

the matrices $\begin{bmatrix} 2 & 0 \\ 0 & 0 \end{bmatrix}$, $\begin{bmatrix} -2 & 0 \\ 0 & 0 \end{bmatrix}$, $\begin{bmatrix} 2 & 0 \\ 0 & -2 \end{bmatrix}$, and $\begin{bmatrix} 0 & -2 \\ 2 & 0 \end{bmatrix}$.

$\qquad \uparrow \qquad\quad \uparrow \qquad\quad \uparrow \qquad\qquad \uparrow$

$\quad$ in (I) $\quad$ in (II) $\quad$ in (III) $\qquad$ in (IV)

It follows that throughout these four regions, (I), (II), (III), and (IV), at least one of the eigenvalues will have a modulus exceeding one.

The point $(\operatorname{tr}A, \det A)$ is in the shaded triangle if $\det(A) < 1$, $\det(A) > \operatorname{tr}(A) - 1$ and $\det(A) > -\operatorname{tr}(A) - 1$. This means that $|\operatorname{tr}A| - 1 < \det(A) < 1$, as claimed.

33. $\lambda_{1,2} = 0.99 \pm (0.01)i$ with eigenvector $\begin{bmatrix} 0 \\ 1 \end{bmatrix} + i \begin{bmatrix} 1 \\ 0 \end{bmatrix}$ for λ_1, so $\vec{w} = \begin{bmatrix} 1 \\ 0 \end{bmatrix}$, $\vec{v} = \begin{bmatrix} 0 \\ 1 \end{bmatrix}$, $\phi = \arctan$

$\left(\dfrac{0.01}{0.99} \right) \approx 0.01$, $r \approx 0.99$. Hence $\vec{x}(0) = \begin{bmatrix} 100 \\ 0 \end{bmatrix} = 100\vec{w} + 0\vec{v}$ and

$\vec{x}(t) \approx 0.99^t \begin{bmatrix} 1 & 0 \\ 0 & 1 \end{bmatrix} \begin{bmatrix} \cos(0.01t) & -\sin(0.01t) \\ \sin(0.01t) & \cos(0.01t) \end{bmatrix} \begin{bmatrix} 100 \\ 0 \end{bmatrix} = 0.99^t \cdot 100 \begin{bmatrix} \cos(0.01t) \\ \sin(0.01t) \end{bmatrix}$

i.e. $\vec{x}(t)$ spirals in.

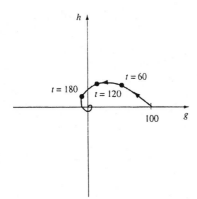

Hence, both glucose and excess insulin oscillate with damped oscillations until all of the excess sugar has been eliminated.

35. a. Let $\vec{v}_1, \ldots, \vec{v}_n$ be an eigenbasis for A. Then $\vec{x}(t) = \sum_{i=1}^{n} c_i \lambda_i^t \vec{v}_i$ and

$$\|\vec{x}(t)\| = \left\| \sum_{i=1}^{n} c_i \lambda_i^t \vec{v}_i \right\| \leq \sum_{i=1}^{n} \|c_i \lambda_i^t \vec{v}_i\| = \sum_{i=1}^{n} |\lambda_i|^t \|c_i \vec{v}_i\| \leq \sum_{i=1}^{n} \|c_i \vec{v}_i\|.$$
$$\underset{\leq 1}{\uparrow}$$

The last quantity, $\sum_{i=1}^{n} \|c_i \vec{v}_i\|$, gives the desired bound M.

b. $A = \begin{bmatrix} 1 & 1 \\ 0 & 1 \end{bmatrix}$ represents a shear parallel to the x-axis, with $A \begin{bmatrix} k \\ 1 \end{bmatrix} = \begin{bmatrix} k+1 \\ 1 \end{bmatrix}$, so that $\vec{x}(t) = A^t \begin{bmatrix} 0 \\ 1 \end{bmatrix} = \begin{bmatrix} t \\ 1 \end{bmatrix}$ is not bounded. This does not contradict part a, since there is no eigenbasis for A.

37. a. Write $Y(t+1) = Y(t) = Y, C(t+1) = C(t) = C, I(t+1) = I(t) = I.$

$$\begin{vmatrix} Y = C + I + G_0 \\ C = \gamma Y \\ I = 0 \end{vmatrix} \rightarrow \begin{array}{c} Y = \gamma Y + G_0 \\ Y = \dfrac{G_0}{1-\gamma} \end{array}$$

$$Y = \frac{G_0}{1-\gamma}, C = \frac{\gamma G_0}{1-\gamma}, I = 0$$

b. $y(t) = Y(t) - \dfrac{G_0}{1-\gamma}, c(t) = C(t) - \dfrac{\gamma G_0}{1-\gamma}, i(t) = I(t)$

Substitute to verify the equations.

$$\begin{bmatrix} C(t+1) \\ i(t+1) \end{bmatrix} = \begin{bmatrix} \gamma & \gamma \\ \alpha\gamma - \alpha & \alpha\gamma \end{bmatrix} \begin{bmatrix} c(t) \\ i(t) \end{bmatrix}$$

  c. $A = \begin{bmatrix} 0.2 & 0.2 \\ -4 & 1 \end{bmatrix}$ eigenvalues $0.6 \pm 0.8i$
     not stable

  d. $A = \begin{bmatrix} \gamma & \gamma \\ \gamma - 1 & \gamma \end{bmatrix}$, $\text{tr} A = 2\gamma$, $\det A = \gamma$, stable (use Exercise 31)

  e. $A = \begin{bmatrix} \gamma & \gamma \\ \alpha\gamma - \alpha & \alpha\gamma \end{bmatrix}$ $\text{tr} A = \gamma(1 + \alpha) > 0$, $\det A = \alpha\gamma$
    Use Exercise 31; stable if $\det(A) = \alpha\gamma < 1$ and $\text{tr} A - 1 = \alpha\gamma + \gamma - 1 < \alpha\gamma$.
    The second condition is satisfied since $\gamma < 1$.
    Stable if $\gamma < \dfrac{1}{\alpha}$
    $\left(\text{eigenvalues are real if } \gamma \geq \dfrac{4\alpha}{(1+\alpha)^2} \right)$

39. Use Exercise 38: $\vec{v} = (I_2 - A)^{-1}\vec{b} = \begin{bmatrix} 0.9 & -0.2 \\ -0.4 & 0.7 \end{bmatrix}^{-1} \begin{bmatrix} 1 \\ 2 \end{bmatrix} = \begin{bmatrix} 2 \\ 4 \end{bmatrix}$.

   $\begin{bmatrix} 2 \\ 4 \end{bmatrix}$ is a stable equilibrium since the eigenvalues of A are 0.5 and -0.1.

41. Find the 2×2 matrix A that transforms $\begin{bmatrix} 8 \\ 6 \end{bmatrix}$ into $\begin{bmatrix} -3 \\ 4 \end{bmatrix}$ and $\begin{bmatrix} -3 \\ 4 \end{bmatrix}$ into $\begin{bmatrix} -8 \\ -6 \end{bmatrix}$:

   $A\begin{bmatrix} 8 & -3 \\ 6 & 4 \end{bmatrix} = \begin{bmatrix} -3 & -8 \\ 4 & -6 \end{bmatrix}$ and $A = \begin{bmatrix} -3 & -8 \\ 4 & -6 \end{bmatrix} \begin{bmatrix} 8 & -3 \\ 6 & 4 \end{bmatrix}^{-1} = \dfrac{1}{50} \begin{bmatrix} 36 & -73 \\ 52 & -36 \end{bmatrix}$.
   There are many other correct answers.

True or False

1. T, by Fact 7.2.2

3. F; If $\begin{bmatrix} 1 & 1 \\ 0 & 1 \end{bmatrix}$, then eigenvalue 1 has geometric multiplicity 1 and algebraic multiplicity. 2.

5. T; $A = AI_n = A[\vec{e}_1 \dots \vec{e}_n] = [\lambda_1\vec{e}_1 \dots \lambda_n\vec{e}_n]$ is diagonal.

7. T; Consider a diagonal 5×5 matrix with only two distinct diagonal entries.

9. T, by Summary 7.1.4

11. F; Consider $A = \begin{bmatrix} 1 & 1 \\ 0 & 1 \end{bmatrix}$

13. T; If $A\vec{v} = 3\vec{v}$, then $A^2\vec{v} = 9\vec{v}$.

15. T, by Fact 7.5.5

17. T, by Example 6 of Section 7.5

19. T; If $S^{-1}AS = D$, then $S^T A^T (S^T)^{-1} = D$.

21. F; Consider $A = \begin{bmatrix} 0 & 1 \\ 0 & 0 \end{bmatrix}$, with $A^2 = \begin{bmatrix} 0 & 0 \\ 0 & 0 \end{bmatrix}$.

23. F; Let $A = \begin{bmatrix} 1 & 0 \\ 1 & 1 \end{bmatrix}$, for example.

25. T; If $S^{-1}AS = D$, then $S^{-1}A^{-1}S = D^{-1}$ is diagonal

27. T; The sole eigenvalue, 7, must have geometric multiplicity 3.

29. F; Consider the zero matrix.

31. F; Consider the identity matrix.

33. F; Let $A = \begin{bmatrix} 1 & 1 \\ 0 & 1 \end{bmatrix}$ and $\vec{v} = \begin{bmatrix} 1 \\ 0 \end{bmatrix}$, for example.

35. F; Let $A = \begin{bmatrix} 2 & 0 \\ 0 & 3 \end{bmatrix}$, $\vec{v} = \begin{bmatrix} 1 \\ 0 \end{bmatrix}$, and $\vec{w} = \begin{bmatrix} 0 \\ 1 \end{bmatrix}$, for example.

37. T; The eigenvalues are 3 and -2.

39. T, by Fact 7.3.5

41. F; Consider a rotation through $\pi/2$.

43. F; Consider $\begin{bmatrix} 1 & 0 \\ 0 & 1 \end{bmatrix}$ and $\begin{bmatrix} 1 & 1 \\ 0 & 1 \end{bmatrix}$.

45. T; There is an eigenbasis $\vec{v}_1, \ldots, \vec{v}_n$, and we can write $\vec{v} = c_1\vec{v}_1 + \cdots + c_n\vec{v}_n$. The vectors $c_i\vec{v}_i$ are either eigenvectors or zero.

47. T, by Fact 7.3.8

49. T; Recall that the rank is the dimension of the image. If $\vec{v}$ is in the image of A, then $A\vec{v}$ is in the image of A as well, so that $A\vec{v}$ is parallel to $\vec{v}$.

51. T; If $A\vec{v} = \lambda\vec{v}$ for a nonzero $\vec{v}$, then $A^4\vec{v} = \lambda^4\vec{v} = \vec{0}$, so that $\lambda^4 = 0$ and $\lambda = 0$.

53. T; If the eigenvalue associated with $\vec{v}$ is $\lambda = 0$, then $A\vec{v} = \vec{0}$, so that $\vec{v}$ is in the kernel of A; otherwise $\vec{v} = A\left(\frac{1}{\lambda}\vec{v}\right)$, so that $\vec{v}$ is in the image of A.

55. T; Either $A\vec{u} = 3\vec{u}$ or $A\vec{u} = 4\vec{u}$.

57. T; Suppose $A\vec{v}_i = \alpha_i\vec{v}_i$ and $B\vec{v}_i = \beta_i\vec{v}_i$, and let $S = [\vec{v}_1 \ldots \vec{v}_n]$. Then $ABS = BAS = [\alpha_1\beta_1\vec{v}_1 \ldots \alpha_n\beta_n\vec{v}_n]$, so that $AB = BA$.

Chapter 8

8.1

1. $\vec{e}_1$, $\vec{e}_2$ is an orthonormal eigenbasis.

3. $\dfrac{1}{\sqrt{5}}\begin{bmatrix} 2 \\ 1 \end{bmatrix}$, $\dfrac{1}{\sqrt{5}}\begin{bmatrix} -1 \\ 2 \end{bmatrix}$ is an orthonormal eigenbasis.

5. Eigenvalues -1, -1, 2

   Choose $\vec{v}_1 = \dfrac{1}{\sqrt{2}}\begin{bmatrix} -1 \\ 1 \\ 0 \end{bmatrix}$ in E_{-1} and $\vec{v}_2 = \dfrac{1}{\sqrt{3}}\begin{bmatrix} 1 \\ 1 \\ 1 \end{bmatrix}$ in E_2 and let $\vec{v}_3 = \vec{v}_1 \times \vec{v}_2 = \dfrac{1}{\sqrt{6}}\begin{bmatrix} 1 \\ 1 \\ -2 \end{bmatrix}$.

7. $\dfrac{1}{\sqrt{2}}\begin{bmatrix} 1 \\ 1 \end{bmatrix}$, $\dfrac{1}{\sqrt{2}}\begin{bmatrix} 1 \\ -1 \end{bmatrix}$ is an orthonormal eigenbasis, so $S = \dfrac{1}{\sqrt{2}}\begin{bmatrix} 1 & 1 \\ 1 & -1 \end{bmatrix}$ and $D = \begin{bmatrix} 5 & 0 \\ 0 & 1 \end{bmatrix}$.

9. $\dfrac{1}{\sqrt{2}}\begin{bmatrix} 1 \\ 0 \\ 1 \end{bmatrix}$, $\dfrac{1}{\sqrt{2}}\begin{bmatrix} -1 \\ 0 \\ 1 \end{bmatrix}$, $\begin{bmatrix} 0 \\ 1 \\ 0 \end{bmatrix}$ is an orthonormal eigenbasis, with $\lambda_1 = 3$, $\lambda_2 = -3$, and $\lambda_3 = 2$, so

   $$S = \dfrac{1}{\sqrt{2}}\begin{bmatrix} 1 & -1 & 0 \\ 0 & 0 & \sqrt{2} \\ 1 & 1 & 0 \end{bmatrix} \text{ and } D = \begin{bmatrix} 3 & 0 & 0 \\ 0 & -3 & 0 \\ 0 & 0 & 2 \end{bmatrix}.$$

11. $\dfrac{1}{\sqrt{2}}\begin{bmatrix} 1 \\ 0 \\ 1 \end{bmatrix}$, $\dfrac{1}{\sqrt{2}}\begin{bmatrix} -1 \\ 0 \\ 1 \end{bmatrix}$, $\begin{bmatrix} 0 \\ 1 \\ 0 \end{bmatrix}$ is an orthonormal eigenbasis, with $\lambda_1 = 2$, $\lambda_2 = 0$, and $\lambda_3 = 1$, so

   $$S = \dfrac{1}{\sqrt{2}}\begin{bmatrix} 1 & -1 & 0 \\ 0 & 0 & \sqrt{2} \\ 1 & 1 & 0 \end{bmatrix} \text{ and } D = \begin{bmatrix} 2 & 0 & 0 \\ 0 & 0 & 0 \\ 0 & 0 & 1 \end{bmatrix}.$$

13. Yes; if $\vec{v}$ is an eigenvector of A with eigenvalue λ, then $\vec{v} = I_3\vec{v} = A^2\vec{v} = \lambda^2\vec{v}$, so that $\lambda^2 = 1$ and $\lambda = 1$ or $\lambda = -1$. Since A is symmetric, E_1 and E_{-1} will be orthogonal complements, so that A represents the reflection in E_1.

15. Yes, if $A\vec{v} = \lambda\vec{v}$, then $A^{-1}\vec{v} = \dfrac{1}{\lambda}\vec{v}$, so that an orthonormal eigenbasis for A is also an orthonormal eigenbasis for A^{-1} (with reciprocal eigenvalues).

17. If A is the $n \times n$ matrix with all 1's, then the eigenvalues of A are 0 (with multiplicity $n - 1$) and n. Now $B = qA + (p - q)I_n$, so that the eigenvalues of B are $p - q$ (with multiplicity $n - 1$) and $qn + p - q$. Thus $\det(B) = (p - q)^{n-1}(qn + p - q)$.

19. Let $L(\vec{x}) = A\vec{x}$. Then $A^T A$ is symmetric, since $(A^T A)^T = A^T (A^T)^T = A^T A$, so that there is an orthonormal eigenbasis $\vec{v}_1, \ldots, \vec{v}_n$ for $A^T A$. Then the vectors $A\vec{v}_1, \ldots, A\vec{v}_n$ are orthogonal, since
$$A\vec{v}_i \cdot A\vec{v}_j = (A\vec{v}_i)^T A\vec{v}_j = \vec{v}_i^T A^T A\vec{v}_j = \vec{v}_i \cdot (A^T A\vec{v}_j) = \vec{v}_i \cdot (\lambda_j \vec{v}_j) = \lambda_j(\vec{v}_i \cdot \vec{v}_j) = 0 \text{ if } i \neq j.$$

21. For each eigenvalue there are two unit eigenvectors: $\pm\vec{v}_1$, $\pm\vec{v}_2$, and $\pm\vec{v}_3$. We have 6 choices for the first column of S, 4 choices remaining for the second column, and 2 for the third.
Answer: $6 \cdot 4 \cdot 2 = 48$.

23. The eigenvalues are real (by Fact 8.1.3), so that the only possible eigenvalues are ± 1 (by Fact 7.1.2). Since A is symmetric, E_1 and E_{-1} are orthogonal complements. Thus A represents a *reflection* in E_1.

25. Note that A is symmetric an orthogonal, so that the eigenvalues of A are 1 and -1.
$$E_1 = \text{span}\left(\begin{bmatrix} 1 \\ 0 \\ 0 \\ 0 \\ 1 \end{bmatrix}, \begin{bmatrix} 0 \\ 1 \\ 0 \\ 1 \\ 0 \end{bmatrix}, \begin{bmatrix} 0 \\ 0 \\ 1 \\ 0 \\ 0 \end{bmatrix}\right), \quad E_{-1} = \text{span}\left(\begin{bmatrix} 1 \\ 0 \\ 0 \\ 0 \\ -1 \end{bmatrix}, \begin{bmatrix} 0 \\ 1 \\ 0 \\ -1 \\ 0 \end{bmatrix}\right)$$

The columns of S must form an eigenbasis for $A : S = \dfrac{1}{\sqrt{2}}\begin{bmatrix} 1 & 0 & 0 & 1 & 0 \\ 0 & 1 & 0 & 0 & 1 \\ 0 & 0 & \sqrt{2} & 0 & 0 \\ 0 & 1 & 0 & 0 & -1 \\ 1 & 0 & 0 & -1 & 0 \end{bmatrix}$ is one possible choice.

27. If n is even, then this matrix is $J_n + I_n$, for the J_n introduced in Exercise 26, so that the eigenvalues are 0 and 2, with multiplicity $\dfrac{n}{2}$ each. E_2 is the span of all $e_i + e_{n+1-i}$, for $i = 1, \ldots, \dfrac{n}{2}$, and E_0 is spanned by all $e_i - e_{n+1-i}$. If n is odd, then E_2 is spanned by all $\vec{e}_i + \vec{e}_{n+1-i}$, for $i = 1, \ldots, \dfrac{n-1}{2}$; E_0 is spanned by all $\vec{e}_i - \vec{e}_{n+1-i}$, for $i = 1, \ldots, \dfrac{n-1}{2}$, and E_1 is spanned by $\vec{e}_{\frac{n+1}{2}}$.

29. By Fact 5.4.1 $(\text{im } A)^\perp = \ker(A^T) = \ker(A)$, so that $\vec{v}$ is orthogonal to $\vec{w}$.

31. True; A is diagonalizable, that is, A is similar to a diagonal matrix D; then A^2 is similar to D^2. Now $\text{rank}(D) = \text{rank}(D^2)$ is the number of nonzero entries on the diagonal of D (and D^2). Since similar matrices have the same rank (by Fact 7.3.8b) we can conclude that $\text{rank}(A) = \text{rank}(D) = \text{rank}(D^2) = \text{rank}(A^2)$.

33. The angles must add up to 2π, so $\alpha = \dfrac{2\pi}{3} = 120°$.

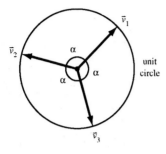

Algebraically, we can see this as follows: let $A = \begin{bmatrix} \vec{v}_1 & \vec{v}_2 & \vec{v}_3 \end{bmatrix}$, a 2×3 matrix.

Then $A^T A = \begin{bmatrix} 1 & \cos\alpha & \cos\alpha \\ \cos\alpha & 1 & \cos\alpha \\ \cos\alpha & \cos\alpha & 1 \end{bmatrix}$ is a noninvertible 3×3 matrix, so that $\cos\alpha = \dfrac{1}{1-3} = -\dfrac{1}{2}$,

by Exercise 32, and $\alpha = \dfrac{2\pi}{3} = 120°$.

35. Let $\vec{v}_1, \ldots, \vec{v}_{n+1}$ be these vectors. Form $A = \begin{bmatrix} \vec{v}_1 & \cdots & \vec{v}_{n+1} \end{bmatrix}$, an $n \times (n+1)$ matrix.

Then $A^T A = \begin{bmatrix} 1 & \cos\alpha & \cdots & \cos\alpha \\ \cos\alpha & 1 & \cdots & \cos\alpha \\ \vdots & & \ddots & \\ \cos\alpha & & \cdots & 1 \end{bmatrix}$ is a noninvertible $(n+1) \times (n+1)$ matrix with 1's on

the diagonal and $\cos\alpha$ outside, so that $\cos\alpha = \dfrac{1}{1-n}$, by Exercise 32, and $\alpha = \arccos\left(\dfrac{1}{1-n}\right)$.

37. a. If $S^{-1}AS$ is upper triangular then the first column of S is an eigenvector of A. Therefore, any matrix without real eigenvectors fails to be triangulizable over $\mathbb{R}$, for example, $\begin{bmatrix} 0 & -1 \\ 1 & 0 \end{bmatrix}$.

b. Proof by induction on n: For an $n \times n$ matrix A we can choose a complex invertible $n \times n$ matrix P whose first column is an eigenvector for A. Then $P^{-1}AP = \begin{bmatrix} \lambda & \vec{v} \\ 0 & B \end{bmatrix}$.

By induction, B is triangulizable, that is, there is an invertible $(n-1) \times (n-1)$ matrix Q such that $Q^{-1}BQ = T$ is upper triangular.

Now let $R = \begin{bmatrix} 1 & 0 \\ 0 & Q \end{bmatrix}$. Then $R^{-1}\begin{bmatrix} \lambda & \vec{v} \\ 0 & B \end{bmatrix} R = \begin{bmatrix} 1 & 0 \\ 0 & Q^{-1} \end{bmatrix}\begin{bmatrix} \lambda & \vec{v} \\ 0 & B \end{bmatrix}\begin{bmatrix} 1 & 0 \\ 0 & Q \end{bmatrix} = \begin{bmatrix} \lambda & \vec{v}Q \\ 0 & T \end{bmatrix}$ is

upper triangular. $R^{-1}\begin{bmatrix} \lambda & \vec{v} \\ 0 & B \end{bmatrix} R = R^{-1}P^{-1}APR = S^{-1}AS$, where $S = PR$, proving our claim.

39. a. For all i, j, $\left| \displaystyle\sum_{k=1}^{n} a_{ik}b_{kj} \right| \leq \displaystyle\sum_{k=1}^{n} |a_{ik}b_{kj}| = \displaystyle\sum_{k=1}^{n} |a_{ik}||b_{kj}|$

$\uparrow$
triangle inequality

b. By induction on t: $|A^t| = |A^{t-1}A| \leq |A^{t-1}||A| \leq |A|^{t-1}|A| = |A|^t$

$\uparrow$ part a $\uparrow$ by induction

41. Let λ be the largest $|r_{ii}|$; note that $\lambda < 1$. Then $|R| = \begin{bmatrix} |r_{11}| & & * \\ & \ddots & \\ 0 & & |r_{nn}| \end{bmatrix} \leq \begin{bmatrix} \lambda & & * \\ & \ddots & \\ 0 & & \lambda \end{bmatrix} =$

$\lambda \begin{bmatrix} 1 & & * \\ & \ddots & \\ 0 & & 1 \end{bmatrix} = \lambda(I_n + U)$, and $|R^t| \leq |R|^t \leq \lambda^t(I_n + U)^t \leq \lambda^t t^n (I_n + U + \cdots + U^{n-1})$.

We learn in Calculus that $\lim_{t \to \infty}(\lambda^t t^n) = 0$, so that $\lim_{t \to \infty}(R^t) = 0$.

8.2

1. $A = \begin{bmatrix} 6 & -\frac{7}{2} \\ -\frac{7}{2} & 8 \end{bmatrix}$

3. $A = \begin{bmatrix} 3 & 0 & 3 \\ 0 & 4 & \frac{7}{2} \\ 3 & \frac{7}{2} & 5 \end{bmatrix}$

5. $A = \begin{bmatrix} 1 & 2 \\ 2 & 1 \end{bmatrix}$, indefinite (since $\det(A) < 0$)

7. $A = \begin{bmatrix} 0 & 0 & 2 \\ 0 & 3 & 0 \\ 2 & 0 & 0 \end{bmatrix}$, indefinite (eigenvalues $2, -2, 3$)

9. a. $(A^2)^T = (A^T)^2 = (-A)^2 = A^2$, so that A^2 is symmetric.

   b. $q(\vec{x}) = \vec{x}^T A^2 \vec{x} = \vec{x}^T AA\vec{x} = -\vec{x}^T A^T A\vec{x} = -(A\vec{x}) \cdot (A\vec{x}) = -\|A\vec{x}\|^2 \leq 0$ for all $\vec{x}$, so that A^2 is negative semi-definite.

   c. If $\vec{v}$ is a complex eigenvector of A with eigenvalue λ, then $A^2\vec{v} = \lambda^2\vec{v}$, and $\lambda^2 \leq 0$, by part b. Therefore, λ is *imaginary*, that is, $\lambda = bi$ for a real b. Thus, the zero matrix is the only skew-symmetric matrix that is diagonalizable over $\mathbb{R}$.

11. The eigenvalues of A^{-1} are the reciprocals of those of A, so that A and A^{-1} have the same definiteness.

13. $q(\vec{e}_i) = \vec{e}_i \cdot A\vec{e}_i = a_{ii} > 0$

15. $A = \begin{bmatrix} 6 & 2 \\ 2 & 3 \end{bmatrix}$; eigenvalues $\lambda_1 = 7$ and $\lambda_2 = 2$

orthonormal eigenbasis $\vec{v}_1 = \dfrac{1}{\sqrt{5}}\begin{bmatrix} 2 \\ 1 \end{bmatrix}$, $\vec{v}_2 = \dfrac{1}{\sqrt{5}}\begin{bmatrix} -1 \\ 2 \end{bmatrix}$

$\lambda_1 c_1^2 + \lambda_2 c_2^2 = 1$ or $7c_1^2 + 2c_2^2 = 1$

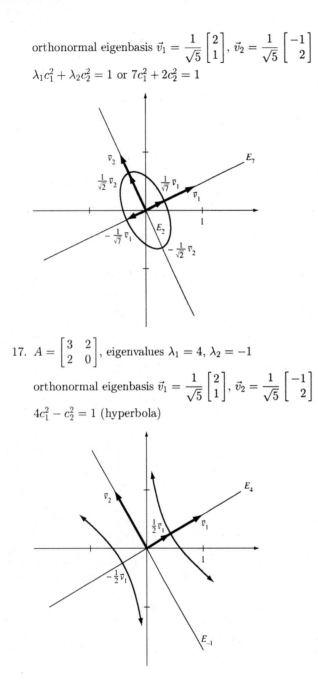

17. $A = \begin{bmatrix} 3 & 2 \\ 2 & 0 \end{bmatrix}$, eigenvalues $\lambda_1 = 4$, $\lambda_2 = -1$

orthonormal eigenbasis $\vec{v}_1 = \dfrac{1}{\sqrt{5}}\begin{bmatrix} 2 \\ 1 \end{bmatrix}$, $\vec{v}_2 = \dfrac{1}{\sqrt{5}}\begin{bmatrix} -1 \\ 2 \end{bmatrix}$

$4c_1^2 - c_2^2 = 1$ (hyperbola)

19. $A = \begin{bmatrix} 1 & 2 \\ 2 & 4 \end{bmatrix}$; eigenvalues $\lambda_1 = 5$, $\lambda_2 = 0$

   eigenvectors $\vec{v}_1 = \dfrac{1}{\sqrt{5}} \begin{bmatrix} 1 \\ 2 \end{bmatrix}$, $\vec{v}_2 = \dfrac{1}{\sqrt{5}} \begin{bmatrix} -2 \\ 1 \end{bmatrix}$

   $5c_1^2 = 1$ (a pair of lines)

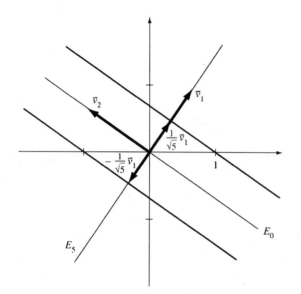

   Note that $(x_1^2 + 4x_1 x_2 + 4x_2^2) = (x_1 + 2x_2)^2 = 1$, so that $x_1 + 2x_2 = \pm 1$, and the two lines are

   $x_2 = \dfrac{1 - x_1}{2}$ and $x_2 = \dfrac{-1 - x_1}{2}$.

21. a. In each case, it is informative to think about the intersections with the three coordinate planes: $x_1 - x_2$, $x_1 - x_3$, and $x_2 - x_3$.

   For the surface $x_1^2 + 4x_2^2 + 9x_3^2 = 1$, all these intersections are *ellipses*, and the surface itself is an *ellipsoid*.

   This surface is connected and bounded; the points closest to the origin are $\pm \begin{bmatrix} 0 \\ 0 \\ \frac{1}{3} \end{bmatrix}$, and those

   farthest $\pm \begin{bmatrix} 1 \\ 0 \\ 0 \end{bmatrix}$.

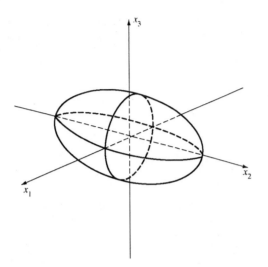

$x_1^2 + 4x_2^2 + 9x_3^2 = 1$ (not to scale)
an *ellipsoid*
In the case of $x_1^2 + 4x_2^2 - 9x_3^2 = 1$, the intersection with the $x_1 - x_2$ plane is an ellipse, and the two other intersections are hyperbolas. The surface is connected and not bounded; the points closest to the origin are $\pm \begin{bmatrix} 0 \\ \frac{1}{2} \\ 0 \end{bmatrix}$.

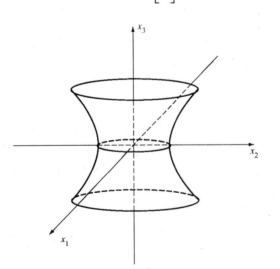

$x_1^2 + 4x_2^2 - 9x_3^2 = 1$ (not to scale)
a *hyperboloid of one sheet*

In the case $-x_1^2 - 4x_2^2 + 9x_3^2 = 1$, the intersection with the $x_1 - x_2$ plane is empty, and the two other intersections are hyperbolas. The surface consists of two pieces and is unbounded. The points closest to the origin are $\pm \begin{bmatrix} 0 \\ 0 \\ \frac{1}{3} \end{bmatrix}$.

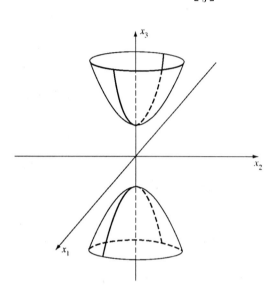

$-x_1^2 - 4x_2^2 + 9x_3^2 = 1$ (not to scale)
a *hyperboloid of two sheets*

b. $A = \begin{bmatrix} 1 & \frac{1}{2} & 1 \\ \frac{1}{2} & 2 & \frac{3}{2} \\ 1 & \frac{3}{2} & 3 \end{bmatrix}$ is positive definite, with three positive eigenvalues $\lambda_1, \lambda_2, \lambda_3$.

Surface is given by $\lambda_1 c_1^2 + \lambda_2 c_2^2 + \lambda_3 c_3^2 = 1$ with respect to principal axes, an *ellipsoid*. To find points closest to and farthest from origin, use technology to find eigenvalues and eigenvectors: eigenvalues: $\lambda_1 \approx 0.56, \lambda_2 \approx 4.44, \lambda_3 = 1$

unit eigenvectors: $\vec{v}_1 \approx \begin{bmatrix} 0.86 \\ 0.19 \\ -0.47 \end{bmatrix}, \vec{v}_2 \approx \begin{bmatrix} 0.31 \\ 0.54 \\ 0.78 \end{bmatrix}, \vec{v}_3 = \frac{1}{\sqrt{6}} \begin{bmatrix} 1 \\ -2 \\ 1 \end{bmatrix}$

Equation: $0.56 c_1^2 + 4.44 c_2^2 + c_3^2 = 1$

Farthest points when $c_1 = \pm \dfrac{1}{\sqrt{0.56}}$ and $c_2 = c_3 = 0$

Closest points when $c_2 = \pm \dfrac{1}{\sqrt{4.44}}$ and $c_1 = c_3 = 0$

$$\text{Farthest points} \approx \pm\frac{1}{\sqrt{0.56}} \begin{bmatrix} 0.86 \\ 0.19 \\ -0.47 \end{bmatrix} \approx \pm \begin{bmatrix} 1.15 \\ 0.26 \\ -0.63 \end{bmatrix}$$

$$\text{Closest points} \approx \pm\frac{1}{\sqrt{4.44}} \begin{bmatrix} 0.31 \\ 0.54 \\ 0.78 \end{bmatrix} \approx \pm \begin{bmatrix} 0.15 \\ 0.26 \\ 0.37 \end{bmatrix}$$

23. Yes; $M = \frac{1}{2}(A + A^T)$ is symmetric, and

$$\vec{x}^T M \vec{x} = \frac{1}{2}\vec{x}^T A \vec{x} + \frac{1}{2}\vec{x}^T A^T \vec{x} = \frac{1}{2}\vec{x}^T A \vec{x} + \frac{1}{2}\vec{x}^T A \vec{x} = \vec{x}^T A \vec{x}$$
$$\uparrow$$

Note that $\vec{x}^T A \vec{x}$ is a 1×1 matrix, so that $\vec{x}^T A \vec{x} = (\vec{x}^T A \vec{x})^T = \vec{x}^T A^T \vec{x}$.

25. $q(\vec{v}) = \vec{v} \cdot A\vec{v} = \vec{v} \cdot (\lambda\vec{v}) = \lambda(\vec{v} \cdot \vec{v}) = \lambda$
$$\uparrow$$
$$\vec{v} \text{ is a unit vector}$$

27. Let $\vec{v}_1, \ldots, \vec{v}_n$ be an orthonormal eigenbasis for A with $A\vec{v}_i = \lambda_i\vec{v}_i$. We know that $q(\vec{v}_i) = \lambda_i$ (see Exercise 25), so that $q(\vec{v}_1) = \lambda_1$ and $q(\vec{v}_n) = \lambda_n$ are in the image.

We claim that all numbers between λ_n and λ_1 are in the image as well. To see this, apply the Intermediate Value Theorem to the continuous function $f(t) = q((\cos t)\vec{v}_n + (\sin t)\vec{v}_1)$ on $\left[0, \frac{\pi}{2}\right]$ (note that $f(0) = q(\vec{v}_n) = \lambda_n$ and $f\left(\frac{\pi}{2}\right) = q(\vec{v}_1) = \lambda_1$).

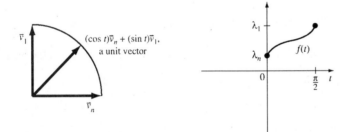

The Intermediate Value Theorem tells us that for any c between λ_n and λ_1, there is a t_0 such that $f(t_0) = q((\cos t_0)\vec{v}_n + (\sin t_0)\vec{v}_1) = c$. Note that $(\cos t_0)\vec{v}_n + (\sin t_0)\vec{v}_1$ is a unit vector. Now we will show that, conversely, $q(\vec{v})$ is on $[\lambda_n, \lambda_1]$ for all unit vectors $\vec{v}$. Write $\vec{v} = c_1\vec{v}_1 + \cdots + c_n\vec{v}_n$ and note that $\|\vec{v}\|^2 = c_1^2 + \cdots + c_n^2 = 1$. Then $q(\vec{v}) = \lambda_1 c_1^2 + \lambda_2 c_2^2 + \cdots + \lambda_n c_n^2 \leq \lambda_1 c_1^2 + \lambda_1 c_2^2 + \cdots + \lambda_1 c_n^2 = \lambda_1$. Likewise, $q(\vec{v}) \geq \lambda_n$. We have shown that the image of S^{n-1} under q is the closed interval $[\lambda_n, \lambda_1]$.

29. From Example 1 we have $S = \frac{1}{\sqrt{5}}\begin{bmatrix} 2 & 1 \\ -1 & 2 \end{bmatrix}$ and $D = \begin{bmatrix} 9 & 0 \\ 0 & 4 \end{bmatrix}$, so that $D_1 = \begin{bmatrix} 3 & 0 \\ 0 & 2 \end{bmatrix}$ and $B = SD_1 = \frac{1}{\sqrt{5}}\begin{bmatrix} 6 & 2 \\ -3 & 4 \end{bmatrix}$.

31. $S = \dfrac{1}{\sqrt{5}} \begin{bmatrix} 2 & 1 \\ -1 & 2 \end{bmatrix}$ and $D_1 = \begin{bmatrix} 3 & 0 \\ 0 & 2 \end{bmatrix}$ (see Exercise 29), so that $B = SD_1S^{-1} = \begin{bmatrix} 2.8 & -0.4 \\ -0.4 & 2.2 \end{bmatrix}$.

33. Use the formulas for x, y, z derived in Exercise 32.

$$x = \sqrt{a} = \sqrt{8} = 2\sqrt{2}$$

$$y = \frac{b}{\sqrt{a}} = -\frac{2}{2\sqrt{2}} = -\frac{1}{\sqrt{2}}$$

$$z = \sqrt{\frac{ac - b^2}{a}} = \sqrt{\frac{36}{8}} = \frac{3}{\sqrt{2}}, \text{ so that}$$

$$L = \begin{bmatrix} 2\sqrt{2} & 0 \\ -\frac{1}{\sqrt{2}} & \frac{3}{\sqrt{2}} \end{bmatrix}.$$

35. Solve the system $\begin{bmatrix} 4 & -4 & 8 \\ -4 & 13 & 1 \\ 8 & 1 & 26 \end{bmatrix} = \begin{bmatrix} x & 0 & 0 \\ y & w & 0 \\ z & t & s \end{bmatrix} \begin{bmatrix} x & y & z \\ 0 & w & t \\ 0 & 0 & s \end{bmatrix}$

$$\left. \begin{array}{l} x^2 = 4, \text{ so } x = 2 \\ 2y = -4, \text{ so } y = -2 \\ 2z = 8, \text{ so } z = 4 \\ 4 + w^2 = 13, \text{ so } w = 3 \\ -8 + 3t = 1, \text{ so } t = 3 \\ 16 + 9 + s^2 = 26, \text{ so } s = 1 \end{array} \right\} L = \begin{bmatrix} 2 & 0 & 0 \\ -2 & 3 & 0 \\ 4 & 3 & 1 \end{bmatrix}$$

37. $\dfrac{\partial q}{\partial x_1} = 2ax_1 + bx_2$ and $\dfrac{\partial q}{\partial x_2} = bx_1 + 2cx_2$, so that $q_{11} = \dfrac{\partial^2 q}{\partial x_1^2} = 2a$, $q_{22} = \dfrac{\partial^2 q}{\partial x_2^2} = 2c$, and $q_{12} = \dfrac{\partial^2 q}{\partial x_1 \partial x_2} = b$, and $D = \det \begin{bmatrix} q_{11} & q_{12} \\ q_{12} & q_{22} \end{bmatrix} = \det \begin{bmatrix} 2a & b \\ b & 2c \end{bmatrix} = 4ac - b^2 > 0$.

The matrix $A = \begin{bmatrix} a & \frac{b}{2} \\ \frac{b}{2} & c \end{bmatrix}$ of q is positive definite, since $a > 0$ and $\det(A) = \frac{1}{4}D > 0$. This means, by definition, that q has a minimum at $\vec{0}$, since $q(\vec{x}) > 0 = q(\vec{0})$ for all $\vec{x} \neq \vec{0}$.

39. If $\vec{v}_1, \ldots, \vec{v}_n$ is such a basis consisting of unit vectors, and we let $A = [\vec{v}_1 \cdots \vec{v}_n]$, then

$$A^T A = \begin{bmatrix} 1 & \cos\alpha & \cdots & \cos\alpha \\ \cos\alpha & \vdots & \cdots & \cos\alpha \\ \vdots & \vdots & \ddots & \vdots \\ \cos\alpha & \cos\alpha & \cdots & 1 \end{bmatrix} \text{ is positive definite, so that } 1 - \cos\alpha > 0 \text{ and } 1 + (n-1)$$

$\cos\alpha > 0$ or $1 > \cos\alpha > \dfrac{1}{1-n}$ or $0 < \alpha < \arccos\left(\dfrac{1}{1-n}\right)$.

Conversely, if α is in this range, then the matrix $\begin{bmatrix} 1 & \cos\alpha & \cdots & \cos\alpha \\ \cos\alpha & \vdots & & \cos\alpha \\ \vdots & \vdots & \ddots & \vdots \\ \cos\alpha & \cos\alpha & \cdots & 1 \end{bmatrix}$ is positive definite, so that it has a Cholesky factorization LL^T. The columns of L^T give us a basis with the desired property.

41. The functions x_1^2, x_1x_2, x_2^2 form a basis of Q_2, so that $\dim(Q_2) = 3$.

43. Note that $T(ax_1^2 + bx_1x_2 + cx_2^2) = ax_1^2$ (we let $x_2 = 0$). Thus $\text{im}(T) = \text{span}(x_1^2)$, $\text{rank}(T) = 1$, $\ker(T) = \text{span}(x_1x_2, x_2^2)$, $\text{nullity}(T) = 2$.

45. Note that $T(ax_1^2 + bx_2^2 + cx_3^2 + dx_1x_2 + ex_1x_3 + fx_2x_3) = ax_1^2 + b + c + dx_1 + ex_1 + f$ (we let $x_2 = x_3 = 1$). Thus $\text{im}(T) = P_2$ and $\text{rank}(T) = 3$. The kernel of T consists of the quadratic forms with $a = 0$, $d + e = 0$, and $b + c + f = 0$ (consider the coefficients of x_1^2, x_1, and 1). The general element of the kernel is $q(x_1, x_2, x_3) = (-c - f)x_2^2 + cx_3^2 - ex_1x_2 + ex_1x_3 + fx_2x_3 = c(x_3^2 - x_2^2) + e(x_1x_3 - x_1x_2) + f(x_2x_3 - x_2^2)$. Thus $\ker(T) = \text{span}(x_3^2 - x_2^2, x_1x_3 - x_1x_2, x_2x_3 - x_2^2)$ and $\text{nullity}(T) = 3$.

47. $T(A + B)(\vec{x}) = \vec{x}^T(A + B)\vec{x} = \vec{x}^T A\vec{x} + \vec{x}^T B\vec{x}$ equals $(T(A) + T(B))(\vec{x}) = T(A)(\vec{x}) + T(B)(\vec{x}) = \vec{x}^T A\vec{x} + \vec{x}^T B\vec{x}$. The verification of the second axiom of linearity is analogous.

By definition of a quadratic form, $\text{im}(T) = Q_n$: For every quadratic form q in Q_n there is a *symmetric* $n \times n$ matrix A such that $q = T(A)$. Thus, the rank of T is $\dim(Q_n) = n(n + 1)/2$ (see Exercise 42).

By the rank nullity theorem,

$$\text{nullity}(T) = \dim(\mathbb{R}^{n \times n}) - \text{rank}(T) = n^2 - \frac{n(n + 1)}{2} = \frac{n(n - 1)}{2}$$

Next, let's think about the kernel of T. In our solution to Exercise 23 we observed that $T(A) = T(\frac{1}{2}(A + A^T))$; note that matrix $\frac{1}{2}(A + A^T)$ is symmetric. Now $\frac{1}{2}(A + A^T) = 0$ if (and only if) $A^T = -A$, that is, if A is skew-symmetric. Thus the skew-symmetric matrices are in the kernel of T. Since the space of skew-symmetric matrices has the same dimension as $\ker(T)$, namely, $n(n - 1)/2$, we can conclude that $\ker(T)$ consists of all skew-symmetric $n \times n$ matrices.

49. The matrix of T with respect to the basis x_1^2, x_1x_2, x_2^2 is $A = \begin{bmatrix} 1 & 0 & 0 \\ 0 & 2 & 0 \\ 0 & 0 & 4 \end{bmatrix}$, with the eigenvalues 1,2,4 and corresponding eigenvectors $\begin{bmatrix} 1 \\ 0 \\ 0 \end{bmatrix}, \begin{bmatrix} 0 \\ 1 \\ 0 \end{bmatrix}, \begin{bmatrix} 0 \\ 0 \\ 1 \end{bmatrix}$. Thus x_1^2, x_1x_2, x_2^2 are eigenfunctions with eigenvalues 1, 2, and 4, respectively. Yes, T is diagonalizable, since there is an eigenbasis.

51. If B is negative definite, then $A = -B$ is positive definite, so that the determinants of all principal submatrices $A^{(m)}$ are positive. Thus $\det(B^{(m)}) = \det(-A^{(m)}) = (-1)^m \det(A^{(m)})$ is positive for even m and negative for odd m.

8.3

1. $\sigma_1 = 2, \sigma_2 = 1$

3. $A^T A = I_n$; the eigenvalues of $A^T A$ are all 1, so that the singular values of A are all 1.

5. $A^T A = \begin{bmatrix} p^2 + q^2 & 0 \\ 0 & p^2 + q^2 \end{bmatrix}$, with eigenvalues $\lambda_1 = \lambda_2 = p^2 + q^2$. The singular values of A are $\sigma_1 = \sigma_2 = \sqrt{p^2 + q^2}$. A represents a rotation-dilation, with dilation factor $\sqrt{p^2 + q^2}$, so that the image of the unit circle is a circle with radius $\sqrt{p^2 + q^2}$.

7. $A^T A = \begin{bmatrix} 1 & 0 \\ 0 & 4 \end{bmatrix}$

   $\lambda_1 = 4, \lambda_2 = 1$; $\sigma_1 = 2, \sigma_2 = 1$

   eigenvectors of $A^T A$: $\vec{v}_1 = \begin{bmatrix} 0 \\ 1 \end{bmatrix}$, $\vec{v}_2 = \begin{bmatrix} 1 \\ 0 \end{bmatrix}$, $\vec{u}_1 = \frac{1}{\sigma_1}(A\vec{v}_1) = \begin{bmatrix} 0 \\ -1 \end{bmatrix}$, $\vec{u}_2 = \frac{1}{\sigma_2}(A\vec{v}_2) = \begin{bmatrix} 1 \\ 0 \end{bmatrix}$, so that

   $U = \begin{bmatrix} 0 & 1 \\ -1 & 0 \end{bmatrix}$, $\sum = \begin{bmatrix} 2 & 0 \\ 0 & 1 \end{bmatrix}$, $V = \begin{bmatrix} 0 & 1 \\ 1 & 0 \end{bmatrix}$.

9. $A^T A = \begin{bmatrix} 5 & 10 \\ 10 & 20 \end{bmatrix}$ (See Exercise 6)

   $\lambda_1 = 25$, $\lambda_2 = 0$; $\sigma_1 = 5$, $\sigma_2 = 0$; eigenvectors of $A^T A$: $\vec{v}_1 = \frac{1}{\sqrt{5}} \begin{bmatrix} 1 \\ 2 \end{bmatrix}$, $\vec{v}_2 = \frac{1}{\sqrt{5}} \begin{bmatrix} -2 \\ 1 \end{bmatrix}$, $\vec{u}_1 = \frac{1}{\sigma_1} A\vec{v}_1 = \frac{1}{\sqrt{5}} \begin{bmatrix} 1 \\ 2 \end{bmatrix}$, $\vec{u}_2 = $ a unit vector orthogonal to

   $\vec{u}_1 = \frac{1}{\sqrt{5}} \begin{bmatrix} -2 \\ 1 \end{bmatrix}$ so that $U = V = \frac{1}{\sqrt{5}} \begin{bmatrix} 1 & -2 \\ 2 & 1 \end{bmatrix}$, $\sum = \begin{bmatrix} 5 & 0 \\ 0 & 0 \end{bmatrix}$.

11. $A^T A = \begin{bmatrix} 1 & 0 \\ 0 & 4 \end{bmatrix}$; $\lambda_1 = 4, \lambda_2 = 1$; $\sigma_1 = 2, \sigma_2 = 1$

    eigenvectors of $A^T A$: $\vec{v}_1 = \begin{bmatrix} 0 \\ 1 \end{bmatrix}$, $\vec{v}_2 = \begin{bmatrix} 1 \\ 0 \end{bmatrix}$, $\vec{u}_1 = \frac{1}{\sigma_1} A\vec{v}_1 = \begin{bmatrix} 0 \\ 1 \\ 0 \end{bmatrix}$, $\vec{u}_2 = \frac{1}{\sigma_2} A\vec{v}_2 = \begin{bmatrix} 1 \\ 0 \\ 0 \end{bmatrix}$, $\vec{u}_3 = \begin{bmatrix} 0 \\ 0 \\ 1 \end{bmatrix}$,

    $U = \begin{bmatrix} 0 & 1 & 0 \\ 1 & 0 & 0 \\ 0 & 0 & 1 \end{bmatrix}$, $\sum = \begin{bmatrix} 2 & 0 \\ 0 & 1 \end{bmatrix}$, $V = \begin{bmatrix} 0 & 1 \\ 1 & 0 \end{bmatrix}$.

13. $A^T A = \begin{bmatrix} 37 & 16 \\ 16 & 13 \end{bmatrix}$; $\lambda_1 = 45, \lambda_2 = 5$; $\sigma_1 = 3\sqrt{5}, \sigma_2 = \sqrt{5}$

    eigenvectors of $A^T A$: $\vec{v}_1 = \frac{1}{\sqrt{5}} \begin{bmatrix} 2 \\ 1 \end{bmatrix}$, $\vec{v}_2 = \frac{1}{\sqrt{5}} \begin{bmatrix} -1 \\ 2 \end{bmatrix}$, $\vec{u}_1 = \frac{1}{\sigma_1} A\vec{v}_1 = \begin{bmatrix} 1 \\ 0 \end{bmatrix}$, $\vec{v}_2 = \frac{1}{\sigma_2} A\vec{v}_2 = \begin{bmatrix} 0 \\ 1 \end{bmatrix}$,

    so that
    $U = \begin{bmatrix} 1 & 0 \\ 0 & 1 \end{bmatrix}$, $\sum = \begin{bmatrix} 3\sqrt{5} & 0 \\ 0 & \sqrt{5} \end{bmatrix}$, $V = \frac{1}{\sqrt{5}} \begin{bmatrix} 2 & -1 \\ 1 & 2 \end{bmatrix}$.

15. If $A\vec{v}_1 = \sigma_1 \vec{u}_1$ and $A\vec{v}_2 = \sigma_2 \vec{u}_2$, then $A^{-1} \vec{u}_1 = \frac{1}{\sigma_1} \vec{v}_1$ and $A^{-1} \vec{u}_2 = \frac{1}{\sigma_2} \vec{v}_2$, so that the singular values of A^{-1} are the reciprocals of the singular values of A. See Exercise 16 for a more detailed explanation.

17. We need to check that $A\left(\dfrac{\vec{b}\cdot\vec{u}_1}{\sigma_1}\vec{v}_1 + \cdots + \dfrac{\vec{b}\cdot\vec{u}_n}{\sigma_n}\vec{v}_n\right) = \mathrm{proj}_{\mathrm{im}A}\vec{b}$ (see page 214 of the text).

But $A\left(\dfrac{\vec{b}\cdot\vec{u}_1}{\sigma_1}\vec{v}_1 + \cdots + \dfrac{\vec{b}\cdot\vec{u}_n}{\sigma_n}\vec{v}_n\right) = \dfrac{\vec{b}\cdot\vec{u}_1}{\sigma_1}A\vec{v}_1 + \cdots + \dfrac{\vec{b}\cdot\vec{u}_n}{\sigma_n}A\vec{v}_n = (b\cdot\vec{u}_1)\vec{u}_1 + \cdots + (\vec{b}\cdot\vec{u}_n)\vec{u}_n$

$= \mathrm{proj}_{\mathrm{im}A}\vec{b}$, since $\vec{v}_1,\ldots,\vec{v}_n$ is an orthonormal basis of $\mathrm{im}(A)$ (see Fact 5.1.6).

19. $\vec{x} = c_1\vec{v}_1 + \cdots + c_n\vec{v}_n$ is a least-squares solution if $A\vec{x} = c_1 A\vec{v}_1 + \cdots + c_n A\vec{v}_n = c_1\sigma_1\vec{u}_1 + \cdots + c_r\sigma_r\vec{u}_r = \mathrm{proj}_{\mathrm{im}A}\vec{b}$. But $\mathrm{proj}_{\mathrm{im}A}\vec{b} = (\vec{b}\cdot\vec{u}_1)\vec{u}_1 + \cdots + (\vec{b}\cdot\vec{u}_r)\vec{u}_r$, since $\vec{u}_1,\ldots,\vec{u}_r$ is an orthonormal basis of $\mathrm{im}(A)$. Comparing the coefficients of $\vec{u}_i$ above we find that it is required that $c_i\sigma_i = \vec{b}\cdot\vec{u}_i$ or $c_i = \dfrac{\vec{b}\cdot\vec{u}_i}{\sigma_i}$, for $i = 1,\ldots,r$, while no condition is imposed on $c_{r+1},\ldots,c_n$. The least-squares solutions are of the form $\vec{x}^* = \dfrac{b\cdot\vec{u}_1}{\sigma_1}\vec{v}_1 + \cdots + \dfrac{\vec{b}\cdot\vec{u}_r}{\sigma_r}\vec{v}_r + c_{r+1}\vec{v}_{r+1} + \cdots c_n\vec{v}_n$, where $c_{r+1},\ldots,c_n$ are arbitrary (see Exercise 17 for a special case).

21. $A = \underbrace{\dfrac{1}{\sqrt{5}}\begin{bmatrix} 1 & 2 \\ -2 & 1 \end{bmatrix}}_{U}\underbrace{\begin{bmatrix} 10 & 0 \\ 0 & 5 \end{bmatrix}}_{\Sigma}\underbrace{\left(\dfrac{1}{\sqrt{5}}\begin{bmatrix} 2 & -1 \\ 1 & 2 \end{bmatrix}\right)}_{V^T}$

$= \underbrace{\dfrac{1}{\sqrt{5}}\begin{bmatrix} 1 & 2 \\ -2 & 1 \end{bmatrix}\left(\dfrac{1}{\sqrt{5}}\begin{bmatrix} 2 & -1 \\ 1 & 2 \end{bmatrix}\right)}_{U \quad\quad V^T}\underbrace{\left(\dfrac{1}{\sqrt{5}}\begin{bmatrix} 2 & 1 \\ -1 & 2 \end{bmatrix}\right)}_{V}\underbrace{\begin{bmatrix} 10 & 0 \\ 0 & 5 \end{bmatrix}}_{\Sigma}\underbrace{\left(\dfrac{1}{\sqrt{5}}\begin{bmatrix} 2 & -1 \\ 1 & 2 \end{bmatrix}\right)}_{V^T}$

$= \underbrace{\dfrac{1}{5}\begin{bmatrix} 4 & 3 \\ -3 & 4 \end{bmatrix}}_{Q}\underbrace{\begin{bmatrix} 9 & -2 \\ -2 & 6 \end{bmatrix}}_{S}$

23. $AA^T U = U\sum V^T V\sum^T U^T U = U\sum\sum^T$, since $V^T V = I_n$ and $U^T U = I_m$, so that

$AA^T\vec{u}_i = \begin{cases} \sigma_i^2\vec{u}_i & \text{for } i = 1,\ldots,r \\ \vec{0} & \text{for } i = r+1,\ldots,m \end{cases}$

The *nonzero* eigenvalues of $A^T A$ and AA^T are the same.

25.

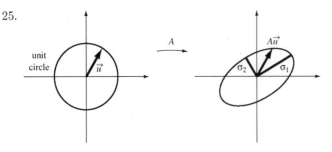

Algebraically: Write $\vec{u} = c_1\vec{v}_1 + c_2\vec{v}_2$ and note that $\|\vec{u}\|^2 = c_1^2 + c_2^2 = 1$.
Then $A\vec{u} = c_1\sigma_1\vec{u}_1 + c_2\sigma_2\vec{u}_2$, so that $\|A\vec{u}\|^2 = c_1^2\sigma_1^2 + c_2^2\sigma_2^2 \geq c_1^2\sigma_2^2 + c_2^2\sigma_2^2 = \sigma_2^2$ and $\|A\vec{u}\| \geq \sigma_2$. Likewise $\|A\vec{u}\| \leq \sigma_1$.

27. Let $\vec{v}$ be a unit eigenvector with eigenvalue λ and use Exercise 26.

29. $$A = U\sum V^T = [\vec{u}_1 \cdots \vec{u}_r \cdots] \begin{bmatrix} \sigma_1 & & & & 0 \\ & \ddots & & & \\ & & \sigma_r & & \\ & & & \ddots & \\ 0 & & & & 0 \end{bmatrix} \begin{bmatrix} \vec{v}_1^T \\ \vdots \\ \vec{v}_r^T \\ \vdots \end{bmatrix} = [\vec{u}_1 \cdots \vec{u}_r \cdots] \begin{bmatrix} \sigma_1\vec{v}_1^T \\ \vdots \\ \sigma_r\vec{v}_r^T \\ 0 \end{bmatrix}$$

$$= \sigma_1\vec{u}_1\vec{v}_1^T + \cdots + \sigma_r\vec{u}_r\vec{v}_r^T$$

31. The formula $A = \sigma_1\vec{u}_1\vec{v}_1^T + \cdots + \sigma_r\vec{u}_r\vec{v}_r^T$ gives such a representation.

33. *Yes*; since A^TA is diagonalizable and has only 1 as an eigenvalue, we must have $A^TA = I_n$.

35. We will freely use the diagram on page 392 (with $r = n$). We have $A^TA\vec{v}_i = A^T(\sigma_i\vec{u}_i) = \sigma_i^2\vec{v}_i$ and therefore $(A^TA)^{-1}\vec{v}_i = \frac{1}{\sigma_i^2}\vec{v}_i$ for $i = 1,\ldots,n$. Then $(A^TA)^{-1}A^T\vec{u}_i = (A^TA)^{-1}(\sigma_i\vec{v}_i) = \frac{1}{\sigma_i}\vec{v}_i$ for $i = 1,\ldots,n$ and $(A^TA)^{-1}A^T\vec{u}_i = \vec{0}$ for $i = n+1,\ldots,m$ since $\vec{u}_i$ is in $\ker(A^T)$ in this case. Note that $(A^TA)^{-1}A^T\vec{u}_i$ is the least-squares solution of the equation $A\vec{x} = \vec{u}_i$; for $i = 1,\ldots,n$ this is the exact solution since $\vec{u}_i$ is in $\text{im}(A)$.

True or False

1. T, by the spectral theorem (Fact 8.1.1)

3. F. The orthogonal matrix $A = \begin{bmatrix} 0 & -1 \\ 1 & 0 \end{bmatrix}$ fails to be diagonalizable (over $\mathbb{R}$).

5. F. The last term, $5x_2$, does not have the form required in Definition 8.2.1

7. T, by Fact 8.2.4.

9. T. If $D = \begin{bmatrix} \lambda_1 & . & 0 \\ . & . & . \\ 0 & . & \lambda_n \end{bmatrix}$, then $D^TD = D^2 = \begin{bmatrix} \lambda_1^2 & . & 0 \\ . & . & . \\ 0 & . & \lambda_n^2 \end{bmatrix}$. The eigenvalues of D^TD are $\lambda_1^2,\ldots,\lambda_n^2$, and the singular values of D are $\sqrt{\lambda_1^2} = |\lambda_1|,\ldots,\sqrt{\lambda_n^2} = |\lambda_n|$.

11. F. Consider $A = \begin{bmatrix} 0 & -1 \\ 1 & 0 \end{bmatrix}$.

13. T, by Fact 8.2.4: all the eigenvalues are positive.

15. F. Consider the shear matrix $A = \begin{bmatrix} 1 & 1 \\ 0 & 1 \end{bmatrix}$. The unit circle isn't mapped into itself, so that the singular values fail to be 1, 1.

17. T, by Fact 8.3.2

19. T, by Fact 8.1.2

21. F. As a counterexample, consider $A = B = 2I_n$.

23. T. By Fact 7.3.8, matrices A and B have the same eigenvalues. Now use Fact 8.2.4.

25. F. Let $A = I_2$, $\vec{v} = \begin{bmatrix} 1 \\ 0 \end{bmatrix}$, $\vec{w} = \begin{bmatrix} 1 \\ 1 \end{bmatrix}$.

27. T. By the spectral theorem, A is diagonalizable: $S^{-1}AS = D$ for some invertible S and a diagonal D. Now $D^n = S^{-1}A^nS = S^{-1}0S = 0$, so that $D = 0$ (since D is diagonal). Finally, $A = SDS^{-1} = S0S^{-1} = 0$, as claimed.

29. T. The eigenvalues $\lambda_1, \ldots, \lambda_n$ of A are nonzero, since A is invertible, so that the eigenvalues $\lambda_1^2, \ldots, \lambda_n^2$ of A^2 are positive. Now use Fact 8.2.4.

31. F. For example, $(x_1^2)(x_2 x_3)$ fails to be a quadratic form.

33. F. Consider $A = \begin{bmatrix} -1 & 0 & 0 \\ 0 & 1 & 0 \\ 0 & 0 & 1 \end{bmatrix}$, which is indefinite.

35. T, since $\vec{x} \cdot A\vec{x}$ is positive, so that $\cos\alpha$ is positive, where α is the angle enclosed by $\vec{x}$ and $A\vec{x}$.

37. F. Consider $A = \begin{bmatrix} 0 & 1 \\ 0 & 0 \end{bmatrix}$.

39. F. Let $A = \begin{bmatrix} 0 & 1 \\ 0 & 0 \end{bmatrix}$ and $B = \begin{bmatrix} 1 & 0 \\ 0 & 0 \end{bmatrix}$. Then 1 is a singular value of BA but not of AB

41. T. The quadratic form $q(x_1, x_2) = \begin{bmatrix} x_1 & 0 & x_2 \end{bmatrix} \begin{bmatrix} a & b & c \\ b & d & e \\ c & e & f \end{bmatrix} \begin{bmatrix} x_1 \\ 0 \\ x_2 \end{bmatrix} = ax_1^2 + 2cx_1 x_2 + fx_2^2$ is positive definite. The matrix of this quadratic form is $A = \begin{bmatrix} a & c \\ c & f \end{bmatrix}$, and $\det(A) = af - c^2 > 0$ since A is positive definite. Thus $af > c^2$, as claimed.

43. F. Consider the indefinite matrix $A = \begin{bmatrix} 1 & 0 \\ 0 & -1 \end{bmatrix}$.

45. T, since $\vec{x}^T A^2 \vec{x} = -\vec{x}^T A^T A \vec{x} = -(A\vec{x})^T A\vec{x} = -\|A\vec{x}\|^2 \leq 0$ for all $\vec{x}$.

47. F. Note that the columns of S must be unit eigenvectors of A. There are two distinct real eigen-values, λ_1, λ_2, and for each of them there are two unit eigenvectors, $\pm\vec{v}_1$ (for λ_1) and $\pm\vec{v}_2$ (for λ_2). (Draw a sketch!) Thus there are 8 matrices S, namely $S = [\pm\vec{v}_1 \quad \pm\vec{v}_2]$ and $S = [\pm\vec{v}_2 \quad \pm\vec{v}_1]$

49. F. Some eigenvalues of A may be negative.

51. T. Let $\vec{v}_1, \vec{v}_2$ be an orthonormal eigenbasis, with $A\vec{v}_1 = \vec{v}_1$ and $A\vec{v}_2 = 2\vec{v}_2$. Consider a nonzero vector $\vec{x} = c_1\vec{v}_1 + c_2\vec{v}_2$; then $A\vec{x} = c_1\vec{v}_1 + 2c_2\vec{v}_2$. If $c_1 = 0$, then $\vec{x} = c_2\vec{v}_2$ and $A\vec{x} = 2c_2\vec{v}_2$ are parallel, and we are all set. Now consider the case when $c_1 \neq 0$. Then the angle between $\vec{x}$ and $A\vec{x}$ is $\arctan(2c_2/c_1) - \arctan(c_2/c_1)$; to see this, subtract the angle between $\vec{v}_1$ and $\vec{x}$ from the angle between $\vec{v}_1$ and $A\vec{x}$ (draw a sketch). Let $m = c_2/c_1$ and use calculus to see that the function $f(m) = \arctan(2m) - \arctan(m)$ assumes its global maximum at $m = \dfrac{1}{\sqrt{2}}$. The maximal angle between $\vec{x}$ and $A\vec{x}$ is $\arctan(\sqrt{2}) - \arctan(1/\sqrt{2}) < 0.34 < \pi/6$.

53. T. We need to show that each entry $a_{ij} = a_{ji}$ off the diagonal is smaller than some entry on the diagonal. Now $(\vec{e}_i - \vec{e}_j)^T A(\vec{e}_i - \vec{e}_j) = a_{ii} + a_{jj} - 2a_{ij} > 0$, so that $a_{ii} + a_{jj} > 2a_{ij}$. Thus the larger of the diagonal entries a_{ii} and a_{jj} must exceed a_{ij}.

Chapter 9

9.1

1. $x(t) = 7e^{5t}$, by Fact 9.1.1.

3. $P(t) = 7e^{0.03t}$, by Fact 9.1.1.

5. $y(t) = -0.8e^{0.8t}$, by Fact 9.1.1.

7. $x^{-2}\,dx = dt$
   $-x^{-1} = t + C$
   $-\dfrac{1}{x} = t + C$, and $-1 = 0 + C$, so that
   $-\dfrac{1}{x} = t - 1$
   $x(t) = \dfrac{1}{1-t}$; note that $\lim_{x \to 1^-} x(t) = \infty$.

9. $x^{-k}\,dx = dt$
   $\dfrac{1}{1-k}x^{1-k} = t + C$, and $\dfrac{1}{1-k} = C$, so that
   $\dfrac{1}{1-k}x^{1-k} = t + \dfrac{1}{1-k}$
   $x^{1-k} = (1-k)t + 1$
   $x(t) = ((1-k)t + 1)^{1/1-k}$.

11. $\dfrac{dx}{1+x^2} = dt$
    $\arctan(x) = t + C$ and $C = 0$.
    $x(t) = \tan(t)$ for $|t| < \dfrac{\pi}{2}$.

13. a. The debt in millions is $0.45(1.06)^{212} \approx 104245$, or about 100 billion dollars.

    b. The debt in millions is $0.45e^{0.06 \cdot 212} \approx 150466$, or about 150 billion dollars.

15. If $P(t) = P_0 \cdot e^{\frac{k}{100}t}$, then the doubling time T satisfies the equation $P(T) = P_0 \cdot e^{\frac{k}{100}T} = 2P_0$ or $e^{\frac{k}{100}T} = 2$ or $\dfrac{k}{100}T = \ln(2)$ or $T = \dfrac{100}{k} \cdot \ln(2) \approx \dfrac{69}{k}$ since $\ln(2) \approx 0.69$.

17.

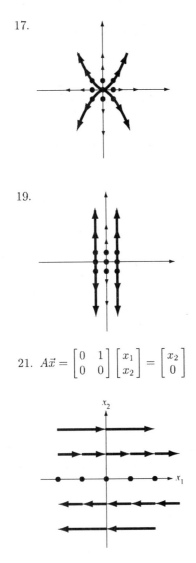

19.

21. $A\vec{x} = \begin{bmatrix} 0 & 1 \\ 0 & 0 \end{bmatrix} \begin{bmatrix} x_1 \\ x_2 \end{bmatrix} = \begin{bmatrix} x_2 \\ 0 \end{bmatrix}$

The trajectories will be horizontal lines. If we start at $\begin{bmatrix} p \\ q \end{bmatrix}$, then the horizontal velocity will be q, so that $\vec{x}(t) = \begin{bmatrix} x_1(t) \\ x_2(t) \end{bmatrix} = \begin{bmatrix} p + qt \\ q \end{bmatrix}$. We can verify that $\dfrac{d\vec{x}}{dt} = \begin{bmatrix} q \\ 0 \end{bmatrix}$ equals $\begin{bmatrix} 0 & 1 \\ 0 & 0 \end{bmatrix} \vec{x}(t) = \begin{bmatrix} q \\ 0 \end{bmatrix}$, as claimed.

23. We are told that $\dfrac{d\vec{x}_1}{dt} = A\vec{x}_1$. Let $\vec{x}(t) = k\vec{x}_1(t)$. Then $\dfrac{d\vec{x}}{dt} = \dfrac{d}{dt}(k\vec{x}_1) = k\dfrac{d\vec{x}_1}{dt} = kA\vec{x}_1 = A(k\vec{x}_1) = A\vec{x}$, as claimed.

25. We are told that $\frac{d\vec{x}}{dt} = A\vec{x}$. Let $\vec{c}(t) = \vec{x}(kt)$. Using the chain rule we find that $\frac{d\vec{c}}{dt} = \frac{d}{dt}(\vec{x}(kt)) =$
$k\frac{d\vec{x}}{dt}\Big|_{kt} = kA(\vec{x}(kt)) = kA\vec{c}(t)$, as claimed.
    To get the vector field $kA\vec{c}$ we scale the vectors of the field $A\vec{x}$ by k.

27. Use Fact 9.1.2.
    The eigenvalues of $A = \begin{bmatrix} -4 & 3 \\ 2 & -3 \end{bmatrix}$ are $\lambda_1 = -6$ and $\lambda_2 = -1$, with associated eigenvectors $\vec{v}_1 = \begin{bmatrix} -3 \\ 2 \end{bmatrix}$ and $\vec{v}_2 = \begin{bmatrix} 1 \\ 1 \end{bmatrix}$. The coordinates of $\vec{x}(0) = \begin{bmatrix} 1 \\ 0 \end{bmatrix}$ with respect to $\vec{v}_1$ and $\vec{v}_2$ are $c_1 = -\frac{1}{5}$ and $c_2 = \frac{2}{5}$.
    By Fact 9.1.2 the solution is $\vec{x}(t) = -\frac{1}{5}e^{-6t}\begin{bmatrix} -3 \\ 2 \end{bmatrix} + \frac{2}{5}e^{-t}\begin{bmatrix} 1 \\ 1 \end{bmatrix}$.

29. $\lambda_1 = 0,\ \lambda_2 = 5;\ \vec{v}_1 = \begin{bmatrix} -2 \\ 1 \end{bmatrix},\ \vec{v}_2 = \begin{bmatrix} 1 \\ 2 \end{bmatrix};\ c_1 = -2,\ c_2 = 1,$ so that $\vec{x}(t) = -2\begin{bmatrix} -2 \\ 1 \end{bmatrix} + e^{5t}\begin{bmatrix} 1 \\ 2 \end{bmatrix} = \begin{bmatrix} 4 \\ -2 \end{bmatrix} + e^{5t}\begin{bmatrix} 1 \\ 2 \end{bmatrix}$.

31. $\lambda_1 = 1,\ \lambda_2 = 6,\ \lambda_3 = 0;\ \vec{v}_1 = \begin{bmatrix} 1 \\ -2 \\ 1 \end{bmatrix}$. Since $\vec{x}(0) = \vec{v}_1$ we need not find $\vec{v}_2$ and $\vec{v}_3$.
    $c_1 = 1, c_2 = c_3 = 0$, so that $\vec{x}(t) = e^t\begin{bmatrix} 1 \\ -2 \\ 1 \end{bmatrix}$.

    In Exercises 32 to 35, find the eigenvalues and eigenspaces. Then determine the direction of the flow along the eigenspaces (outward if $\lambda > 0$ and inward if $\lambda < 0$). Use Figure 11 of Section 9.1 as a guide to sketch the other trajectories.

33.

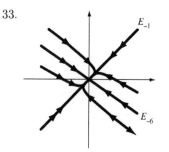

See Exercise 27.

35.

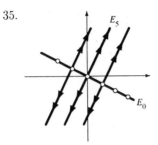

See Exercises 29 and 30.
In Exercises 36 to 39, find the eigenvalues and eigenspaces (the eigenvalues will always be positive). Then determine the direction of the flow along the eigenspaces (outward if $\lambda > 1$ and inward if $1 > \lambda > 0$). Use Figure 11 of Section 7.1 as a guide to sketch the other trajectories.

37.

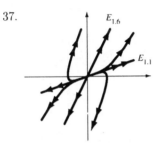

39.

41. The trajectories are of the form $\vec{x}(t) = c_1 e^{\lambda_1 t}\vec{v}_1 + c_2 e^{\lambda_2 t}\vec{v}_2 = c_1\vec{v}_1 + c_2 e^{\lambda_2 t}\vec{v}_2$.

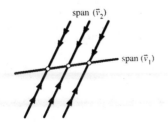

43. a. These two species are *competing* as each is hindered by the other (consider the terms $-y$ and $-2x$).

   b.

   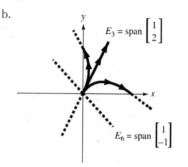

   Although only the first quadrant is relevant for our model, it is useful to consider the phase portrait in the other quadrants as well.

   c. If $\dfrac{y(0)}{x(0)} > 2$ then species y wins (x will die out); if $\dfrac{y(0)}{x(0)} < 2$ then x wins. If $\dfrac{y(0)}{x(0)} = 2$ then both will prosper and $\dfrac{y(t)}{x(t)} = 2$ for all t.

45. a. Species y has the more vicious fighters, since they kill members of species x at a rate of 4 per time unit, while the fighters of species x only kill at a rate of 1.

   b.

   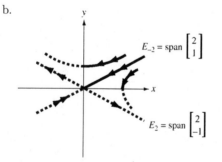

   c. If $\dfrac{y(0)}{x(0)} < \dfrac{1}{2}$ then x wins; if $\dfrac{y(0)}{x(0)} > \dfrac{1}{2}$ then y wins; if $\dfrac{y(0)}{x(0)} = \dfrac{1}{2}$ nobody will survive the battle.

47. a. The two species are in symbiosis: Each is helped by the other (consider the terms kx and ky).

   b. $\lambda_{1,2} = \dfrac{-5 \pm \sqrt{9 + 4k^2}}{2}$

   Both eigenvalues are negative if $\sqrt{9 + 4k^2} < 5$ or $9 + 4k^2 < 25$ or $4k^2 < 16$ or $k < 2$ (recall that k is positive).

If $k = 2$ then the eigenvalues are -5 and 0.

If $k > 2$ then there is a positive and a negative eigenvalue.

c.

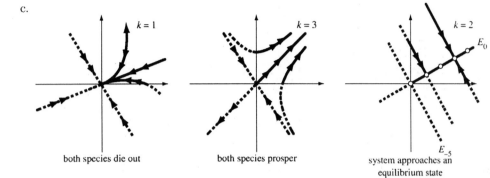

both species die out　　　both species prosper　　　system approaches an equilibrium state

49. $A = \begin{bmatrix} -1 & -0.2 \\ 0.6 & -0.2 \end{bmatrix}$, $\lambda_1 = -0.4$, $\lambda_2 = -0.8$

$E_{-0.4} = \text{span} \begin{bmatrix} -1 \\ 3 \end{bmatrix}$, $E_{-0.8} = \text{span} \begin{bmatrix} 1 \\ -1 \end{bmatrix}$

$\begin{bmatrix} g(0) \\ h(0) \end{bmatrix} = 15 \begin{bmatrix} -1 \\ 3 \end{bmatrix} + 45 \begin{bmatrix} 1 \\ -1 \end{bmatrix}$, so that $c_1 = 15, c_2 = 45$.

$\begin{bmatrix} g(t) \\ h(t) \end{bmatrix} = 15e^{-0.4t} \begin{bmatrix} -1 \\ 3 \end{bmatrix} + 45e^{-0.8t} \begin{bmatrix} 1 \\ -1 \end{bmatrix}$, so that

$g(t) = -15e^{-0.4t} + 45e^{-0.8t}$

$h(t) = 45e^{-0.4t} - 45e^{-0.8t}$.

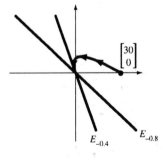

51. ith component of $\frac{d}{dt}(S\vec{x}) = \frac{d}{dt}(s_{i1}x_1(t) + s_{i2}x_2(t) + \cdots + s_{in}x_n(t))$

$= s_{i1}\frac{dx_1}{dt} + s_{i2}\frac{dx_2}{dt} + \cdots + s_{in}\frac{dx_n}{dt}$

$= i$th component of $S\frac{d\vec{x}}{dt}$

53. For the initial value $\begin{bmatrix} 1 \\ 0 \end{bmatrix}$, the system $\dfrac{d\vec{x}}{dt} = \begin{bmatrix} 0 & -1 \\ 1 & 0 \end{bmatrix} \vec{x}$ has the solution $\vec{x}(t) = \begin{bmatrix} \cos(t) \\ \sin(t) \end{bmatrix}$, by Exercise 20; the system $\dfrac{d\vec{x}}{dt} = \begin{bmatrix} 0 & -q \\ q & 0 \end{bmatrix}$ has the solution $\vec{x}(t) = \begin{bmatrix} \cos(qt) \\ \sin(qt) \end{bmatrix}$, by Exercise 25; and the system $\dfrac{d\vec{x}}{dt} = \begin{bmatrix} p & -q \\ q & p \end{bmatrix} \vec{x}$ has the solution $\vec{x}(t) = e^{pt} \begin{bmatrix} \cos(qt) \\ \sin(qt) \end{bmatrix}$, by Exercise 24 $\left(\text{write } \begin{bmatrix} p & -q \\ q & p \end{bmatrix} = pI_2 + \begin{bmatrix} 0 & -q \\ q & 0 \end{bmatrix} \right)$.

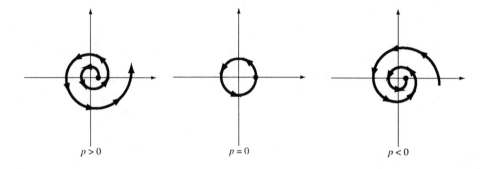

$p > 0$ $p = 0$ $p < 0$

55. $A = \begin{bmatrix} 0 & 1 \\ -p & -q \end{bmatrix}$, $\lambda_{1,2} = \dfrac{1}{2} \left(-q \pm \sqrt{q^2 - 4p} \right)$; note that both eigenvalues are negative. $E_{\lambda_1} = \text{span} \begin{bmatrix} 1 \\ \lambda_1 \end{bmatrix}$ and $E_{\lambda_2} = \begin{bmatrix} 1 \\ \lambda_2 \end{bmatrix}$.

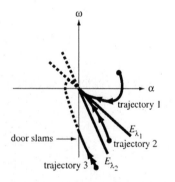

In the case of trajectory 3 the door will slam: Initially the door is opened just a little (α is small) and given a strong push to close it (ω is large negative). More generally, the door will slam if the point $\begin{bmatrix} \alpha(0) \\ \omega(0) \end{bmatrix}$ representing the initial state is located below the line $E_{\lambda_2} = \text{span} \begin{bmatrix} 1 \\ \lambda_2 \end{bmatrix}$, that is, if $\dfrac{\omega(0)}{\alpha(0)} < \lambda_2$.

9.2

1. By Euler's formula (Fact 9.2.2), $e^{2\pi i} = \cos(2\pi) + i\sin(2\pi) = 1$.

3.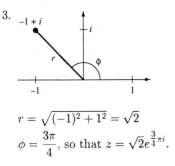

$$r = \sqrt{(-1)^2 + 1^2} = \sqrt{2}$$

$\phi = \dfrac{3\pi}{4}$, so that $z = \sqrt{2}e^{\frac{3}{4}\pi i}$.

5. $e^{-0.1t - 2it} = e^{-0.1t}e^{-2it} = e^{-0.1t}(\cos(2t) - i\sin(2t))$ spirals inward, in clockwise direction

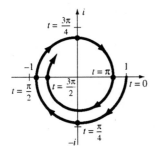

7. $\det(A) = -2$, so that the zero state is not stable, by Fact 9.2.5

9. The eigenvalues are conjugate complex, $\lambda_{1,2} = p \pm iq$, and $\text{tr}(A) = 2p < 0$, so that p is negative. By Fact 9.2.4, the zero state is stable.

11. a. $q(\vec{x}) = 2a_{i1}x_ix_1 + 2a_{i2}x_ix_2 + \cdots + a_{ii}x_i^2 + \cdots + 2a_{in}x_ix_n +$ terms not involving x_i, so that

$$\frac{\partial q}{\partial x_i} = 2a_{i1}x_1 + 2a_{i2}x_2 + \cdots + 2a_{ii}x_i + \cdots + 2a_{in}x_n \text{ and } \frac{d\vec{x}}{dt} = \text{grad}(q) = 2A\vec{x}.$$

The matrix of the system is $B = 2A$.

    d. The zero state is a stable equilibrium solution of the system $\dfrac{d\vec{x}}{dt} = \text{grad}(q) = 2A\vec{x}$ if (and only if) all the eigenvalues of $2A$ are negative. This means that the quadratic form $q(\vec{x}) = \vec{x} \cdot A\vec{x}$ is negative definite.

13. Recall that the zero state is stable if (and only if) the real parts of all eigenvalues are negative. Now the eigenvalues of A^{-1} are the reciprocals of those of A; the real parts have the same sign $\left(\text{if } \lambda = p + iq, \text{ then } \dfrac{1}{\lambda} = \dfrac{1}{p + iq} = \dfrac{p - iq}{p^2 + q^2}\right)$.

15. The eigenvalues are $\lambda_1 = \text{tr}(A) > 0$ and $\lambda_2 = 0$.

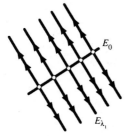

17. If $A = \begin{bmatrix} -1 & k \\ k & -1 \end{bmatrix}$ then $\text{tr}(A) = -2$ and $\det(A) = 1 - k^2$. By Fact 9.2.5, the zero state is stable if $\det(A) = 1 - k^2 > 0$, that is, if $|k| < 1$.

19. False, consider $A = \begin{bmatrix} 1 & 0 & 0 \\ 0 & 2 & 0 \\ 0 & 0 & -4 \end{bmatrix}$.

21. a. $\begin{vmatrix} \frac{db}{dt} = 0.05b+ & s \\ \frac{ds}{dt} = & 0.07s \end{vmatrix}$ and $\begin{bmatrix} b(0) \\ s(0) \end{bmatrix} = \begin{bmatrix} 1000 \\ 1000 \end{bmatrix}$

    b. $\lambda_1 = 0.07, \lambda_2 = 0.05; \vec{v}_1 = \begin{bmatrix} 50 \\ 1 \end{bmatrix}, \vec{v}_2 = \begin{bmatrix} 1 \\ 0 \end{bmatrix}; \vec{x}(0) = 1000\vec{v}_1 - 49000\vec{v}_2$; so that

    $b(t) = 50000e^{0.07t} - 49000e^{0.05t}$ and $s(t) = 1000e^{0.07t}$.

23. $\lambda_{1,2} = -\frac{1}{2} \pm i, r > 1$, so that trajectory spirals outwards. Choose II.

25. $\lambda_{1,2} = -\frac{1}{2} \pm i$; real part is negative so that trajectories spiral inwards in the counterclockwise direction

    $\left(\text{if } \vec{x} = \begin{bmatrix} 1 \\ 0 \end{bmatrix} \text{ then } \frac{d\vec{x}}{dt} = \begin{bmatrix} -1.5 \\ 2 \end{bmatrix} \right)$. Choose IV.

27. $\lambda_{1,2} = \pm 3i$, $E_{3i} = \text{span}\left(\begin{bmatrix} 1 \\ 0 \end{bmatrix} + i \begin{bmatrix} 0 \\ -1 \end{bmatrix} \right)$, so that $p = 0, q = 3, \vec{w} = \begin{bmatrix} 0 \\ -1 \end{bmatrix}, \vec{v} = \begin{bmatrix} 1 \\ 0 \end{bmatrix}$.
    Now use Fact 9.2.6

    $\vec{x}(t) = e^{0t} \begin{bmatrix} 0 & 1 \\ -1 & 0 \end{bmatrix} \begin{bmatrix} \cos(3t) & -\sin(3t) \\ \sin(3t) & \cos(3t) \end{bmatrix} \begin{bmatrix} a \\ b \end{bmatrix} = \begin{bmatrix} \sin(3t) & \cos(3t) \\ -\cos(3t) & \sin(3t) \end{bmatrix} \begin{bmatrix} a \\ b \end{bmatrix}$

    There are other ways to write these solutions; for an example see page 470 of the text.

29. $\lambda_{1,2} = 2 \pm 4i$, $E_{2+4i} = \text{span}\left(\begin{bmatrix} 1 \\ 0 \end{bmatrix} + i \begin{bmatrix} 0 \\ 1 \end{bmatrix} \right)$, so that

    $\vec{x}(t) = e^{2t} \begin{bmatrix} 0 & 1 \\ 1 & 0 \end{bmatrix} \begin{bmatrix} \cos(4t) & -\sin(4t) \\ \sin(4t) & \cos(4t) \end{bmatrix} \begin{bmatrix} a \\ b \end{bmatrix} = e^{2t} \begin{bmatrix} \sin(4t) & \cos(4t) \\ \cos(4t) & -\sin(4t) \end{bmatrix} \begin{bmatrix} a \\ b \end{bmatrix}$.

    See page 470 of the text for another representation of the answer.

31. $\lambda_{1,2} = -1 \pm 2i$, $E_{-1+2i} = \text{span}\left(\begin{bmatrix} 1 \\ 0 \end{bmatrix} + i \begin{bmatrix} 0 \\ -1 \end{bmatrix}\right)$, so that $p = -1, q = 2, \vec{w} = \begin{bmatrix} 0 \\ -1 \end{bmatrix}, \vec{v} = \begin{bmatrix} 1 \\ 0 \end{bmatrix}$.

Now $\begin{bmatrix} 1 \\ -1 \end{bmatrix} = \vec{x}(0) = \vec{w} + \vec{v}$, so that $a = 1$ and $b = 1$.

Then $\vec{x}(t) = e^{-t} \begin{bmatrix} 0 & 1 \\ -1 & 0 \end{bmatrix} \begin{bmatrix} \cos(2t) & -\sin(2t) \\ \sin(2t) & \cos(2t) \end{bmatrix} \begin{bmatrix} 1 \\ 1 \end{bmatrix} = e^{-t} \begin{bmatrix} \sin(2t) + \cos(2t) \\ \sin(2t) - \cos(2t) \end{bmatrix}$.

33. $\lambda_{1,2} = \pm i$, $E_i = \text{span}\left(\begin{bmatrix} 1 \\ 1 \end{bmatrix} + i \begin{bmatrix} 0 \\ 1 \end{bmatrix}\right)$

$a = 1, b = 0$, so that $\vec{x}(t) = \begin{bmatrix} 0 & 1 \\ 1 & 1 \end{bmatrix} \begin{bmatrix} \cos(t) & -\cos(t) \\ \sin(t) & \cos(t) \end{bmatrix} \begin{bmatrix} 1 \\ 0 \end{bmatrix} = \begin{bmatrix} \sin(t) \\ \sin(t) + \cos(t) \end{bmatrix}$

$= \cos(t) \begin{bmatrix} 0 \\ 1 \end{bmatrix} + \sin(t) \begin{bmatrix} 1 \\ 1 \end{bmatrix}$.

35. $A = \begin{bmatrix} 0 & 1 \\ -b & -c \end{bmatrix}$ and $f_A(\lambda) = \lambda^2 + c\lambda + b$, with eigenvalues $\lambda_{1,2} = \dfrac{-c \pm \sqrt{c^2 - 4b}}{2}$.

a. If $c = 0$ then $\lambda_{1,2} = \pm i\sqrt{b}$. The trajectories are ellipses.

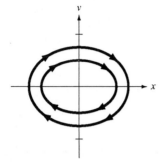

The block *oscillates harmonically*, with period $\dfrac{2\pi}{\sqrt{b}}$. The zero state is not asymptotically stable.

b. $\lambda_{1,2} = \dfrac{-c \pm i\sqrt{4b - c^2}}{2}$

The trajectories spiral inwards, since $\operatorname{Re}(\lambda_1) = \operatorname{Re}(\lambda_2) = -\dfrac{c}{2} < 0$. This is the case of a *damped oscillation*. The zero state is asymptotically stable.

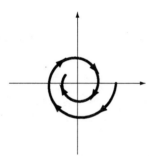

c. This case is discussed in Exercise 9.1.55. The zero state is stable here.

37. a. $\dfrac{1}{z(t)}$ is differentiable when $z(t) \neq 0$, since both the real and the imaginary parts are differen-

tiable $\left(\text{if } z = p + iq \text{ then } \dfrac{1}{z} = \dfrac{p - iq}{p^2 + q^2}\right)$. To find $\left(\dfrac{1}{z}\right)'$, apply the product rule to the equation

$z\left(\dfrac{1}{z}\right) = 1$: $z'\left(\dfrac{1}{z}\right) + z\left(\dfrac{1}{z}\right)' = 0$, so that $\left(\dfrac{1}{z}\right)' = -\dfrac{z'}{z^2}$.

b. $\left(\dfrac{z}{w}\right)' = \left(z\dfrac{1}{w}\right)' = z'\dfrac{1}{w} + z\left(\dfrac{1}{w}\right)' = \dfrac{z'}{w} - \dfrac{zw'}{w^2} = \dfrac{z'w - zw'}{w^2}$

39. Let $A = \begin{bmatrix} \lambda & 1 & 0 \\ 0 & \lambda & 1 \\ 0 & 0 & \lambda \end{bmatrix}$. We first solve the system $\dfrac{d\vec{c}}{dt} = (A - \lambda I_3)\vec{c} = \begin{bmatrix} 0 & 1 & 0 \\ 0 & 0 & 1 \\ 0 & 0 & 0 \end{bmatrix}\vec{c}$, or $\dfrac{dc_1}{dt} = c_2(t), \dfrac{dc_2}{dt} = c_3(t), \dfrac{dc_3}{dt} = 0$.

$c_3(t) = k_3$, a constant, so that $\dfrac{dc_2}{dt} = k_3$ and $c_2(t) = k_3 t + k_2$. Likewise $c_1(t) = \dfrac{k_3}{2}t^2 + k_2 t + k_1$.

Applying Exercise 9.1.24, with $k = -\lambda$, we find that $\vec{c}(t) = e^{-\lambda t}\vec{x}(t)$ or $\vec{x}(t) = e^{\lambda t}\vec{c}(t)$

$$= e^{\lambda t} \begin{bmatrix} k_1 + k_2 t + \dfrac{k_3}{2}t^2 \\ k_2 + k_3 t \\ k_3 \end{bmatrix} \text{ where } k_1, k_2, k_3 \text{ are arbitrary constants. The zero state is stable if (and}$$

only if) the real part of λ is negative.

9.3

1. The characteristic polynomial of this differential equation is $\lambda - 5$, so that $\lambda_1 = 5$. By Fact 9.3.8 the general solution is $f(t) = Ce^{5t}$, where C is an arbitrary constant.

3. Use Fact 9.3.13, where $a = -2$ and $g(t) = e^{3t}$:
$$f(t) = e^{-2t}\int e^{2t}e^{3t}\,dt = e^{-2t}\int e^{5t}\,dt = e^{-2t}\left(\frac{1}{5}e^{5t} + C\right) = \frac{1}{5}e^{3t} + Ce^{-2t}, \text{ where } C \text{ is a constant.}$$

5. Using Fact 9.3.13, $f(t) = e^t \int e^{-t}t\,dt = e^t(-te^{-t} - e^{-t} + C) = Ce^t - t - 1$, where C is an arbitrary constant.

7. By Definition 9.3.6, $p_T(\lambda) = \lambda^2 + \lambda - 12 = (\lambda + 4)(\lambda - 3)$.
Since $p_T(\lambda)$ has distinct roots $\lambda_1 = -4$ and $\lambda_2 = 3$, the solutions of the differential equation are of the form $f(t) = c_1 e^{-4t} + c_2 e^{3t}$, where c_1 and c_2 are arbitrary constants (by Fact 9.3.8).

9. $p_T(\lambda) = \lambda^2 - 9 = (\lambda - 3)(\lambda + 3) = 0$
$f(t) = c_1 e^{3t} + c_2 e^{-3t}$, where c_1, c_2 are arbitrary constants.

11. $p_T(\lambda) = \lambda^2 - 2\lambda + 2 = 0$ has roots $\lambda_{1,2} = 1 \pm i$. By Fact 9.3.9, $x(t) = e^t(c_1 \cos(t) + c_2 \sin(t))$, where c_1, c_2 are arbitrary constants.

13. $p_T(\lambda) = \lambda^2 + 2\lambda + 1 = (\lambda + 1)^2 = 0$ has the double root $\lambda = -1$. Following the strategy on page 436, we find $f(t) = e^{-t}(c_1 t + c_2)$, where c_1, c_2 are arbitrary constants.

15. By integrating twice we find $f(t) = c_1 + c_2 t$, where c_1, c_2 are arbitrary constants.

17. By Fact 9.3.10, the differential equation has a particular solution of the form $f_p(t) = P\cos(t) + Q\sin(t)$. Plugging f_p into the equation we find $(-P\cos(t) - Q\sin(t)) + 2(-P\sin(t) + Q\cos(t)) + P\cos(t) + Q\sin(t) = \sin(t)$ or $\begin{vmatrix} 2Q = 0 \\ -2P = 1 \end{vmatrix}$, so $\begin{array}{l} P = -\frac{1}{2} \\ Q = 0 \end{array}$.

Therefore, $f_p(t) = -\frac{1}{2}\cos(t)$.

Next we find a basis of the solution space of $f''(t) + 2f'(t) + f(t) = 0$. In Exercise 13 we see that $f_1(t) = e^{-t}$, $f_2(t) = te^{-t}$ is such a basis.

By Fact 9.3.4, the solutions of the original differential equation are of the form $f(t) = c_1 f_1(t) + c_2 f_2(t) + f_p(t) = c_1 e^{-t} + c_2 te^{-t} - \frac{1}{2}\cos(t)$, where c_1, c_2 are arbitrary constants.

19. We follow the approach outlined in Exercises 16 and 17.

  - Particular solution $x_p(t) = \cos(t)$

  - Solutions of $\dfrac{d^2 x}{dt^2} + 2x = 0$ are $x_1(t) = \cos(\sqrt{2}t)$ and $x_2(t) = \sin(\sqrt{2}t)$.

  - The solutions of the original differential equation are of the form $x(t) = c_1 \cos(\sqrt{2}t) + c_2 \sin(\sqrt{2}t) + \cos(t)$, where c_1 and c_2 are arbitrary constants.

21. $p_T(\lambda) = \lambda^3 + 2\lambda^2 - \lambda - 2 = (\lambda - 1)(\lambda + 1)(\lambda + 2) = 0$ has roots $\lambda_1 = 1, \lambda_2 = -1, \lambda_3 = -2$.
    By Fact 9.3.8, the general solution is $f(t) = c_1 e^t + c_2 e^{-t} + c_3 e^{-2t}$, where c_1, c_2, c_3 are arbitrary constants.

23. General solution $f(t) = Ce^{5t}$
    Plug in: $3 = f(0) = Ce^0 = C$, so that $f(t) = 3e^{5t}$.

25. General solution $f(t) = Ce^{-2t}$
    Plug in: $1 = f(1) = Ce^{-2}$, so that $C = e^2$ and $f(t) = e^2 e^{-2t} = e^{2-2t}$.

27. General solution $f(t) = c_1 \cos(3t) + c_2 \sin(3t)$ (Fact 9.3.9)
    Plug in: $0 = f(0) = c_1$ and $1 = f\left(\dfrac{\pi}{2}\right) = -c_2$, so that $c_1 = 0, c_2 = -1$, and $f(t) = -\sin(3t)$.

29. General solution $f(t) = c_1 \cos(2t) + c_2 \sin(2t) + \frac{1}{3}\sin(t)$, so that $f'(t) = -2c_1 \sin(2t) + 2c_2 \cos(2t) + \frac{1}{3}\cos(t)$ (use the approach outlined in Exercises 16 and 17)
    Plug in: $0 = f(0) = c_1$ and $0 = f'(0) = 2c_2 + \frac{1}{3}$, so that $c_1 = 0$, $c_2 = -\frac{1}{6}$, and $f(t) = -\frac{1}{6}\sin(2t) + \frac{1}{3}\sin(t)$.

31. $\dfrac{dv}{dt} + \dfrac{k}{m}v = g$
    constant particular solution: $v_p = \dfrac{mg}{k}$
    General solution of $\dfrac{dv}{dt} + \dfrac{k}{m}v = 0$ is $v(t) = Ce^{-\frac{k}{m}t}$.
    General solution of the original differential equation: $v(t) = Ce^{-\frac{k}{m}t} + \dfrac{mg}{k}$
    Plug in: $0 = v(0) = C + \dfrac{mg}{k}$, so that $C = -\dfrac{mg}{k}$ and $v(t) = \dfrac{mg}{k}\left(1 - e^{-\frac{k}{m}t}\right)$
    $\lim\limits_{t \to \infty} v(t) = \dfrac{mg}{k}$ (the "terminal velocity")

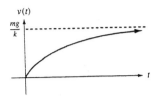

33. By Fact 9.3.9 $x(t) = c_1 \cos\left(\sqrt{\frac{g}{L}}t\right) + c_2 \sin\left(\sqrt{\frac{g}{L}}t\right)$, with period $P = \dfrac{2\pi}{\sqrt{\frac{g}{L}}} = 2\pi\dfrac{\sqrt{L}}{\sqrt{g}}$. It is required

    that $2 = P = 2\pi\dfrac{\sqrt{L}}{\sqrt{g}}$ or $L = \dfrac{g}{\pi^2} \approx 0.994$ (meters).

35. a. $p_T(\lambda) = \lambda^2 + 3\lambda + 2 = (\lambda + 1)(\lambda + 2) = 0$ with roots $\lambda_1 = -1$ and $\lambda_2 = -2$, so $x(t) = c_1 e^{-t} + c_2 e^{-2t}$.

    b. $x'(t) = -c_1 e^{-t} - 2c_2 e^{-2t}$
       Plug in: $1 = x(0) = c_1 + c_2$ and $0 = x'(0) = -c_1 - 2c_2$, so that $c_1 = 2, c_2 = -1$ and $x(t) = 2e^{-t} - e^{-2t}$.

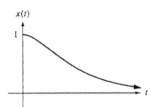

    c. Plug in: $1 = x(0) = c_1 + c_2$ and $-3 = x'(0) = -c_1 - 2c_2$, so that $c_1 = -1, c_2 = 2$, and $x(t) = -e^{-t} + 2e^{-2t}$.

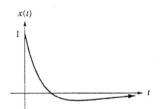

    d. The oscillator in part (b) never reaches the equilibrium, while the oscillator in part (c) goes through the equilibrium once, at $t = \ln(2)$.

37. $f_T(\lambda) = \lambda^2 + 6\lambda + 9 = (\lambda + 3)^2$ has roots $\lambda_{1,2} = -3$.
    Following the method of Example 10, we find the general solution $x(t) = e^{-3t}(c_1 + c_2 t)$ with $x'(t) = e^{-3t}(c_2 - 3c_1 - 3c_2 t)$.
    Plug in: $0 = x(0) = c_1$, and $1 = x'(0) = c_2 - 3c_1$, so that $c_1 = 0, c_2 = 1$, and $x(t) = te^{-3t}$.

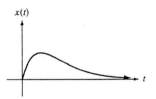

The oscillator does not go through the equilibrium at $t > 0$.

39. $f_T(\lambda) = \lambda^3 + 3\lambda^2 + 3\lambda + 1 = (\lambda + 1)^3 = 0$ has roots $\lambda_{1,2,3} = -1$. In other words, we can write the differential equation as $(D + 1)^3 f = 0$.
    By Exercise 38, part (c), the general solution is $f(t) = e^{-t}(c_1 + c_2 t + c_3 t^2)$.

41. We are looking for functions x such that $T(x) = \lambda x$, or $T(x) - \lambda x = 0$. Now $T(x) - \lambda x$ is an nth-order linear differential operator, so that its kernel is n-dimensional, by Fact 9.3.3. Thus λ is indeed an eigenvalue of T, with an n-dimensional eigenspace.

43. a. Using the approach of Exercises 16 and 17 we find $x(t) = c_1 e^{-2t} + c_2 e^{-3t} + \dfrac{1}{10} \cos t + \dfrac{1}{10} \sin t$.

    b. For large t, $x(t) \approx \dfrac{1}{10} \cos t + \dfrac{1}{10} \sin t$.

45. We can write the system as $\begin{array}{l|l} \frac{dx_1}{dt} = x_1 + 2x_2 & x_1(0) = 1 \\ \frac{dx_2}{dt} = x_2 & x_2(0) = -1 \end{array}$.

    The solution of the second equation, with the given initial value, is $x_2(t) = -e^t$.

    Now the first equation takes the form $\dfrac{dx_1}{dt} - x_1 = -2e^t$.

    Using Example 9 (with $a = 1$ and $c = -2$) we find $x_1(t) = e^t(-2t + C)$.

    plug in: $1 = x_1(0) = C$, so that $x_1(t) = e^t(1 - 2t)$ and $\vec{x}(t) = e^t \begin{bmatrix} 1 - 2t \\ -1 \end{bmatrix}$.

47. a. We start with a *preliminary remark* that will be useful below: If $f(t) = p(t)e^{\lambda t}$, where $p(t)$ is a polynomial, then $f(t)$ has an antiderivative of the form $q(t)e^{\lambda t}$, where $q(t)$ is another polynomial. We leave this remark as a calculus exercise.

    The function $x_n(t)$ satisfies the differential equation $\dfrac{dx_n}{dt} = a_{nn}x_n$, so that $x_n = Ce^{a_{nn}t}$, which is of the desired form.

    Now we will show that x_k is of the desired form, assuming that $x_{k+1}, \ldots, x_n$ have this form. x_k satisfies the differential equation $\dfrac{dx_k}{dt} = a_{kk}x_k + a_{k,k+1}x_{k+1} + \cdots + a_{kn}x_n$ or $\dfrac{dx_k}{dt} - a_{kk}x_k = a_{k,k+1}x_{k+1} + \cdots + a_{kn}x_n$.

    Note that by assumption of the function on the right-hand side has the form $p_1(t)e^{\lambda_1 t} + \cdots + p_m(t)e^{\lambda_m t}$. If we set $a_{kk} = a$ for simplicity, we can write $\dfrac{dx_k}{dt} - ax_k = p_1(t)e^{\lambda_1 t} + \cdots + p_m(t)e^{\lambda_m t}$.

By Fact 9.3.13, the solution is

$$x_k(t) = e^{at} \int e^{-at} (p_1(t)e^{\lambda_1 t} + \cdots + p_m(t)e^{\lambda_m t}) \, dt = e^{at} \int (p_1(t)e^{(\lambda_1 - a)t} + \cdots + p_m(t)e^{(\lambda_m - a)t}) \, dt$$

$$= e^{at}(q_1(t)e^{(\lambda_1 - a)t} + \cdots + q_m(t)e^{(\lambda_m - a)t} + C) = q_1(t)e^{\lambda_1 t} + \cdots + q_m(t)e^{\lambda_m t} + Ce^{at} \text{ as claimed (note}$$

that a is one of the λ_i). The constant C is determined by $x_k(0)$. Note that we used the *preliminary remark* in the second to last step.

b. It is shown in introductory calculus classes that $\lim_{t \to \infty} (t^m e^{\lambda t}) = 0$ if and only if λ is negative (here m is a fixed positive integer). In light of part (a), this proves the claim.